THE GPO AND THE EASTER RISING

THE GPO
AND THE
EASTER RISING

KEITH JEFFERY
Queen's University, Belfast

IRISH ACADEMIC PRESS
DUBLIN • PORTLAND, OR

First published in 2006 by
IRISH ACADEMIC PRESS
44, Northumberland Road, Dublin 4, Ireland

and in the United States of America by
IRISH ACADEMIC PRESS
c/o ISBS, Suite 300, 920 NE 58th Avenue
Portland, Oregon 97213-3644

Website: www.iap.ie

British Library Cataloguing in Publication Data
An entry can be found on request

ISBN 0-7165-2827-4 (cloth)
ISBN 0-7165-2828-2 (paper)

Library of Congress Cataloging-in-Publication Data
An entry can be found on request

Typeset in 11 pt on 13 pt Palatino by FiSH Books, Enfield, Middx.
Printed by MPG Books Ltd, Bodmin, Cornwall

Contents

Preface

This book, which combines new accounts with the stories told in *The Sinn Fein Rebellion As They Saw It* (Dublin: Irish Academic Press, 1999), is founded on the proposition that the GPO is central to all narratives of the Rising, but that the actual experiences of those Dubliners and others who were working in the Post Office has been neglected in the subsequent historiography. It reproduces a wealth of hitherto unpublished documents drawn from the treasure-trove of material on the Rising held in the British Post Office Archives, and never before exploited by historians. This material is complemented with other important hitherto unpublished matter from the United Kingdom National Archives, as well as some vivid eyewitness accounts of the events in and around the GPO first published shortly after the Rising.

Many people have helped in the making of this book. At Irish Academic Press I have to thank Frank Cass, who had the original idea, and Lisa Hyde, who has been unfailingly enthusiastic, encouraging and helpful with the project, even though she must have wondered if she would ever see the manuscript. Margaret O'Sullivan of the British Association for Local History first encouraged me to think about what could be done with the Post Office Archives. Paul Arthur, Tom Bartlett, Tom Garvin, Gerard Lyne, James McGuire, Eve Morrison, Eunan O'Halpin and Bill Vaughan all helped in a variety of ways, not all of which were purely scholarly. Lindsay Duguid and John Murray-Browne once again provided generous hospitality in London. Stephen Ferguson of An Post has been very helpful indeed, and generously let me see a pre-publication copy of his wonderful booklet, *G.P.O. Staff in 1916*, for which he also productively quarried the British postal archives. This is the first book I have completed as a member of the School of History and

Anthropology at Queen's University Belfast, and I would like to thank my new colleagues there for the warm welcome they have given me, and the encouragement they provide for all sorts of historical ventures. Finally, my sons Ben and Alex Jeffery did much Trojan work more or less cheerfully keying in text, while Sally Visick and the technical expertise of Designs Matter was, as always, of incalculable assistance.

I am grateful for access to unpublished Crown copyright material reproduced in this volume and held in the United Kingdom National Archives and the British Postal Museum and Archive. Like all other toilers in the historical vineyard, I owe a tremendous debt to the archivists and librarians who tend the raw materials for our history. We are also indebted to the families of witnesses who have preserved and made available precious historical records, and I would like specially to thank Dermot and Dick Humphreys for their help, and the latter for permission to publish his father's memoir. The document containing the narrative by Dick Humphreys reproduced in chapter 6 is the property of the Board of the National Library of Ireland and the text has been reproduced with their permission.

KEITH JEFFERY
Belfast
January 2006

Illustrations

Abbreviations in Text and Notes

BPMA   British Postal Museum and Archive (London)
DBC   Dublin Bread Company
DMP   Dublin Metropolitan Police
DO   District Office
GPO   General Post Office
ICA   Irish Citizen Army
IO   Irish Office
IRA   Irish Republican Army
IRB   Irish Republican Brotherhood
RIC   Royal Irish Constabulary
RIR   Royal Irish Regiment
SE   Superintending Engineer
TNA   The National Archives (United Kingdom)
TS   Telegraph Service
WT   Wireless Telegraphy

Individuals identified by initials in Chapter Four
B.   Paul G. Besson
C.   John J. Coonan
F.   Fred Norway
G.   Grace (Mrs Norway's sister)
H.   Arthur Hamilton Norway
M.N.   Sir Matthew Nathan
N.   Nevil Shute Norway
O'B.   Edmond O'Brien S. Lord Shaw
V.   W. H. F. Verschoyle
W.   William and Elsie Wheeler

1 Introduction

The General Post Office – the GPO – is central to all accounts of the Easter Rising of 1916. It is, perhaps, the most famous post office in the world. William Irwin Thompson refers to it as 'the General Post Office of history',[1] privileging it over all other post offices, general or otherwise. Here Patrick Pearse and James Connolly set up their headquarters, and here the most enduring scenes of patriotic endeavour and heroic rebel defiance took place. The GPO became, as Tim Pat Coogan has observed, 'both the heart and the symbol of the Rising'.[2] In 1935, at the unveiling of Albert Power's sculpture of Cuchulainn as a 1916 memorial, Eamon de Valera declared that 'this was the scene of an event which will ever be counted an epoch in our history – the beginning of one of Ireland's most glorious and sustained efforts for independence'.[3]

The actions of the rebels at the GPO on that first day of the Rising have been comparatively well recorded in both published and unpublished texts. Among the general accounts of the Rising,[4] Desmond Ryan's *The Rising* has particular authority for the events at the GPO as Ryan was a member of the garrison there and very close to Patrick Pearse, who appointed him to be his literary executor. *The Rising*, which F. X. Martin described as 'the first accurate overall picture of what took place during those days in April 1916',[5] was published in the late 1940s, shortly after Desmond FitzGerald, another member of the GPO garrison, wrote his memoirs of the revolutionary period. which were published posthumously in the 1960s.[6] Also published posthumously (in 1957) was a 'report on operations in the G.P.O. garrison area during Easter Week, 1916' in *The I.R.B. and the 1916 Insurrection*, by another GPO veteran, Diarmuid Lynch.[7] Although this 'labour of love' was based on '182 factual statements' which Lynch acquired 'from individual participants',[8] the resulting narrative is unsatisfactorily impressionistic, and lacks any detailed source references.

A few other individual eyewitness accounts of the events at the GPO have been published. That of Father John Flanagan, reproduced below in Chapter 7, was written shortly after the Rising and published in the *Catholic Bulletin* in 1918. Flanagan's account and 'In defence of the G.P.O.', a memoir by two participants which had been first published in *An tOglác* ten years after the Rising,[9] were both re-published in 1966 in Roger McHugh's useful but frustrating (there is, for example, no index) collection of eyewitness accounts, *Dublin 1916*.[10] More recently, a memoir completed in 1961 by W. J. Brennan-Whitmore, who had been among the Volunteers who occupied the GPO and was later 'officer commanding North Earl Street area', was published in an edition meticulously edited and introduced by Pauric Travers.[11]

Noting in the mid-1960s that contemporaneous documents from the revolutionary years were still being discovered, F. X. Martin declared 'how vitally important it is to get at original sources if the real story of 1916 is to be known'.[12] Martin's observation has been the inspiration behind this volume of eyewitness accounts of the Rising from the perspective of the General Post Office. The 'real story of 1916' *must* include the bystanders, the uncommitted, the ordinary workers in the GPO, who were suddenly caught up in the dramatic events of Easter Week. For many of those whose stories are told in this volume (for example, Samuel Guthrie and J. H. Reeves in Chapter 5), their first response to the events of Easter Monday 1916 was to attempt to return to duty as quickly as possible. 'Keeping going' in adverse circumstances was also demonstrated by the female staff at the Telephone Exchange in Crown Alley across the river from the GPO, which the Volunteers did not attack and which continued to operate throughout the week. There need not have been anything particularly 'political' at the time about this decision to carry on working. In later years, however, with the changed political circumstances in Ireland, it is perhaps not surprising that stories of 'soldiering on' or 'derring do' during the Rising, and apparently *against* the rebels, might have been suppressed. But these stories are part of Ireland's history as much as those of the fighting men and women, and it is appropriate that they should be told so that the full history of the Rising may be recorded.

A particular feature of the documents collected here is their closeness to the events described. With the single exception of Arthur Hamilton Norway's 'Irish experiences in war' (written, it seems, in the mid 1920s) all the accounts in this volume (and this distinguishes it from other collections, such as Roger McHugh's) date from within two years of the Rising, and most of the material comes from the year of the Rising itself. Among this is a wealth of records from the British Post Office archives, which previous historians of the Rising have sadly neglected to investigate, even if they have been aware of its existence.[13] Recent scholarly studies of the Rising – for example by Foy and Barton in 1999, and Townshend in 2005 – have simply ignored the treasures of the Post Office archives.

This material falls into three broad categories: precisely contemporary documents; official reports; and published eye-witness accounts. Among the examples of contemporary documents are the gripping first messages sent out by Post Office employees from Dublin and included in Chapter 1. Arthur Hamilton Norway's first two letters reporting on the situation within a few days of the start of the Rising, his more considered official report and his later memoir are included in Chapter 2. Along with this material are official reports, and eye-witness accounts by other Post Office employees reproduced in Chapter 3. Norway's writings on the Rising are complemented by his wife's contemporary letters from Dublin, written in April and May 1916, and published just a couple of months later. Supplementing the material from the Post Office archives are the papers of the 'Wilson-Byrne Committee' in the United Kingdom National Archives (formerly the Public Record Office), another group of records neglected by historians of the Rising. This committee reviewed the cases of Irish civil servants suspected of being complicit in the rebellion. Its report and the papers relating to four individual Post Office employees – chosen as a representative sample – are reproduced in Chapter 9, and illustrate a fascinating range of experience from clear Sinn Féin activism to evident non-involvement.

It was not just Post Office employees who fell under suspicion; officials from every branch of government were investigated, and some departments did their own reviews. All Irish subordinate staff employed by the National Health Insurance Commission, for example, were required to provide a diary of their movements from Saturday 22 April to Monday 1 May. These staff included clerks, typists, book keepers, 'char women etc.', and the 190 diaries which they completed and which are preserved in the British National Archives give an extraordinary and surely unique snap-shot of the lives of 'ordinary' Dubliners during the Rising.[14]

In addition to the 'civil service' material which comprises the majority of the stories in this volume, there is also in Chapter 8 a journalistic account of Easter Week by St John Ervine, the manager of the Abbey Theatre, which gives a sense of how the events in the GPO were seen by an especially observant and thoughtful onlooker. There are also two narratives from the insurgent side: one, 'a rebel's tale' (reproduced in Chapter 6) was written very soon after the Rising by Dick Humphreys, and gives a perspective from inside the building where on the Thursday Humphreys spent some time in the top-floor Telegraph Room which Samuel Guthrie and W A. Pemberton (in Chapter 5) had vacated on the Monday.[15] The other narrative from inside the GPO is by Father John Flanagan (Chapter 7), which gives a glimpse of what it was like in the building at the end of the week.

The 'Secretary's Tales' in Chapter 3 comprise the reports and memoir of Arthur Hamilton Norway (1859–1938), who was Secretary to the Irish Post Office from 1912 to 1916. He was a man of some literary talent and ambitions. During the 1890s he wrote 'two charming additions to the "Highways and Byways Series"',[16] *Devon and Cornwall* (1897) and *Yorkshire* (1899), as well as a *History of the Post-Office Packet Service* (1895), in which he drew on his own Cornish family background. Later on he added a novel (*Parson Peter: A Tale of the Dart*), a travel book (*Naples Past and Present*) and a study of Dante's *Divine Comedy*.[17] Literary gifts appear to have run in the family. His second son, Nevil Shute Norway (1899–1960), writing as 'Nevil Shute', became a best-selling author of popular fiction.

Norway was a well-regarded and successful civil servant. After his death a former colleague wrote of him as 'a man of high character and lofty ideals…combined with a generous and kindly nature, which endeared him to all his colleagues'.[18] He suffered progressively from deafness, which Nevil reckoned kept him from rising to the highest levels of the public service. Indeed he viewed his father's appointment in August 1912 to head the Post Office in Ireland as not so much a promotion – for he remained at the assistant secretary grade – as 'being shunted into a dead end' in view of his increasing disability.[19]

In his own memoir Norway adduced personal reasons concerning the health of his wife and elder son, Fred, as persuading him to move to Ireland. But there was also a political dimension to the appointment. Following the amalgamation of the Irish and British Post Offices in 1831 (apparently because of 'defects in the working of the Irish Post Office'[20]), the secretaryship to the Irish department had generally been filled by 'one of the higher officials' from the London headquarters in St Martin's-le-Grand.[21] Norway's appointment clearly fitted into this pattern, but when considering who should succeed Sir Reginald Egerton, an Englishman who had headed the Irish Post Office since 1898, Herbert Samuel, the Postmaster-General, can hardly have been ignorant of the political ramifications which accompanied appointment to the higher ranks of the civil service in Ireland. It is possible that Samuel had no opportunity for much 'quiet, calm deliberation' about this matter of departmental staffing. At precisely the period when the Dublin job was being settled, Samuel himself was embroiled in defending his public reputation during the 'Marconi scandal', when accusations were made of improper share dealing on his part and that of his ministerial colleagues Lloyd George and Rufus Isaacs.[22] Yet Norway can be seen as well-suited for the Irish job. He was clearly well-qualified, and could be regarded as a 'safe pair of hands' for a potentially difficult position. He was, moreover, 'inclined' to the 'case for Home Rule'.[23] In addition, with his growing deafness (as his son afterwards suspected), he might not have nursed long-term ambitions to stay in Dublin, or even with the civil service. In short, he was able, available, politically sympathetic, and probably amenable to the opportunity of early retirement.

When Norway was being appointed Ireland was apparently well on the road to Home Rule. In April 1912 the third Government of Ireland Bill had been introduced into parliament. The proposed legislation provided for an Irish parliament and executive to take control of all domestic business, while matters such as defence and foreign affairs would remain in the hands of the United Kingdom parliament in London. It was widely assumed (not least among Ulster unionists) that John Redmond, the leader of the Irish parliamentary party, would in due course become the first Prime Minister of Ireland. With this in mind, and also continuing a policy adopted by its Conservative and Unionist predecessor, Asquith's Liberal government had taken to appointing increasing numbers of Catholic Irish nationalists to government positions.[24]

Although under the proposed Home Rule legislation postal services were excluded from the competence of an Irish parliament, Norway's appointment, over the head of an Irish assistant secretary with strong nationalist sympathies, James MacMahon, was widely criticised by nationalists. Some local authorities passed resolutions condemning the appointment of an Englishman who, it was noted, was both a Protestant and a Mason. *The Leader*, a Dublin weekly edited by D. P. Moran which vigorously championed Irish-Ireland ideas, asserted that the affair made a mockery of Home Rule and was a conspiracy fomented by 'the Jew financier' Samuel and 'the intellectual coon' Augustine Birrell (Chief Secretary for Ireland since 1907).[25] The *Sinn Féin Weekly* described the appointment as 'one of the grossest jobs yet perpetrated' and 'an insult to every Irishman in the Post Office'.[26] Nationalist representatives lobbied to change Samuel's decision. The prominent MP Tim Healy wrote to his brother that there was 'great searching of hearts because of the threatened appointment of a Mr. Norway, from London, to succeed Egerton, a Catholic, as secretary to the Post Office. All the bishops, including Dr. O'Donnell, wrote in vain to Redmond and Dillon. Herbert Samuel saw Redmond several times. The action of the Government', he concluded, 'shows that they have no belief that Home Rule will become law.'[27] The question of Norway's position came up again early in 1915 when the Nationalist MP John Dillon raised it with Samuel's successor as Postmaster-General, Charles Hobhouse. Dillon asserted that Samuel had agreed to appoint Norway for only two years, after which he would be replaced by an Irishman. Hobhouse, who had also been lobbied by John Redmond and the Belfast Nationalist MP, Joseph Devlin, denied that any such promise had been made, but he conceded that Norway would only keep his present position until the Home Rule government came in when he would be 'abolished': 'that may be a year hence or two years or three years. We do not want him back in the G.P.O.', he added, 'and he will not be sorry to obtain abolition terms.'[28]

Norway was not unaware of the sensitivities accompanying his public position in Dublin. When Sir Matthew Nathan, his former superior at the Post Office in London, was appointed permanent under-secretary to the Irish Office in August 1914, Norway advised him not to join the Kildare Street Club as 'in the minds of Nationalists it is identified irreparably with a narrow and rather bitter type of Unionism which they resent'. Norway himself had joined the Sackville Street Club, which although a Protestant establishment was less closely identified with political unionism. Evidently drawing on his own experience, he stressed that strongly-held nationalist feelings existed 'to an extent which is worth attention from an Englishman taking up duty here for the first time and hoping, as I presume you do, to occupy a position of friendly relations with both sides'.[29] Such evidence as there is suggests that Norway lived up to this admirable standard. Tim Healy recalled long afterwards that Norway had 'behaved in Dublin most impartially'.[30]

Chapter 4, 'The Wife's Tale' comprises the text of *The Sinn Fein Rebellion as I Saw It*, a set of four letters which Mrs Norway wrote for family consumption beginning on Easter Tuesday, 25 April, the second day of the Rising. Although the final letter was not completed until 26 May, the bulk of the account was written during the Rising itself and constitutes an especially vivid narrative of the Easter week events. It usefully complements other existing contemporary eyewitness accounts written by south Dublin residents, perhaps most importantly that of the writer James Stephens, sympathetic to the Sinn Féin cause,[31] but also the letters of Alfred Fannin, a comfortably-off Protestant businessman.[32] Mrs Norway's perspective combined that of the administration, which she experienced through her husband, and of a comparatively detached middle-class English observer. The reviewer for the *Times Literary Supplement*, indeed, extravagantly concluded that Mrs Norway was 'not one of the Unionist "wreckers" who are said to view the recent rebellion with no sense of proportion, but – judging by her remarks about Sir E. Carson and the Ulster Volunteers – a radical Home Ruler'.[33]

At times the various accounts overlap. Every commentator reported rumours. On the second day of the Rising Stephens wrote that 'the rumours began, and I think it will be many a year before the rumours cease'.[34] Some of these turned out to be completely false – for example that the Pope had committed suicide, which St John Ervine (whose account is reproduced in Chapter 8) heard, or the wild tales reported by Mrs Norway early in the week of widespread insurrection outside Dublin, and that Sir Roger Casement had been shot in London. Some of these, including one that Jacob, the biscuit manufacturer whose factory was occupied by rebels, had declared that he would 'never make another biscuit in Ireland',[35] she corrected in footnotes. Other tales reflected a perhaps understandable misinterpretation of events. Writing on the afternoon of Friday 28 April, Mrs Norway recorded that on Wednesday 'three of the ringleaders' had been caught, 'and it is said they were shot immediately!'[36] This story clearly stemmed from the murder at about 10.15 on Wednesday morning of Francis Sheehy-Skeffington and two journalists on the orders of a deranged British army officer and fellow-Irishman, Captain J. C. Bowen Colthurst. Far from the men being 'ringleaders', Sheehy-Skeffington was a well-known pacifist who had been trying to organise unofficial parties to prevent looting in Dublin and the two other men, Thomas Dickson and Patrick MacIntyre, were editors of 'violently Loyalist papers which had strongly supported John Redmond's recruiting campaign'.[37]

The privations of civilians feature in the contemporary accounts. For some days the city was effectively paralysed and food supplies quickly ran short.[38] Mrs Norway tells a story of how the maidservant of an acquaintance, Mrs Elsie Wheeler, walked forty miles in one day carrying meat and butter.[39] Mrs Wheeler was the wife of William Ireland de Courcy Wheeler, a prominent Dublin surgeon who was knighted in 1919. Wheeler's brother, Major Henry de Courcy Wheeler, was present when Patrick Pearse formally surrendered at the end of the Rising.[40] Elsie Wheeler's father was Lord Shaw of Dunfirmline, a law lord and former Liberal MP, who when he retired from the bench in 1929 became Lord Craigmyle. He appears in Mrs Norway's narrative as 'Lord S.' Shaw was in Dublin recuperating from major surgery (performed by his son-in-law) when he got caught up in the Rising. Like many others in the city he could not resist sight-seeing. 'No military regulation', he wrote in his memoirs, was able to restrain 'the incredulous curiosity of the populace'. Shaw also recalled 'a sense of relief and gratitude' among the people 'when the military was poured into Dublin' and he sentimentally remarked on 'their bravery and good humour and courage, their kindness and friendship towards the soldiery, and their mutual helpfulness'.[41]

Norway describes in his memoir how he had been working at the GPO on the morning of Easter Monday and had been called away to a meeting with the Chief Secretary at Dublin Castle just minutes before the insurgents occupied the building. Norway speculated what might have been his fate had he remained in the building just a few minutes longer. Equipped with his elder son Fred's automatic pistol, which Nevil, anxious about the general situation, had two days previously cleaned and loaded for him, he might 'have tried to hold the staircase, and keep the mob down... The certain result', he continued with fine irony, 'would have been that I should have been shot at once, and the probable result would have been that the Government in London would have declared the whole trouble to have arisen from my wicked folly in firing on a body of peaceful, if armed, citizens.' Mrs Norway's letters reflect the panic and confusion which swept through the administration during the week. On the Wednesday we find her husband peremptorily being summoned to the Vice-Regal Lodge in Phoenix Park, and when no car could be found, the Viceroy resorted to giving Norway instructions over the telephone in incomprehensible French. The next day Sir Matthew Nathan summoned him four times to Dublin Castle 'without', as Norway complained, 'any reason of real advantage'.

There is not much reflection as to the causes of the Rising in Mrs Norway's letters, though, as the *Times Literary Supplement* noticed, she had some caustic words for the Unionists who were preparing armed resistance to Home Rule before the Great War broke out. 'In Ulster', she wrote, 'the wind was sown, and my God, we have reaped the whirlwind!' Her account also reflects the contemporary (and erroneous) British assumption that the Rising owed more to German initiative than Irish. She assumed that Sinn Féin was 'encouraged no doubt by German intrigue and German money', and recorded armed Volunteers marching down Grafton Street singing 'Die Wacht am Rhein'. Nevil followed this line in his memoirs. 'The Germans', he wrote, 'established contact with the Sinn Féin volunteers by submarine and did everything within their power to stimulate a rising'. Their object was 'to cause the diversion of British troops from the Western Front. In this they were successful.'[42]

For Nevil, in Dublin for the school holidays,[43] the Rising was a great adventure. 'This week', wrote his mother, 'has been a wonderful week for N. Never before has a boy of just seventeen had such an experience.' In his autobiography Nevil wrote that about half an hour after the GPO had been seized, he and his mother arrived in Sackville Street, on their way to meet his father for lunch. The street was crowded and 'there was a cordon of volunteers around the Post Office, and trigger-happy young men in green uniforms in great excitement were firing off their revolvers from time to time at nothing in particular'. Having sent his mother away, Nevil witnessed the rebels attack the troop of lancers which came down the street: 'these were the first men that I had seen killed'. He recalled that during the Rising 'I was far more comfortable and at home than my parents. This was my cup of tea I was mentally conditioned for war: it was what I had been bred and trained for for two years.' He joined a Red Cross ambulance service organised by the Royal Irish Automobile Club and served as a stretcher bearer for most of the week.[44]

Although much of his writing has an autobiographical flavour and a number of his early novels clearly draw on his work as an aeronautical engineer, Shute made very little literary use of his Irish experiences. *Beyond the Black Stump*, published in 1956,[45] and sniffily dismissed by the *Times Literary Supplement* as 'a contrived and shallow piece of work',[46] is the only fiction in which he appears to have used any material from his time in Ireland and, even so, only rather tangentially. The novel concerns the relationship between Mollie Regan, one of a successful Irish-Australian family running a substantial sheep business at 'Laragh Station' in the remote north of Western Australia, and Stanton Laird, an American geologist prospecting for oil.

The station is owned by Pat and Tom Regan, both fervent Irish republicans who had fought with the IRA during the Rising and in the subsequent 'Tan War' of 1919–21. When they first emigrated to Australia and settled at Laragh they had, as Shute delicately put it, 'lived somewhat indiscriminately' with the local Aborigines. Pat's favourite, who ranked as the 'chief wife', was known as 'the Countess Markievicz' and there were (among others) two mixed-race sons called James Connolly and Joseph Plunkett. Having come under fire in St Stephen's Green, Dublin, where Constance Markievicz commanded a contingent of Volunteers, in his recollections of the Rising Hamilton Norway wrote of 'the virago, the Countess Markievicz'. Mrs Norway thought Markievicz had been 'one of the most dangerous of the leaders', and hoped that she would 'be treated with the same severity as the men'.[47]

In one passage concerning the Laragh Station 'Countess', Shute appears to have taken his own, quiet revenge for the ill-treatment he believed his family had received at the hands of the 1916 insurgents:

> The Countess was unaccustomed to a lavatory and her table manners had left much to be desired, so the men had fallen into the habit of dining alone while the black women took their meals out in the kitchen, or in any place they wished...The men ate in virtual silence; conversation at meal times was unknown on Laragh Station. The Countess slopped around in bare feet, huge, black, smiling, and shapeless in a cotton frock worn very evidently with nothing underneath it, removing used dishes from the table and carrying them out to wash.[48]

Part of the story of the Regans' haphazard personal relations had an Easter Rising aspect. Mrs Regan, we learn, had originally been married to Tom Regan, by whom she had borne three children but had left him for his brother Pat, by whom she had Mollie. There had been no divorce, since, as Mollie put it, 'We're all Micks here', and her parents' arrangement was merely a common-law situation. Pat had softened Tom's feelings by presenting him with a cherished possession: 'General Shamus O'Brian's own Mauser that he carried at the start of the Troubles, in Easter Week 1916'. Both Regan brothers had, apparently, been with O'Brien when he was killed on the roof of Jacob's biscuit factory.[49] Shute's original intention, however, had been for Pat to give Tom a racehorse, 'Laragh Lad', but this and some other details in the novel were changed after Shute's lawyers warned that his fictional characters might be confused with a real Australian family and a libel action might ensue.[50] To satisfy the lawyers Shute proposed 'to substitue for the racehorse a relic of the Irish rebellion greatly prized by both brothers, such as a Mauser pistol used by Rory O'Connor in his last stand, or a crucifix carried by Pearse. To avoid offence in Ireland a fictitious hero might be used.'[51] So it was to be. Mollie explained the transaction to a baffled Stanton: 'I think perhaps it eased hard feelings when Daddy gave him the Mauser. There were just the three great Irish generals in the Troubles – Edmund [*sic*] Pearse, Rory O'Connor, and Shamus O'Brian, and Uncle Tom always says that O'Brian was the greatest of them all. The Mauser means an awful lot to them.'[52] No great offence on this score seems to have been taken in Ireland. The reviewer for the *Irish Independent* thought the background to *Beyond the Black Stump* was 'highly effective' and ambiguously praised the author's 'excellent knowledge of stage-Irish dialogue'. He was less admiring of Shute's 'muddled knowledge of comparatively recent Irish history', which had resulted in some 'weird and wonderful' results'.[53]

Nevil Shute's eccentric use of Irish rebel doings in a minor and now largely forgotten novel is a curious and evanescent legacy for his father's four-year stewardship of the Post Office in Ireland. If the Rising had never occurred, Norway would have left something much more permanent in the great improvements he supervised at the Dublin GPO. As Mrs Norway noted, when he arrived in Ireland the public office was a 'miserable, dirty little place', and, in her words, Norway '*hustled*' to see that plans were implemented to reconstruct the building, providing a grand new hall with an entrance under the central portico.[54] The building itself, completed in 1818 to a design by Francis Johnson, has an impressive, if severe, granite façade. During the nineteenth century the interior of the building was much altered, and from 1870 there was only a small and inconvenient public office entered from a side street. This was rectified in the 1915-16 improvements which installed 'a large, well lighted, and architecturally imposing new Public Office' with furniture and fittings of Burmese teak, and re-opened the building's main entrance through the central arch of the portico.[55]

Within weeks the newly-remodelled GPO was destroyed, and, as graphically described by Mrs Norway, the building reduced to a smouldering shell. Not everyone was dismayed by the destruction. 'It is greatly to be regretted', asserted George Bernard Shaw, 'that so very little of Dublin has been demolished. The General Post Office was a monument, fortunately not imperishable, of how extremely dull eighteenth-century pseudo-classic architecture can be. Its demolition does not matter. What does matter is that all the Liffey slums have not been demolished.'[56] Since the principal façade survived 1916 comparatively uninjured, however, a decision was taken in 1924 to reconstruct the GPO rather than demolish it.[57] The British royal arms were removed from the pediment, but otherwise the O'Connell Street frontage is essentially as it was in 1916. An even more lavish public office was constructed on the ground floor, though the entrance in the middle was replaced by twin doors on each side of the portico. Inside the contemporary GPO is the sculpture of Cuchulainn, and a series of imaginative paintings depicting scenes from the Rising. Here the rebels are amply commemorated, but of the Post Office employees who were working in the building on Easter Monday 1916 there is no sign. For their stories, and other tales of the Rising, you will have to read on.

Notes

1. William Irwin Thompson, *The Imagination of an Insurrection: Dublin, Easter 1916* (New York: Oxford University Press, 1967), p. 208.
2. Tim Pat Coogan, *1916: The Easter Rising* (London: Phoenix pbk edn, 2005), p. 107.
3. *Irish Times*, 22 Apr. 1935, quoted in Yvonne Whelan, *Reinventing Modern Dublin: Streetscape, Iconography and the Politics of Identity* (Dublin: University College Dublin Press, 2003), p. 166.
4. Of which the best are Desmond Ryan, *The Rising: The Complete Story of Easter Week* (Dublin: Golden Eagle Books, 1949); Max Caulfield, *The Easter Rebellion: Dublin 1916* (London: Muller, 1964); Michael Foy and Brian Barton, *The Easter Rising* (Stroud, Glos.: Sutton, 1999); and Charles Townshend, *Easter 1916: The Irish Rebellion* (London: Penguin, 2005).
5. F. X. Martin, '1916 – myth, fact and mystery', *Studia Hibernica*, no. 7 (1967), p. 33.
6. 'Inside the G.P.O.' was published in a special fiftieth anniversary Supplement to the *Irish Times*, 7 Apr. 1966, and also as part of the *Memoirs of Desmond FitzGerald, 1913-1916* (London: Routledge & Kegan Paul, 1968).
7. Diarmuid Lynch, *The I.R.B. and the 1916 Insurrection*, ed. Florence O'Donoghue (Cork: Mercier Press, 1957).
8. Ibid., pp. xi, 154.
9. M. J. Staines and M. W. Reilly, 'In defence of the G.P.O.', *An tÓglác*, 23 Jan. 1926.
10. London: Arlington Books, 1966
11. W. J. Brennan-Whitmore, *Dublin Burning: The Easter Rising from behind the Barricades* (Dublin: Gill & Macmillan, 1996).
12. F. X. Martin, '1916', p. 41.
13. See my 2003 Phillimore Lecture, delivered to the British Association of Local History, and published as 'Letters, bombs and local history', *The*

Local Historian, vol. 33 no. 4 (Nov. 2003), pp. 207-20, which explores some of the 1916 riches of the Post Office archives. Among historians of the Irish revolution, only the indefatigable Peter Hart has investigated the archives, in his case for evidence concerning Michael Collins's employment in the Post Office in 1906-10 (see Peter Hart, *Mick: The Real Michael Collins* (London: Macmillan, 2005), ch. 3 'Clerk'). Leon Ó Broin used Hamilton Norway's 'Irish experiences in war' in his *Dublin Castle and the 1916 Rising* (Dublin: Helicon, 1966; rev. edn, London: Sidgwick & Jackson, 1970). It is not clear where Dr Ó Broin acquired his copy of the manuscript.

14. These papers, which richly deserve a study on their own account, are in TNA, CO 904/25/2.
15. Michael Collins also spent some time on the top floor of the building (Hart, *Mick*, pp. 93-4).
16. *The Times*, 3 Jan. 1939.
17. First published, respectively, in 1900, 1901 and 1931.
18. *The Times*, 9 Jan. 1939.
19. Nevil Shute, *Slide Rule: Autobiography of an Engineer* (London: Heinemann, 1954), pp. 7, 13.
20. R. B. McDowell, *The Irish Administration* (London: Routledge & Kegan Paul, 1964), pp. 86-7.
21. Maurice Headlam, *Irish Reminiscences* (London: Robert Hale, 1947), p. 63.
22. See Bernard Wasserstein, *Herbert Samuel* (Oxford: Oxford University Press, 1992), pp. 129–46.
23. Statement read by Mr A. H. Norway, 25 May 1916, *Royal Commission on the Rebellion in Ireland: Minutes of Evidence*, p. 61 [Cd. 8311] H. C. 1916, xi, 246.
24. See Lawrence W. McBride, *The Greening of Dublin Castle: The Transformation of Bureaucratic and Judicial Personnel in Ireland, 1892–1922* (Washington D.C.: Catholic University of America Press, 1991).
25. Ó Broin, *Dublin Castle*, pp. 14-15.
26. 10 Aug. 1912 (quoted in McBride, *Greening of Dublin Castle*, p. 164).
27. 16 Aug. 1912, Healy to Maurice Healy (T. M. Healy, *Letters and Leaders of My Day* (London: Thornton Butterworth, 2 vols, 1928), vol. ii, p. 508).
28. Hobhouse to Sir Matthew Nathan, *c.* Feb. 1915 (quoted in Ó Broin, *Dublin Castle*, p. 48).
29. Norway to Nathan, 30 Sept. 1914 (ibid., p. 13).
30. Healy, *Letters and Leaders of My Day*, ii, p. 508.
31. James Stephens, *The Insurrection in Dublin* (Dublin: Maunsel, 1916).
32. *Letters from Dublin, Easter 1916: Alfred Fannin's Diary of the Rising*, ed. Adrian & Sally Warwick-Haller (Dublin: Irish Academic Press, 1995). Mrs Norway's account also illuminates the particular difficulties faced by Dublin hotels and their residents during the Rising. See also Elizabeth Bowen, *The Shelbourne* (London: Harrap, 1951), pp. 151–62.
33. *Times Literary Supplement*, 10 Aug. 1916, p. 375.
34. Stephens, *Insurrection in Dublin*, p. 21. For rumours see also *Letters from Dublin*, pp. 24-5, 42–3.
35. See below p. 85.
36. Ibid., p. 80
37. Max Caulfield, *The Easter Rebellion* (Boulder, Col.: Roberts Reinhart, rev.

edn, 1995), pp. 153-4, 166-7.

38. See Stephens, *Insurrection in Dublin*, pp. 60–1; *Letters from Dublin*, p. 32.

39. See below pp. 93–4.

40. Caulfield, *The Easter Rebellion*, pp. 348, 351.

41. Lord Craigmyle, *Letters to Isabel* (London: Nicholson & Watson, new edn, 1936), pp. 286-90. Lord Macmillan's entry on Craigmyle in the *Dictionary of National Biography 1931–1940* warns that 'so far as it purports to narrate facts and to convey impressions', Craigmyle's memoir ' must be read with considerable reservations'. I am grateful to Professor Alan Bairner, of Dunfirmline and formerly the University of Ulster at Jordanstown, for drawing my attention to this work.

42. Shute, *Slide Rule*, pp. 23-4.

43. He was a pupil at Shrewsbury School in England.

44. Shute, *Slide Rule*, pp. 25-7.

45. London: William Heinemann. Quotations below are taken from the first Australian edition (Melbourne: Heinemann, 1956).

46. 25 May 1956, p. 309.

47. Constance Markievicz in fact was spared execution apparently after pleading with the court-martial on the grounds of being a female (Leon Ó Broin, *W. E. Wylie and the Irish Revolution* (Dublin: Gill & Macmillan, 1989), p. 27).

48. Shute, *Beyond the Black Stump*, p. 81.

49. Ibid., pp. 119, 199.

50. See typescript of *Beyond the Black Stump* and accompanying correspondence (National Library of Australia, Papers of Nevil Shute Norway (MS 2199), series 2, folder 17).

51. Notes by Shute (ibid.).

52. Shute, *Beyond the Black Stump*, p. 200.

53. *Irish Independent*, 2 June 1956.

54. See below p. 90.

55. Christine Casey, *Dublin* (*Buildings of Ireland* series) (London: Yale University Press, 2005), pp. 147-9. The account of the GPO improvements is drawn from a two-part article, 'The General Post Office, Dublin, and the Dublin Greco-Roman period', in *The Irish Builder and Engineer*, vol. 58 nos 7 and 8 (25 Mar. and 8 Apr. 1916), pp. 134-6, and 170–2.

56. 'Neglected morals of the Irish rising', *New Statesman*, 6 May 1916 (quoted in Bernard Shaw, *The Matter with Ireland*, ed. David H. Green and Dan H. Laurence (London: Hart-Davis, 1962), pp. 106-7).

57. Office of Public Works, *Building for Government: The Architecture of State Buildings. OPW: Ireland 1900–2000* (Dublin: Town House and Country House, 1999), pp. 51–3.

2 *The Occupation of the GPO*

In Britain, the first sign that something was wrong in Ireland was when, as the Post Office file of records dealing with the Rising put it, 'all communication with Dublin – telegraph & telephone – ceased at 12.45 p.m.'[1] In this archive file is a series of dramatic messages, reproduced below, which haphazardly describe the extraordinary events during the afternoon of 24 April and vividly communicate the shock and confusion of the day.

First of all is a telegram from 'Nevin', the Post Office Telegraph relay station in North Wales where the GPO lines from Ireland came ashore,[2] received in London at 1.33 p.m. saying:

```
DN [Dublin] informs NV [Nevin] that
Volunteers have taken possession of
Telegraph Office at DN and all links
stopped in consequence.
```

At 2.30 p.m. a telegram came from Amiens Street station, the terminus of the Great Northern line from Belfast (now Connolly Station), sent by Mr Gomersall, head of the Post Office Engineer's Department:

```
To Secretary GPO London
GPO Dublin taken possession of today at
noon by Sinn Féiners. Sorting Office and
instrument room wrecked. Some railway
stations also held.
```

One of the significant things about this message is how it shows that from the very start the Rising was characterised as led by Sinn Féin, which was not in fact the case, but which afterwards powerfully boosted Sinn Féin's public profile in Ireland.

Then, there was the first telephone message. In the Post Office archives is a pencil-written record of a telephone call at 2.50 p.m. from Samuel Guthrie in Dublin. Imagine the scene. Guthrie (as can be followed in his own account in Chapter 5) had been thrown out of his office by armed men, who had occupied the GPO, smashing windows and barricading doors. There was sporadic gunfire, here and at other places across the city. Guthrie and his colleagues stood about for a bit, no doubt wondering what to do, but eventually they walked (maybe they ran) the half mile or so up Talbot Street to the nearest main railway station. There he and other engineers hurriedly set up telegraph communications and sorted out an emergency telephone line to London, where he got through to the superintendent on duty in the Central Telegraph Office, Mr H. T. Phillips. Phillips (we presume) scribbled down Guthrie's astounding message, reaching him over what must have been a crackly, uncertain, long-distance telephone line:

> I am speaking from Amiens St Rl. The GPO has been taken possession of by the Irish Volunteers who have turned out everyone.
>
> I am afraid they are bent on demolishing the inst[rument] room. I tell you in case you may have wondered why you cd not get DN. Will you please advise Secretary & anyone else that it may concern & also advise any Irish Stns [?you] may be right to. Yes I will take Govt work & will do best to deliver it. *The streets are not safe.*[3]

This is real history. Here we have Guthrie's voice speaking to us through a fragment of paper locked up in an archive for nearly ninety years.

The possibility that this might be some sort of hoax appears to have occurred to Phillips who, according to notes in the file 'endeavoured to satisfy himself that Mr Guthrie is the person telegraphing from Amiens Street'. Having confirmed Gurthie's identity, Phillips informed the War Office and the Admiralty of the happenings in Dublin. For the rest of the afternoon the engineers in Ireland worked to restore full communications (as described in their accounts in Chapter 5) and make contact with Arthur Norway, head of the Irish Post Office, as well as the civil and military authorities in Ireland. At 4.15 there was a further message 'from Mr Guthrie':

> I have been trying to reach Mr Norway at
> his town residence, but he was not in.
> They told me he is in the Dublin Castle.
> That being so he is not to be reached as
> the Castle is under siege.
>   Westland Row [Station; now Pearse
> Station] is also in the hands of
> Volunteers.

By the early evening, however, both the Castle and Army Headquarters had been patched into effective communication with London, as is demonstrated by two official cables which have survived in the archives. The first was from Sir Mathew Nathan, the Under-Secretary in the Irish Office, and the most senior civil servant in Ireland.

Headquarters Dublin Irish Office to Birrell, London 6.11 p.m.

> Insurrection broke out noon today in
> Dublin when attack made on Castle but not
> pressed home. Since then large hostile
> parties have occupied Stephen's Green, and
> various parties have held up troops
> marching from barracks firing on them from
> houses. City Hall, Post Office, Four
> Courts, Westland Row Station occupied by
> Sinn Féiners, some Railway Bridges blown
> up and telegraph communication completely
> interrupted. Have information of two
> policemen, one military officer and half
> dozen soldiers killed but casualties may
> be much more numerous.

```
Situation at present not satisfactory but
understand troops now beginning arrive
from Curragh.
```

The second cable is from 'Commandeth Dublin', the telegraphic address of the army high command and it was noted that the message had been 'telephoned from Dublin Castle to a local police station & was sent thence by hand to Amiens Street for London'.

Commandeth Dublin to General Headquarters Home Forces, Horse Guards London 8.58 p.m.

```
Insurgents occupy Municipal buildings in
Parliament Street, Harcourt Street and
Westland Row stations also General Post
Office and are entrenched in Stephens
Green and occupy many scattered corner
houses throughout Dublin. We occupy
Castle, Kingsbridge [Heuston Station],
North Wall, Electric Power Station,
Telephone Exchange and other places and
have recovered Magazine. About 1600 troops
have arrived from Curragh and more are
coming, also four 18 pounder guns from
Athlone. Number of insurgents unknown.
They did not arrive in large formed bodies
but some may have come in Easter traffic.
There has been some looting but
information is scanty owing to interrupted
communications. Casualties reported up to
present under fifty.
```

Despite the rather circuitous routing of this message, the significant fact is that it got through at all, and it is clear that the authorities owed much to the GPO personnel on the ground for restoring and securing communications with Britain. A combination of weakness on the rebel side (in part because of the

confusion over the mobilisation there were simply not enough
Volunteers to go round), and resourcefulness on the part of the
Post Office engineers (along with a good helping of luck), meant
that government communications were not crippled as might
have been hoped, and the Post Office men were able to exploit
the rudiments of a cable link and relatively quickly get wires up
and running. And it is to their side, and what might be called the
'view from the Post Office', we now turn, looking first at the
memoir and contemporary reports of Arthur Hamilton Norway.

Notes

1. BPMA, POST 56/177.
2. Nefyn, on the Lleyn peninsula south-west of Caernarvon.
3. Emphasis added.

3 The Secretary's Tales

Arthur Norway, the Secretary of the Irish Post Office, wrote a number of accounts of the circumstances and events of the Easter Rising, which are all reproduced in this chapter. The first one, 'Irish experiences in war', was the last of these documents to be written. We are not sure when this was, but Norway (who died in 1938) says in the text that 'more than ten years' had passed since 1916. He did not write it for publication, but just 'for the information of my family'. The text below is taken from a photocopy in the papers of Dr Leon Ó Broin in the National Library of Ireland.[1] The document consists of twenty-nine typescript pages and may be incomplete. It ends abruptly at the end of a page, although with a complete sentence. It is presented first in this chapter because Norway sketches in the background to the Rising as he saw it, together with his time as head of the Irish Post Office from September 1912. One advantage of the memoir being written only for private consumption is that Norway is quite frank in his opinions of the men at the top level of the Irish administration. The Viceroy, Lord Aberdeen, was 'a kindly and well meaning man, but dull'; the Chief Secretary, Augustine Birrell, 'a shrewd literary critic, but a negligent and undiscerning politician'; and the Under-Secretary, Sir James Dougherty, 'a man of supine temperament'. Norway was certainly writing with the benefit of hindsight, but his opinions have a refreshing edge to them, and are certainly reflected (though naturally in a less unguarded manner) in his wife's more contemporary observations, which will be found in Chapter 4. Both Norway and his wife, for example, agreed that the government's complacent and permissive attitude towards both Nationalist and Unionist 'sedition' threatened what he called 'forgetfulness of public duty' within his own department, and amounted to a broader abdication of political responsibility on the part of the Irish administration.

The last third or so of 'Irish experiences in war' deals with the events of Easter Monday and after. This text can be compared to Norway's two letters to his Post Office superiors in London, written during Easter Week itself, which include some personal narrative and are reproduced below.

Frustratingly, however, in his letter of Thursday 27 April, Norway deliberately confined himself only to describing matters 'which directly concern the Post Office'. Nevertheless, there are one or two racy anecdotes, and the perilous atmosphere of danger throughout the city – amply confirming Samuel Guthrie's '*The streets are not safe*' in that first telephone conversation – runs through the letters and Norway's own experience of the first two days of the Rising.

The final document in the chapter is Norway's report of June 1916 which describes how the Post Office coped with the loss of the GPO and the main telegraph office. It confirms the importance of the Central Telephone Exchange for the early maintenance of official communications, and describes the strenuous efforts Norway and his staff made to restore other services, such as postal deliveries and the payment of pensions. There is one noteworthy contrast between this report, which commends the devotion of Post Office employees to the maintenance of Post Office work, and Norway's discussion about the political loyalties of his staff in 'Irish experiences in war'. Here he recounts the worries he had about the political pressures some of his 17,000 staff came under – from both Unionist and Nationalist militants. He was concerned, on the one hand, that the military authorities rather too readily condemned potential subversives, and, on the other, that the Dublin Castle authorities refused to take seriously the possibility that there might be any dangerous disaffection among Irish civil servants.

The sensitivities of the situation are illustrated by the fact that Norway felt unable to discuss the matter of extremist political opinion inside the Post Office with his second-in-command, James MacMahon, who was 'deeply involved in Nationalist politics'. During the Rising MacMahon was confined to his bed having suffered a heart attack, and in his letter of 27 April (reproduced below) Norway said that 'otherwise his help would have been invaluable', yet, afterwards in his 22 June report, Norway praised MacMahon (though in rather unspecific terms) for having done 'much useful & valuable work'. MacMahon, in fact, succeeded Norway as head of the Irish Post Office in 1916, and became Under Secretary at the Irish Office in 1918. Here the deteriorating political situation, MacMahon's own nationalist sympathies, and a rather ineffectual personality combined to vitiate any positive contribution he might have been able to make to the better government of Ireland. While 'not devoid of brains', reported a senior English bureaucrat in 1920, MacMahon lacked 'initiative, force and driving power'.[2]

Irish Experiences in War
Arthur Hamilton Norway

It was suggested to me lately, by Sir Andrew Wingate,[3] that a certain public importance attaches to my experiences in Ireland as Secretary of the Post Office in that country, and that they are worth recording, not indeed as possessing consequence at all equal to that of the great and dangerous crises in which England was involved on the Continent of Europe, but rather as illustrating certain tendencies of Government which have, in other generations as well as ours, proved a weakness to our country, and permitted the growth of evils which might have been eradicated if recognised and faced at an early stage.

I have accepted this suggestion half unwillingly, because a doubt obtrudes itself whether I can tell the tale even now that more than ten years have passed, and I am far withdrawn from active life, without some strong feeling which might be inconsistent with the honest tradition of loyalty to their political heads in which British Civil Servants are trained and which becomes the habit of their life. But I do not write for publication. I have kept silence for many years, and if I break it now, it is only in my study, and for the information of my family, and especially of any coming after me who may care to ask themselves what I did in difficult circumstances. They are entitled to this knowledge, if they desire it. And if not, it is but to leave these pages unread or to put them in the fire.

In the year 1912 I was one of the Assistant Secretaries of the Post Office, having then spent rather less than thirty years on the highest grade of the Civil Service; and the Irish appointment was not one lying in my direct way. In fact, it was of rather lower standing, and of the same pay, namely £1200 per annum, so that it could not be offered to me as a promotion. But my dear wife had been subjected to a severe operation, and had recently lost her mother, to whom she was deeply attached; so that I welcomed for her the opportunity of a change of scene. My son Fred, moreover, had had grave ill health at Rugby, and for him too I thought the change to Ireland would be advantageous. So I sought the appointment, and it could scarcely be refused to me, since my standing and influence in the service were high, and would have justified me in seeking any change of work which could be given to me reasonably. And so, after I had put aside various suggestions that I was imperilling my chances of the Second Secretaryship by going out of the line of promotion, the Postmaster General, Sir Herbert Samuel, appointed me, and I took up office in Dublin in September 1912.

The dominant question in Ireland at that time was Home Rule, and it may be well to say that the system of Government denoted by that phrase differed widely from the Dominion status which has now been conferred on Southern Ireland, since it proposed the creation of a purely subordinate legislature in Dublin, subject in all respects to the ultimate control of Parliament at Westminster, which could not only review all acts of the Irish Government, but could, if it thought right, reverse them, and give to the reversed statutes the force of law in Ireland. It is important to remember that this was the extreme length to which the Liberal Party, the only supporters of Home Rule in Great Britain, had ever proposed to go towards satisfying the insistent claims of Irish Nationalists. The idea of conceding Dominion status, or in any other way releasing the acts of an Irish Legislature from British control, was not part of the policy of any British party, and was indeed repudiated by all politicians of responsibility. I was myself a liberal of the imperialist school led by Lord Rosebery, and Sir Edward Grey; and relying on the maintenance of British control, I did not see real danger to the welfare of the British Empire in the concession of Home Rule of the type proposed.

Such however as it was, the proposal was resented fiercely by Conservatives in Great Britain and Ireland, and excited small enthusiasm among Irish Nationalists, who accepted it with the avowed intention of using it to gain more. When I reached Ireland, society was divided very sharply, and little intercourse existed between those who supported Home Rule and those who opposed it, the former indeed having few, if any, representatives above the salt socially, while bitterness between the two was so great that almost the first piece of advice given to me was in no case to engage a parlour maid who was a Roman Catholic, since any talk which touched on politics at the dinner table would be reported to the priests. That this belief was not groundless was demonstrated a little later when a heedless letter from a guest, containing some sharp strictures on Nationalist Roman Catholics, and left carelessly by me upon the desk in my study, was stolen by a cook dismissed for insolence, who quoted some of its phrases in a last interview with my wife, and who did in all probability endeavour to stir up mischief by using it in some of those subterranean ways which are common enough in Ireland. No mischief resulted, however, and we were always on good terms with the priests and nuns in our neighbourhood, as well, of course, as with our own Church.

Lord Aberdeen was Viceroy when I took up duty, a kindly and well meaning man, but dull, and by no means strong enough to deal with the difficult situation which was even then growing up. The Chief Secretary was Mr. Birrell, a shrewd literary critic, but a negligent and undiscerning politician, who did not occupy his Lodge in the Phoenix Park, and visited Ireland rarely. The Under Secretary, whose duty it was to know the country accurately, and to probe its movements deeply, was Sir James Dougherty, a man of supine temperament and narrow, if capable, ideas, to whom one would not look for quick and resolute action on the sudden appearance of a public danger. The Inspector General of the Royal Irish Constabulary was Sir Neville Chamberlain, a distinguished soldier and perhaps alive to the growth of trouble which he did not check. The head of the Dublin Metropolitan Police, an unarmed force, was Sir John Ross of Bladensburg, of whom I think with constant admiration as a fine and resolute man, completely loyal to his subordinates at a time of grave difficulty, of which I will say more later. All these, with the certain exception of the last, were dominated by the strong conviction held by Mr. Birrell, and adopted as a principle of action by the Ministry, that Ireland must be governed according to Irish ideas, by which doctrine they understood that all strong action must be foregone, and everything avoided which might conceivably create friction.

Now the truth about the Irish is that they appreciate strength, despise weakness, and desire to be governed firmly and justly. But this was never known at Westminster, and any efforts to assert it were turned down contemptuously. It was indeed a chief difficulty of the situation that Irish disloyalty was not taken seriously in London, where it was usual to speak of it with contempt as displaying the characteristics of comic opera. It is certainly strange that administrators who well remembered the Phoenix Park murders, and innumerable other crimes committed in the eighties, should have subsided to the easy optimism which had spread through all departments of the Government when I reached Ireland. Everyone believed that the point was off the Irish pikes, and the gunmen had forgotten how to shoot. This was partly true. But it was also true that dangerous men and organisations were stirring in their sleep, while those who should have watched them played golf and dined in peace.

Within a few days of reaching Dublin I called on Sir James Dougherty, the Under Secretary, at the Castle, and naturally asked him about the state of the country. He expressed no anxiety nor did he indicate any source of difficulty likely to present itself to me. He told me, however, that the term Sinn Féin denoted every shade of Nationalism, from innocent enthusiasts for Gaelic literature and Gaelic sports at one end to red-hot Fenians at the other; so that to call a man a Sinn Féiner established nothing about him, until one knew to which section of Sinn Féin he belonged. There was truth in this, as I found later. But it would have been expressed more accurately by saying that the Sinn Féin movement, innocent enough at the outset, had been adopted by dangerous men as a screen, much as they used the Gaelic Athletic Association somewhat later, or perhaps even then, making use of the organisation of both Societies to cloak their meetings, and professing, if questions arose, the simplest enthusiasm for Gaelic sport and literature. I do not know whether Sir James Dougherty suspected this. He certainly gave me no hint of it. I discovered the fact independently of him, and before dropping the point I may say that before the rebellion broke out the dangerous elements in Sinn Féin, no less that in the Gaelic Athletic Association, had eaten up the rest, and the whole of both was to be taken seriously, though wise men need not have feared them. This rather clever policy of screening was, I think, new in Ireland, and to some extent may excuse the singular failure to recognise the approach of danger.

It is scarcely worth while to speak of the attitude of Lord Aberdeen, for I can recall no observation of value which he ever made to me on the condition of the country, or any other matter. In all quarters I found the same light complacency. The country was quiet. Why should it not remain so? But ere long I began to get an occasional police report indicating that a member of my staff was suspected of belonging to the Irish Republican Brotherhood, of which I had not heard before. In my office there was none who could, or would, tell me the nature of the Brotherhood. So I pursued enquiries in the Sackville Street Club, of which I was a member, but at first with no better success, for men seemed disinclined to talk of the matter. At last I asked a Resident Magistrate, one O'Sullivan, whether he knew anything of the Brotherhood. He looked startled, and answered, 'Not now. Formerly of course I did.' 'And what was it, when you knew it?' I continued. 'A black murder Society,' he rapped out, 'and never anything else.' 'Does it exist now?' I went on. 'I hope to God it doesn't,' he replied. 'You would be alarmed?' 'Very much indeed,' he said. And the conversation ended with a promise that he would satisfy himself about the existence of the Brotherhood in his own district, and tell me the result on his next visit to Dublin.

A fortnight later he came up to me in the smoking room, and assured me that he found no trace of it in his neighbourhood. I told him of my police reports, and he became grave, and warned me that the reports were probably indications of coming trouble.

I was sufficiently impressed by this to resolve to satisfy myself whether all the police reports affecting my staff reached me, and on enquiry at the Castle I found that they did not. I saw Sir Neville Chamberlain and Sir John Ross, and with little difficulty arranged that every report affecting in any way a Post Office servant was to be sent to me confidentially. I received them and studied them carefully, drawing conclusions which might have been of use had I succeeded in gaining attention for them. But preconceived ideas were rooted too strongly to admit the recognition of fresh facts by the Irish Govt., or by the Postmaster General.

While this study occupied many weeks, during which I collected as much information as I could about tendencies shaping themselves in the country, difficulty began to present itself for me at Post Offices in the North, where a growing opposition to Home Rule among the people, loyalist as they claimed to be, threatened forgetfulness of public duty no less than in the rest of Ireland. It was evident, of course, that with politics, as such, I, the head of the Post Office, had nothing to do. My duty was to secure that the staff of the Post Office did their work efficiently and impartially, and I began to see that I should have trouble in effecting this, trouble too of a kind for which neither my experience, nor that of any other high officer of the Post Office had any precedent, for sedition in England is too rare to be regarded seriously. There was however beginning to emerge, both North and South, a conviction that loyalty to political ends must override all other loyalties, and among the rest of course loyalty to the Postmaster General. Now this would be serious at any time. But the administrative problem which it threatened to raise was increased enormously by the consideration that the latter loyalty might become ere long of vital consequence to the safety of the Empire. For Army headquarters was uneasy about risks of invasion long before August 1914, and a year before that the danger of war sent important officers to my room with maps to explain in confidence what line would be held if the danger broke. Clearly, all operations would be imperilled if there were not full confidence in the secrecy and honour of the Post Office staff. The same considerations applied of course to any outbreak of rebellion on either side. My problem began to grow acute.

Naturally, I consulted my Chiefs in London, but had in answer only a request for any practicable suggestion. I had but one, of the effectiveness of which I was not sure, but which seemed worth trying. It was to contradict by a public warning to the staff the growing idea, sedulously propagated by both sides, that their duty as Post Office servants might be subordinated to their political action. I drafted a short notice to this effect, and proposed to put it up in all offices, arguing that not only would it serve to remind men and women of their duty, but it would put a useful answer in the hands of weaklings who were puzzled by specious balancings of two loyalties, and who could point to the notice and say, 'No. There is what my employer expects of me.' I still think this notice might have done much to save the situation, for most men and women are honest at heart, and will respond to a clear call. But the call was not given, for the Postmaster General thought the notice provocative, and others in London condemned it as unnecessary. None of them indicated any other step which could be taken, and the situation continued to drift.

In fact the problem of how to keep the growing sedition out of the Irish Post Offices, and secure or maintain the safety of the communications, did not seem in London to be a problem at all, for none there regarded the peace of the country as seriously threatened. I had myself no certain conviction on the subject, materials for judgment being scanty and not always reliable. But I was uneasy, and in particular I wanted more information about the Irish Republican Brotherhood The only chance of obtaining any was through the Irish Government and to Dublin Castle accordingly I went. I told the Under Secretary that I heard disquieting things about the Brotherhood, and referred in particular to the police reports. A memorandum was obtained from the secret Intelligence Department, and sent on to me. It was to the effect that the Brotherhood had been troublesome in former days, but had subsided much in consequence, and might be regarded as dormant, and in fact negligible, comprising in its membership perhaps a thousand persons in all parts of Ireland. Nothing was said about the aims of the organisation, nor any warning given of its dangerous character. I did not see that I could do more. I locked the memorandum in my safe. This was some months before the war. The exact date I forget.

I am not writing history in detail, and I need only say that as the outbreak of war approached the Ulster Unionists drew closer towards armed rebellion, and their unpunished creation of an armed force was imitated most unhappily by the institution of the Irish Volunteers on the Nationalist side. Stories of gun running were rife, and at last in July a cargo of rifles was landed at Howth, and brought by road towards Dublin. Nothing was known, of course, at the Castle almost at the moment of landing. Quick and resolute action was needed to prevent the rifles from reaching Dublin. The Under Secretary was, I think, in England. The Lord Chancellor hesitated and lost time. Mr. Harrell, second in command to Sir John Ross at the Dublin Metropolitan police, and son of a former Under Secretary, summoned a company of the K.O.B.[4] from the Barracks, acting largely on his own responsibility. The act cost him dear. He got the rifles. But in return to Dublin the soldiers were mobbed by an ugly crowd, and stone throwing began, not without injury to the soldiers, who fired on the crowd, killing and wounding several. The panic was terrible, and the city filled itself with a fierce anger which did much to increase the danger of the situation. Politicians, both Nationalist and Liberal, whipped up the indignation. The fatal word 'provocative' was applied to Mr. Harrell's resolute action, even by those whose experience should have shown them the acute risk of allowing the rifles to reach an already excited city. A Commission presided over by Lord Shaw of Dunfermline was appointed to investigate the occurrences of that unhappy morning, and to placate Irish opinion, which was done by dismissing Mr. Harrell, notwithstanding the firm support of Sir John Ross, his chief, support which he renewed with great courage before Lord Hardinge's Commission,[5] which investigated the outbreak of the rebellion, and of which I shall speak later.

It could not be supposed that the passions on which these and other grave incidents were the indication or the cause would fail to sap the loyalty of some of the 17,000 men and women under my authority at Irish Post Offices. My anxieties for the safety of the communications in my charge were not relieved by the fact that none in London shared them. I could not but wonder at times whether the easy confidence shown across the Channel were not the wiser attitude, and the consequent distrust of my own judgment did not make my position easier, though I do not see that it led me to omit any possible precaution. There was none with whom I could take counsel in Ireland, for all were extreme on one side or the other, so fiercely passionate in denouncing the motives and acts of those who disagreed with them that consultation darkened counsel, and I was driven back on my own imperfect opportunities of deducing the truth. There were those in Dublin who were fond of saying, – the 'Irish Times' was among them – that the Post Office was full of Sinn Féiners, and that no steps were taken to discourage their activities. But of these critics none even once approached me with their evidence. Nor do I even now see that facts were in my possession at that time which would have justified me in holding that membership of Sinn Féin created a danger to the State, or rendered an officer less competent to serve the Postmaster General efficiently. Certainly, neither of these points was ever urged by the Irish Government, in whose custody, and not in mine, lay the safety of the country.

While I was groping for a clear conception of my duty in this maze of uncertainties, the war broke, like a blaze of light, bringing out in sharp relief every risk which had occurred to me; and others which had not, all suddenly turned vital, and invested with reality. I had gone to London, after much hesitation, to attend a large farewell dinner to my old friend, Sir Alexander King, who was resigning the Secretaryship of the Post Office. I had scarcely reached London when the storm broke, and the precautionary stage was declared. I went at once to the Postmaster General, Mr. Charles Hobhouse, who while agreeing that my presence was needed at my office, insisted that I should stay for the dinner. I did, and sat next to Sir Matthew Nathan, with whom, as Secretary of the Post Office, my relations had not been free from friction.[6] We met that night with cordiality, and he told me that he was to be the new Under Secretary in Dublin. He was a man of charming manners, to dine with whom was a very agreeable experience, since he was a courteous and polished host and had the instinct for entertaining. But he was not discerning, nor resolute. 'What is the use,' he said to me once, 'of contending against the stream of tendency?' 'That is fatalism,' I said. 'No,' he answered, 'it is good sense.' And his conception of loyalty was not to tell his political chief when he thought him wrong, but to help him in his policy without remonstrance, – wherein, I think, he acted rather as becomes a soldier than a Civil Servant occupying an important post.

It would be idle to attempt to recapture the impressions under which official life went on at the outset of the war. Embarkation was going on secretly and swiftly at many points in Ireland, and as it was of great importance that details of the units embarking should not leak out, the question what dependence could be placed on the Post Office staff leapt into the front, that is in Ireland, though in London the same easy confidence reigned unbroken. At Army headquarters in Dublin it did not. The first Post Office servant to fall under their ban was Hegarty, Postmaster of Queenstown, at which port many secret things were happening. A high officer called on me to say that Hegarty must not remain at Queenstown, or indeed in Ireland. I asked why, seeing that his official reputation was high and he held the complete confidence of Sir Andrew Ogilvie,[7] and other old colleagues of mine in the Secretariat, where he had worked for years before going to Queenstown. The answer was guarded, but explicit in this point, that Hegarty was known to have been in very recent communication with the German Ambassador. This was not all, for much suspicion rested on him. But relations of any sort with the German Ambassador at that moment served to show unsuitability for control of the Queenstown Office in war; and after receiving my assurance that I would act at once, the officer left me, remarking casually that in war time proved traitors were shot.

I found great difficulty about this case in London where Ogilvie, and others acquainted with Hegarty, were most indig-nant that any one could doubt his loyalty, and fought stoutly against my reports. But I carried my point. Hegarty was transferred at once to the Postmastership of Whitchurch in Shropshire, where he remained throughout the war, giving rise to no further official trouble. But I may say, if only to show how baseless was the confidence felt in him by Ogilvie and others, and how just the unproved suspicions of the military Intelligence, that Hegarty has now written a book, in which he reveals that fact that even when he was earning golden opinions in the Secretariat he was already not only a secret member of the Irish Republican Brotherhood, but one of its chief directors, & that he continued to direct it actively from Whitchurch. Of this I had not the least inkling.

The moment was so critical, and the military judgment so clear, that the case of Hegarty caused me little trouble. It was otherwise with the next which occurred almost simultaneously. The towns in Ireland were placarded with recruiting posters, and a sorter in the Waterford Post Office was arrested by soldiers in the act of tearing down one of these. The evidence was clear, and the disloyalty of the act especially disgraceful in a servant of the State. How the military authorities would have dealt with the prisoner I do not know. For he had scarcely been arrested when one Michael Murphy, Nationalist member for Tramore, went to General Friend, Commander in Chief in Ireland, and threatened him that if the man was punished recruiting in Waterford would stop at once. General Friend yielded, and released the man. At once he claimed to resume duty, and that was where I came in. For it was obvious that the man was disloyal, and that his restoration to duty unpunished would be of the worst example to the staff, some of whom were wavering, both at Waterford and elsewhere. I went to Army headquarters, where I was assured that the General regretted already that he had released the man, that he saw the danger of restoring him to duty,. and wished that I could do any thing to keep him out. He could not, however, arrest the man again. I thereupon went to the Castle, where I saw Sir Matthew Nathan, and suggested to him that he, as head of the permanent staff of the Irish Government, could, under the Defence of the Realm Act, keep this disloyal man out of any Irish Post Office. He did not dispute that he could do so, but refused, on the mere ground that General Friend had released the man. I then, having failed to move the military or the Civil authority in Ireland, reported to the Postmaster General my anxieties about the staff, contending that as a purely postal question, within his sole responsibility, it was undesirable to replace this man on duty. Apparently, my fears were considered, for I had no decision for three weeks, after which I was instructed to replace the man on duty, paying his wages for the whole period of his absence. I fear this case did not go unnoted.

About this time I noted in the police reports more frequent references than before to the I.R.B., which seemed to be more widely active than before; and desiring to know whether the Castle was aware of any growth of this evil organisation, I asked for another memorandum. This was obtained, and was to the effect that the I.R.B. was not quite so dormant, nor quite so insignificant in numbers, as at the date of the former memorandum. But is might still be regarded as unimportant and giving rise to no anxiety. Such was the last advice, which I received from the Irish Government on this grave matter. And as a comment on it, I transcribe here a few clauses from the proclamation of the Irish Republic posted in Dublin at the outbreak scarce a year later.

'Irishmen and Irishwomen. In the name of God and of the dead generations from which she receives her old tradition of Nationhood, Ireland, through us, summons her children to her flag, and strikes for her freedom.

Having organised and trained her manhood through her secret revolutionary organisation, the Irish Republican Brotherhood...and supported by gallant Allies in Europe, but relying in the first on her own strength, she strikes in full confidence of victory.'

Thus, the I.R.B. was at the heart of the matter, and the complacent assurances of the Castle were fatally wrong. A determined effort to stamp out this dangerous body, versed as it has always been in murder and intrigue, might have cost many lives but would have freed Ireland from a terror whence no good thing can come, and saved the British Government from a failure more disgraceful than can easily be found in its great history.

Nothing known to me, or I think to others, at the time suggested the great part of the Brotherhood on the conspiracy. But it was clear enough that some organisation was using terror as a weapon, and in illustration of this I may note the case of another Hegarty, brother of the Postmaster of Queenstown, who was a sorter in the Cork Post Office, but fell under the ban of the active military Intelligence, who applied to me for his removal form Cork. The evidence pointed clearly enough to association with dangerous and disloyal men, but established no fact which could be said to justify punishment. Thus the case could only be met by transfer to an equivalent position out of Ireland, and I notified to Hegarty that he must go and work in England for a time, retaining his pay, and receiving in addition a subsistence allowance of a guinea a week. He protested. 'For what am I being punished?' he asked. 'You are not being punished,' I replied. 'But of what am I suspected?' 'No charge is made against you,' I said: 'but the Postmaster General decides in his discretion, as your employer, to employ you out of Ireland for the present.' 'Then' said he, 'I refuse to leave Ireland.' 'In that case you will be dismissed,' I answered. 'And why? What have I done to deserve dismissal? I am entitled to know my offence.' 'I have told you,' I said, 'that no offence is charged against you now. If you refuse to obey orders, you will be dismissed, but for disobedience.' He did refuse, and he was dismissed for disobedience.

Some weeks later – I forget how many – , he was arrested on the double charge of having in his possession a quantity of dynamite, presumably for unlawful purposes, and a large amount of violently seditious literature. He was arrested in bed, the dynamite and the pamphlets were in his bedroom. He was brought to trial first on the charge of possessing dynamite, and was defended by Tim Healy, afterwards Governor General. Healy pressed with great ingenuity the point that no evidence existed to show what Hegarty meant to do with the dynamite, and so impressed the jury that they acquitted him. As he left the Court, the Crown arrested him on the seditious literature charge. Again he was defended by Healy, who this time induced the jury to disagree. A third trial followed, with the same counsel, and on that occasion Healy, or some other power, was even more successful, for Hegarty was acquitted, and the prosecutions ended. The next morning, as I was walking down to my Office, I met Sir Neville Chamberlain walking up towards the Castle. I stopped him, and said, 'Have you heard that Hegarty is acquitted?' 'No, how did that happen', he said, 'I thought the evidence so clear.' 'It was,' I said, 'but the point is this, – not the diabolical cleverness of Healy, but the fact that the acquittal was by a mixed jury, five Protestants, I believe, and seven Catholics.' 'It is odd that a mixed jury should acquit,' he said; 'they were more likely to disagree.' 'Yes,' I answered, 'One would say that in agreeing to acquit they must have been under the influence of some strong motive.' 'Such as what?' he asked, though I think he knew well enough. 'Why, only two would be strong enough,' I answered, 'bribery and fear.' 'Fear, then,' answered Chamberlain, dropping his voice, 'but of what?' 'The I.R.B.' I answered, and we went each his way. This was the first occasion on which, at this fresh crisis of Irish affairs, I had cause to suspect the use of terror as a political resource. But of course terror was no new thing in Ireland.

It would have been hard to miss the significance of cases such as these, even if the public risks which they suggested had not been present to my mind already. My difficulty was how to form an idea of the extent to which my large staff had yielded to disloyalty. To show alarm, or doubt, seemed likely to increase the mischief. Intentional treachery is rare. Most men and women are honest to their duty, once undertaken. But some were not. How was I to discover them? Police and Army reports gave me my only basis of fact, and even those had to be used with caution, since they were often uncertain in tone and judgment, so that they supplied rather starting points for enquiry than definite conclusions, and to take their implications as proved would have been unjust. Army Intelligence was shrewd, as I have shown, but not immune from hasty suspicion. I felt my duty was double, – first to secure the public interest, but next, and not less, to protect my staff from punishment due to unjust suspicion. To strike at the guilty, and strike hard, was the one chance of holding my staff steady. To strike at the loyal in error would be fatal. But who was loyal, and who disloyal? It was vital to know.

I took the Police and Army reports, and classified them in three groups, labelling the first 'Dangerous', the second 'Potentially dangerous,' the third 'Probably negligible.' The first group was small, at no time containing more than a dozen names. These were selected from the reports, and comprised all members of the staff whom I found to be in more than casual communication with the small group of men in Dublin whom I knew to be dangerous plotters. These men were known in Dublin to all who cared to know of them, and I may say that all were shot after the rebellion among the group of sixteen rebels for whom there was no pardon. This fact shows that my principle of classification was not wrong, for men in frequent intercourse with rebels must be presumed to be in sympathy with them. But, granting the soundness of the principle, I was still far from being able to purge the Irish Post Office, for I had still to convince my chief and colleagues in London that there was danger in the situation, and this they refused resolutely to admit, telling me I had let myself be frightened by heady police officers and soldiers, and that no movement in Ireland need cause a moment's anxiety. Strong Unionists were as contemptuous as Liberals. All alike scouted the idea that Ireland could give serious trouble, and in this view my apprehensions and suggestions broke idly and spent themselves in vain.

My problem, in fact, was, as I said, no problem at all in the eyes of those at St Martin's le Grand,[8] who naturally accepted Mr. Birrell's optimism, and as there was no problem, it followed that no instructions were needed for my guidance. I saw this well enough. But it seemed right to make an effort to discover whether what I was doing was all that could be done, and accordingly I made a full copy of my classified list of suspects in the Post Office, and attached a covering memorandum setting forth the principles on which I framed it, and explaining in each case what I had done, and what discussions I had held with the Under Secretary, so as to assure myself that in all matters of importance the Irish Government and the Post Office were not at variance. I sent this up with a personal note asking whether it was regarded as a complete discharge of my duty in unfamiliar circumstances. No reply whatever reached me. I waited three months, during which the tension in Ireland increased, and then wrote again, asking once more to be told whether my action was approved, or whether there was anything else that I could do. This time a note from the Private Secretary reached me, saying the matter was under consideration, and I should hear further. But neither at that time, some three months before the rebellion, nor at any subsequent period, was I told whether I was right or wrong, and still less was any other course of action suggested to me. Nor, to this day, do I know what the Postmaster General thought, if he thought at all.

I do not think however that my labour was wasted. For the time was to come in which the reputation of the Post Office would have been deeply prejudiced, had I proved unable to clear it of the reproach of negligence in a vital matter. Even at the moment, and unable as I was to see what was approaching, I felt the advantage of having clarified my ideas by thorough study of the facts available to me. I was conscious of having done my best, and though I often wished for a confidant, I saw none, even in my own office, whom I could confide in. My second in command, James MacMahon, was deeply involved in Nationalist politics, the intimate friend of many Irish members, and in close relations with the Roman Catholic bishops. Priests, in fact, haunted his office, and I could not but feel that it was not to him that I ought to confide my anxieties at that critical time, when it was not safe to trust men freely. There were sound men among his subordinates, but I could not go past him to consult them, and so I kept my counsel. I do not now think that I was wrong.

Hampered as I was by indifference in London, I set myself steadily to use every occasion which presented itself of perfecting my list of suspects, and proceeding against any of those included in the dangerous class whose actions gave me the material. Cautious as they were, I got it sometimes. But hardly ever could I convince the Postmaster General of the desirability of action. In my memory there rises up the case of Cornelius Collins, a clerk in the Accountant's Office, known to be of extreme and dangerous views, but so clever that his tracks were always covered. At last the police reports gave me evidence not only that he was in frequent communication with men afterwards shot as rebel leaders, but that he had been present at a highly seditious meeting held in the south. One must remember that this was wartime, when sedition and treason are not far apart. I knew also that Collins was drawing into his net one after another of his colleagues who, but for him, would have run straight. The man in fact was dangerous, and I recommended that he be sent to London in an equivalent position, – a light recommendation, of which, on looking back, I scarcely approved. Probably I thought at the time that it would be useless to suggest sharper courses, and indeed I had always to remember that my one chance of getting anything done was to be studiously moderate.

Light as the discipline was, however, it was too heavy for the Postmaster General, who instructed me to warn Collins personally of the effect on his career of continuing his association with disloyal organisations. I did so, and Collins at once began to fence with me. 'What are these associations?' he asked indignantly. 'I specify none,' I answered, 'I warn you in terms which are quite general, and it is for you to interpret them, remembering that the warning is meant seriously, and that this is wartime.' 'But evidently,' he insisted, 'you mean that I must drop my connexion with the Gaelic Athletic Association. May I not take interest in Irish sport.' 'I did not mention the Gaelic Athletic Association,' I replied, 'I warned you in general terms.' 'But you meant that?' he went on. 'I do not intend to be more explicit,' I replied. He continued to press me, but with no result. This was a few weeks before the rebellion broke out. When it did, one of the first persons arrested was Cornelius Collins, who was caught in Kerry, endeavouring to join Sir Roger Casement, and who had in his possession incriminating papers relating to the Irish Republican Brotherhood. Evidently, he was near the heart of the movement. My recommendation that he be removed from Ireland erred in leniency, if at all, and the refusal to accept it was a grave error.

It was rather fortunate that I had by this time gained the trust and confidence of large sections of my staff, who had convinced themselves of my intention to be just. They had warrant for this, but that story would be too long to tell. I did not, even at this time of suspicion, lose their confidence and a conspicuous proof of it was given, when a deputation of the staff at Cork asked to see me, and laid before me, temperately and quietly, the fears under which they worked when they saw Army suspicions falling first on one and then on another, so that no man's career was safe. I heard them out, and saw in them sincerity. I thought them honest. Accordingly, I told them that I sat there to distinguish just from unjust suspicion. That from the latter I would protect them to the utmost of my power, and that I felt sure of support from the Postmaster General. But, I added none among them who gave cause for just suspicion or failed in loyalty, or associated with seditious persons, would have help or protection from me. I told them there was but one line of safety, to be loyal and honest in their duty. So long as they were, but so long only, I was on their side. They thanked me, and went away.

It is difficult to recall the stages of the deepening conviction of those days that some outbreak was impending. The greater anxieties of the war deadened our minds even then. It even seemed to matter little, when the greater hazard was at stake. I remember that Lord Granard wrote to me from Gallipoli, asking for my opinion as to what was coming in Ireland, and I replied that barricades were coming, and that I thought we should see grape shot in the streets of Dublin ere long. I remember, too, that two days before the outbreak my son Nevil came into my room at the Post Office, saying he did not like the look of things in Dublin, and would be happier about me if I were armed. Accordingly, he induced me to take from my safe the Colt Automatic which my son Fred used in the few weeks of splendid service which preceded his mortal wound near Armentières. He cleaned it, charged the magazine and four other clips, and laid the whole in a short drawer of my desk, saying 'Now you have thirty shots, and I feel happier about you.' And there the automatic lay on the morning of Easter Monday. I wonder often what I should have done with it, had I been still in my office when the rebels rushed it, instead of missing that crisis by something less than half an hour.

There was no great tension in the air during that week end in Dublin. I was aware personally of some anxiety, for Sir Matthew Nathan told me on the Saturday at the Castle that a prisoner of consequence had been taken in Kerry, and that some risk existed of an attempt at rescue as he was brought through Dublin on his way to London. He did not mention a name, nor did I ask, though I surmised that it must be Sir Roger Casement. Sir Matthew hinted at military precautions in the south, and possible restrictions on the use of postal services by the public. But said nothing of any outbreak in Dublin, nor can I think he had in his mind any serious apprehension of what occurred. If he had, more precautions would certainly have been taken; nor can I think that being in confidential talk with me, he would have omitted such a word of warning as would have put me on my guard, and given me a chance of protecting the Post Office, not to mention the private property which he knew me to have stored there when I gave up my house, after Fred's death, when the associations of it became too keenly painful. But we parted without hint of danger, and for me the Sunday passed quietly.

That night, Sunday, a dance was given by the Gaelic Athletic Association, largely attended by those classes from which the rebellion derived its strength. The dance stood in some close relation to the outbreak. Many of those present were in the secret, and I know of a servant girl, who being faithful, like many of her class, to her master, and even more to her master's children, woke her young mistress early on the Monday morning, and begged her earnestly to stay within doors, since something terrible was about to happen. If, however, some few were warned, they were few indeed. The city bore its usual aspect that Monday morning as I went down after breakfast to the Sackville Street club, where I read the papers, and then went into my office, a few houses away, intending to write letters, and remain till lunch. I was still in the midst of my first letter, when my telephone rang, and Sir Matthew Nathan spoke, asking me to go up to the Castle. He gave no reason, but I surmised some need for such steps as he had suggested two days before. I locked my desk, gave the key of my room to the porter, who was the only person on duty, the day being a bank holiday, and left, saying I should be back in half an hour. I never saw my room again till the whole building was gutted and burnt to a shell.

I saw nothing unusual as I walked up to the Castle. Nathan had with him Major Price, the Army Intelligence Officer. He turned to me as I came in, and told me there was serious trouble in Kerry, where a ship had been seized with German Officers on board, and material for a rising. Casement, however, whom he then named, had been conveyed to London under guard, with no attempt at rescue. The position was serious, and he desired me to take immediate steps for denying the use of the Telephone and Telegraph service over large areas of Southern Ireland to all but military and Naval use. I said that was too important a matter to be settled verbally, and I must have it in writing. 'Very well,' he said, 'You write out what you want, and I will sign it.' I was just finishing the necessary order, when a volley of musketry crashed out beneath the window. I looked up. 'What's that?' I asked. 'Oh, that's probably the long promised attack on the Castle,' cried Nathan, jumping up, and leaving the room, while Major Price shouted from the window to some person below, after which he too ran off. I waited for a few minutes, and then went down stairs in search of some explanation. At the foot of the staircase I found all the messengers huddled together in a frightened crowd. They had just seen the policeman at the gate shot through the heart. They were badly shaken.

They had however got the gate of the Upper Castle yard shut. The gate of the lower yard also had been shut. No attack was proceeding, and I found Nathan with the Store keeper breaking open the armoury in the hope of arming the handful of constables of the Dublin Metropolitan Police who formed the only guard of the Castle. He found some revolvers, but no cartridges; so that the constables remained of little use, while the rebels, declaring themselves without opposition ranged at will about the city, seizing one important building after another, and posting their proclamation of the Irish Republic wherever they would. In the handsome building of the General Post Office, which I had left so short a while before, the Union Jack was hauled down, and the green flag of the Irish Republic floated in its place. The Office in fact was rushed twenty minutes after I had left it, my room being appropriated for the rebel head-quarters. The guard of soldiers at the door of the Instrument room did their best, but for some military reason, which I never heard, they had been deprived of ammunition, without my knowledge. Their rifles being empty, they retreated inside and barricaded the door. But the rebels fired through it, shot the sergeant in the face, and, the post being untenable, the men surrendered. Had I not been rung up by the Under Secretary, I should have been the only man armed upon the premises. What then should I have done? I presume I ought to have tried to hold the staircase, and keep the mob down. I hope I should have done so. The certain result would have been that I should have been shot at once, and the probable result would have been that the Government in London would have declared the whole trouble to have arisen from my wicked folly in firing upon a body of peaceful, if armed, citizens. So much one sees clearly, for politicians in a difficulty are never fair, and still less generous. But all else is dark.

Sir Matthew Nathan had no intention of extricating me from an approaching danger, in the existence of which he did not in fact believe. He had formed the habit, possibly on instructions from Mr. Birrell, of consulting John Dillon upon every step he took, and viewing everything through the eyes of that old and inveterate rebel. Under this fatal influence, and on the accepted policy of avoiding all measures which might be provocative, he had omitted all precautions, making no arrests, and leaving the city during that critical week end denuded so far of troops that when the Castle gates were shut on himself, the Attorney General (afterwards Sir James O'Connor[9]) and me, there was no force nearer than the Curragh which could be used to restore us to freedom. The rebels had posted snipers in the upper windows of houses commanding the exits from the Castle, and were firing on all who left it. It was perhaps worth while for one who had led a very sheltered life to become suddenly one of a besieged garrison, and I do not know that the disquiet of the situation was much relieved by the fact that no attack developed, and that the sounds of fighting were still distant. I remember drawing Nathan's attention to the fact that the small courtyard up and down which he was pacing was commanded by the windows of houses accessible from the street, and could not be considered safe. He agreed, but replied that there were no soldiers to occupy those houses, so that we must take our chance. Why the Castle was not attacked I do not know. The afternoon wore on, and at dusk a battalion of the South Staffords marched in, having come up by train from the Curragh, and lost seven men, – so we were told – on the way from Kingsbridge to the Castle. Besieged we may not have been, in a true sense; but the relief with which we watched the cheerful smiles of officers and men as they stacked their arms in the lower courtyard was considerable, for it is clear enough that the rebels could have made us prisoners without loss, and the lot of prisoners during the rebellion was not always comfortable or even safe.

Safe as we felt, in the presence of our own troops, there was enough in the streets of Dublin that night of wild passion and fierce hope to convince the most careless of us that the country stood on the edge of some abyss, and as dark fell the thought recurred oftener than one wished that this sudden outbreak was formidable, and might be timed to coincide with some German stroke, possibly an invasion – for if that was in fact impossible we had no assurance of it then. When it grew quite dark, the troops attacked the City Hall, at the gate of the Upper Castle yard, which the rebels had occupied, and barricaded. I stood in the lower yard with the Attorney General, listening to the noise of fighting. The rifle volleys came in crashes, mingled with the tapping of machine guns, and the shattering burst of bombs, so near that they seemed close beside us. The yard was lit by torches, and crowded with men and soldiers, among whom from time to time a woman was carried in, caught in the act of carrying ammunition to the rebels, and fighting like trapped cats. It was a strange and awful scene. I turned to the Attorney

General, and said, 'This seems to be the death knell of Home Rule.' Now he was a sane and moderate Nationalist. But he said thoughtfully, 'Upon my soul, I don't know are we fit for it after all.' And then, after a little interval, 'The man I am sorry for is John Redmond.'

It was late before the noise of fighting died away, and not till after midnight did I prevail on the soldiers at the Castle gate to open it sufficiently to let me slip out, and whisk round into a side lane, expecting to get a sniper's bullet between my shoulders as I ran. But nothing happened, and I got back safely to the Royal Hibernian Hotel in Dawson street, where my wife waited for me in considerable anxiety. She has herself told the story of that day in the admirable letters published in a separate volume, and I shall try not to repeat what she says but only to supplement it. She was invaluable to me in the days which followed, and it is not too much to say that throughout the week of active fighting she and I, with one of my Principal clerks who, at great risk, managed to reach me day by day, – I refer to my friend Mr. J. J. Coonan, – constituted the General Post Office, for with very few exceptions the staff were unable to pass the cordons of rebels and of soldiers, and we saw nothing of them. One conspicuous officer, Mr. Gomersall, the Superintending Engineer, rendered admirable and very plucky service. For the rebels having cut the Telegraph and Telephone wires, with the intention of isolating Dublin from the rest of Ireland, and so from England, the Engineer took a car and drove round the outskirts of the city, picking up the ends of the cables, and leading them in to private circuits which he commandeered for the purpose; and this he did with such success that our communications were kept open throughout the rebellion.

It is perhaps worth while to record, since I have referred to the Irish Republican Brotherhood, to say that while I was sitting with Sir Matthew Nathan during the afternoon of this first day of the rebellion, a constable brought in one of the placards which the rebels were posting as they seized one after another important buildings in the city. It is this placard, or proclamation, from which I quote on page [33] of the present notes, and Sir Matthew passed it across the table for me to see. I had in mind the latest report sent to me from the Intelligence Dept in the Castle, by Nathan's orders, and especially the assertion in this report that the I.R.B. was probably dormant, and might be regarded as negligible. I put my finger on the paragraph which I have quoted, and passed it back to Sir Matthew, with the remark, 'It seems that the I.R.B. is not so dormant after all.' Sir Matthew smiled uncomfortably, but said nothing.

His manner and actions were those of a man who was not cool and steady, but rather bewildered. Nor is this surprising, for it was, and is, manifest that he, as permanent head of the Irish service, and Responsible adviser of Mr. Birrell, the Chief Secretary, who as I have said visited Dublin rarely, must bear the blame for neglecting to suppress dangerous associations, and for giving his confidence to those who did not deserve it, such as John Dillon, with whom he used to discuss many matters of consequence, and who dined with him at regular intervals. I think his intercourse with Dillon may have been imposed on him by Mr. Birrell, and if so, it is improbable that Sir Matthew would have exercised his own judgment on the point at all, for that would have run counter to his conception of loyalty, expounded more than once by him to me, – a conception differing vitally from that traditional in the Civil Service, which enjoins that the political Head should always know what his chief advisers think. 'What I want from you,' said Lord Buxton to me, as Postmaster General, 'is to give me your best opinion. I may reject it, but I always want to know it.' He was right. But Sir Matthew's view was that his duty lay in finding out what his Chief wished to do, and in helping him to do it without discussion. Any degree of contention, or discussion even, was in his opinion disloyalty.

I dwell on this since it throws light on the events of the previous day, I mean the Sunday before the outbreak, when there was still a last chance of preserving peace. My information was derived from Lord Wimborne, who had replaced Lord Aberdeen as Lord Lieutenant, and with whom my wife and I were lunching at the Vice-regal Lodge a few weeks after the Rebellion. There was, it seems, a Council on that day at the Lodge, and during the discussion Lord Wimborne urged strongly the immediate arrest of the well known dangerous persons who were the mainsprings of the rebellious movement, and most of whom, if not all, were subsequently shot. But Lord Wimborne was not in the Cabinet, and Mr. Birrell, who was, but was in London, had empowered Sir Matthew, as his represent-ative, to oppose the Lord Lieutenant, following out to the last the fatal doctrine that nothing must be done which could possibly create friction. The Cabinet authority prevailed, – one wonders whether the voice behind was not John Dillon's. Lord Wimborne, who spoke to me about it with indignation, did not press his view, though I still think that he, as representative of the King, might have brought into play reserve powers, and compelled the arrests. He was not strong enough to do that, and there were no arrests. The consequence that a new and deadly risk was added to the dangers in which England stood, at that grave moment of the war.

If, then, Sir Matthew, whose action had prevented the arrest of ring leaders while there was still time, was shaken and bewildered at the moment of the outbreak, it is little wonder. His reputation was gone. His counsellor had betrayed him. The things he did not believe in were before him. He had failed to guard England from added danger. I do him the justice of believing the perception to have been very bitter to him.

The City Hall, and other important buildings which the rebels had seized, were not recaptured that night. After 10 p.m. the sound of fighting died away; and first the Attorney General (James O'Connor) and then I slipped out of the lower Castle Yard into a lane on the right, and so, through silent streets, I reached the Hibernian Hotel in Dawson Street, where my wife and son were much relieved to see me. Next day, it was obvious at an early hour that to reach the Post Office, on the further side of the river, was impossible; the bridges being held strongly by rebels, while the Post Office itself was known to have been seized a quarter of an hour after I left it, and the green flag of the revolt was flying from its roof. And here I may say that at the outbreak of the war, being uneasy about the risk of a German agent gaining access to the Instrument room, and destroying the Telegraph system by throwing a bomb into the test box, I applied for a guard of soldiers, and such a guard was posted in my presence, the orders being that the sentries were to keep their magazines full, but the cut off close, and were to shoot to stop any unidentified person who approached the Instrument Room. But for some reason, and at some later date, though when or why, I could not discover, in the post-rebellion confusion, the sentinels had been deprived of ammunition, and left at their posts with empty rifles. On the rebel attack, they retreated into the Instrument Room, barricading the door. But the rebels fired through, shooting the Sergeant in the face. There was no alternative but to surrender. The soldiers were helpless, and the blame lies with those, probably civilians, who disarmed them. If I, who had a revolver with thirty shots, had been still in the Office, and had attempted, as I hope I should, to hold the staircase, I should have been shot at once, and what is worse, I should have been blamed by a frightened Government seeking for a scapegoat.

I have said that by the courageous enterprise of Mr. Gomersall the adverse effect of the loss of the Telegraph Office was neutralised, the wires being led into Amiens Street, which was, and remained in our hands. The Telephone office, off Dame Street, was also ours. But with those exceptions there was no Post Office, save the room which I had commandeered at the Hibernian Hotel, and the Telephone circuit which I had appropriated. At that Telephone, my wife, or I, sat all day long. Her cool pluck, and excellent good sense, were invaluable to me, and indeed to the public interest.

Shortly after breakfast the next morning the Police rang me up, by direction of the Under Secretary, asking me to go to the Castle. I asked by what route. 'By Dame Street,' was the answer, 'That is quite safe today.' I was surprised, but to Dame Street I went, and was just turning into it, opposite to Trinity College, when a storm of bullets swept down the street, evidently from rebel rifles, and was answered by sharp successive volleys from Trinity College. The police were wrong; and I give this incident to show that even they were quite unable to foretell from hour to hour where the fighting would break out. The bearing of the fact will be seen as I proceed. I reached the Castle by devious back lanes and found, on that as on other mornings, that Sir Matthew Nathan had little to say to me which could not have been said over the telephone, without calling me away from the only point at which I could be of service, or exposing me to the quite real risks of the streets. Indeed, knowing that my only substitute at the telephone was my wife, he summoned me the next day to the Castle four times, at some personal risk, and much interruption, without any reason of real advantage.

It is the less necessary to relate in detail the events of the following eight days because my wife has told them vividly in her published letters. I shall set down merely what supplements her tale. It was difficult to discover what was happening. For instance, I had occasion that morning to see the Engineer, and as he had incurred some risk a few hours before in coming down from Terenure to see me, I thought it unfair to bring him down again, and set out to visit him. I went up Grafton Street to the corner of St Stephen's Green, whence looking up towards Harcourt Street I could see a barricade of upturned motors etc about half way along the Green, near the College of Surgeons. There was a brisk exchange of rifle and machine gun fire going on between the rebels entrenched at the further side of the Green, and our own soldiers in the Shelbourne Hotel; and with this sound ringing through the air, it was difficult to look trustfully on a barricade, though it seemed abandoned. I asked a few people what the position was, and as they were assuring me the fighting at that point was over, I saw a man walk through the barricade towards us. If he could pass, it was clear I could; so I went on and entered Harcourt street, which was the direct and only way to Terenure. I had not gone far however when the whole street was blocked by a crowd of people swept back by soldiers, and finding it impossible to go on, I turned again into Stephen's Green, and walked back the way I came. As I drew near the College of Surgeons, I noticed several windows broken by rifle bullets, and in the same moment a bullet flew past my nose and broke a window on my left. I then saw for the first time that the College of Surgeons was held by rebels, and it was under heavy cross fire from the Shelbourne Hotel. It was in fact the command of that virago the Countess Markiewicz, and I was at that moment crossing the line of fire. This may serve to show the difficulty of ascertaining where one could go in safety; for clearly the information given by those I questioned in Grafton Street was wrong.

I set these two illustrations of the uncertainties in Dublin side by side because they throw a curious light on proposals made to me authoritatively either on that day, or the next. Sir Matthew rang me up and asked me to go down to the Castle. When I arrived he said he wanted to know from me whether I could not restore postal services over at least some part of the area of Dublin. I asked 'What part?' 'That is what I want you to tell me,' he said. 'But how can I?' I asked. 'I have no official information whatever, and no staff, as you are aware. You, on the other hand, as head of the Civil Government of Ireland, have full reports of police, and perhaps of military. Surely, I might ask you to indicate the districts which you think safe enough to justify me in putting postmen in uniform upon the streets.' 'It is useless to ask me that,' he said, 'for that is what I want from you.' 'I must press you,' I said, 'that I have no means whatever of forming a sound opinion. Will you not at least give me the reports you have, and let me study them.' 'No,' he said, 'I want your sole judgment, and I want it in writing by four o'clock.' I protested that this was scarcely fair, but in vain. Finding it was impossible to move Sir Matthew, I returned to my hotel, and had scarcely reached it when the Lord Lieutenant rang me up, and put the same question. Half an hour later the Irish Office in London pressed the same point on me, and it seemed obvious that the Government, being pressed in the House of Commons, wanted to get up and declare that the rising in Dublin had been exaggerated, that some degree of order was restored, and that postal deliveries had been resumed over considerable areas of the City. The fact that the rebels were firing on any one who wore uniform, even the Fire Brigade, and that the postmen would certainly have been shot, was either unknown to them, or treated as of no importance. To me it was the governing consideration. I had no member of my staff to consult with. But the case seemed clear. I rang up the mail cart Contractor, and asked him whether he felt justified in sending out his vans and drivers into any part of Dublin. He said, rather indignantly, 'You must know the answer to that question. Why do you put it to me? 'Because it is pressed on me,' I said. 'May I take it that you will not send out the vans?' 'You may,' he answered. I then wrote at once a short report to the effect that being asked for my opinion as to the practicability of resuming normal postal services over some part of Dublin, and having at my command no official information about the state of the City, I could only say that my own observation led me to the conclusion that no such steps were practicable at the time, and that the lives of postmen would be in great danger if they appeared upon the streets. I therefore declined respectfully to order them to go out.

I took this myself to Sir Matthew Nathan, who received it ungraciously, not concealing his opinion that my attitude was obstructive. I had not, however, nor have I now, the least doubt that I was right.

As I conceived my duty in the difficult and changing circumstances, and in the absence of any guidance whatever from my Chiefs in London, who left me throughout to take my own line, I was bound in reason both to protect the interests of the Crown and public, so far as I could, and also to protect honest members of the Post Office staff against punishment which could not be shown or presumed with probability to be deserved, for they had no other protector. The fair and just discharge of these two functions was not easy. Both however were vitally important, and mistakes were likely to be disastrous. I thought it of the first consequence to act both firmly and justly. How difficult that was may be seen from what happened in the latter days of the rebellion. Sir John Maxwell was then in command, having replaced General Friend. The revolt was broken, and the soldiers were arresting large numbers of men of whom some certainly had been fighting, though their rifles were cast away, while others had been only curious spectators. The crowds were such that discrimination was impossible, and the arrests were wholesale. There were accordingly in my hands long lists of Post Office men, and some women, under arrest, and detained. The problem was to decide which were guilty, for it was clear that none who had fought against the Crown ought to be restored to the service of the Crown, having in fact dismissed themselves. The trouble lay in finding evidence of guilt.

As I was beginning to work at that problem, an officer from Army Headquarters was shown in. 'The General understands,' he said, 'that you are able to indicate certain members of your staff who have taken part in the rebellion.' 'That is not so,' I said, 'I have lists of officers arrested and detained. But their cases must in justice be examined before they can be pronounced guilty, and dismissed; for some among them may probably be innocent.' He agreed that the conditions in the streets were such as to render just distinctions difficult. 'But,' he said, 'if you will give me your list I will tell the General what you say, and you shall be consulted before anything is done.' I gave him the lists, impressing on him clearly that they could not be regarded as anything more than the starting point of an enquiry. The next morning the lists were returned to me, marked in the General's own hand 'Dismiss,' opposite some score of names, or more, but without any indication of evidence justifying the sentences. I did not see my way to dismiss men and women without evidence. The declaration of military law did not seem to justify the abandonment of any effort to distinguish guilt from innocence. I went up to Army Headquarters. The General was absent from Dublin, and the officers I saw could only say that in his absence nothing could be done. 'You mean,' I said, 'that I must at once dismiss these men?' 'Since military law is declared, you must indeed,' was the reply. 'Well, gentlemen,' I said, 'the Post Office does not dismiss men without evidence that it is acting justly. I shall suspend these instructions. But I will go to London tonight, lay the matter before the Postmaster General, whose authority is supreme in his Department, and take his instructions.' It seemed to them unheard of that any one should hesitate to carry out the order of the General. I did as I had said, however, and early the next morning I put the whole case before the Postmaster General, Mr. Pease, and Sir Evelyn Murray, the Secretary. They approved what I had done and as the result of somewhat protracted negotiations, a small Committee was sent to Dublin, consisting of Sir Guy Fleetwood Wilson,[10] and Sir William Byrne,[11] who investigated the various cases, rather perfunctorily, and assumed the responsibility of indicating who were to be dismissed, – a number, I may add, considerably less than had been indicated by the General. The procedure created at least some protection against injustice.[12]

Arthur Hamilton Norway to The Secretary of the GPO[13]

Thursday, 27 April 1916[14]

I take the opportunity created by the departure for England of Lord Shaw of Dunfermline to report briefly on the events of the last three days in so far as they affect my responsibilities, premising only that the report is written in haste, under constant interruption & with information which is necessarily imperfect.

Although the obviously increasing armed strength of the Irish Volunteers has appeared to me for many months a serious danger, I saw no reason to anticipate an outbreak. On Monday morning Dublin appeared in its usual condition. I went to my office about 11 a.m. to do some work, & had hardly sat down when my telephone bell rang & the Under Sec. asked me to go up to the Castle. The streets were in their usual condition. I was with Sir M. Nathan for some 20 minutes, & had just made a written note of some instructions which he gave me & which were never carried out, when shots were heard, & quite unexpectedly the attack on the Castle began.

I do not conceive it to be proper for me to attempt to describe events other than those which directly concern the Post Office. I found it impossible to leave the Castle for more than 12 hours. About 11 p.m. I was able to regain my hotel.

So far as I can ascertain, the Post Office was rushed about a quarter of an hour after I left my room. The Instrument room was guarded by soldiers, as since the first days of the war, but the soldiers had, at some subsequent time, without my knowledge, been deprived of cartridges, & were accordingly powerless. They appear to have made some fight & the sergeant was wounded, but I believe not dangerously. The original instructions, given in my presence in the early days of August 1914, were that each man of the guard should have his magazine charged, & cut off closed, & should fire to stop any unauthorized person. I had no reason to suspect any alteration of these instructions.

A the moment of writing (noon) the Post Office is still in hands of rebels, & I am without information as to how long it may be so.

Possible resumption of postal services

This was of course considered on Tuesday, but I decided that nothing of the kind was practicable in the then state of the City. About the justice of this conclusion I have no doubt whatsoever.

Yesterday I was pressed on the same subject by the Lord Lieutenant, & separately by the Under Secretary. I held a conference with such of my staff as I could collect, & decided once more that the thing is impossible. On ringing up the mail cart contractors, I received an assurance that they would let no mail cart leave the yard. Apart from that, the streets are in such a condition that all use of them in almost any direction is dangerous. I have myself narrowly escaped being shot – twice yesterday – and I cannot accept any responsibility of ordering Postmen to attempt either collections or deliveries at present.

As this matter may be brought up in London, I should add that there is no authority who can indicate with certainty what routes or districts are safe at the moment, or will be safe an hour hence. The Metropolitan Police misled me grossly on this subject yesterday; and Lord Shaw of Dunfermline, leaving this hotel by a route which was safe an hour previously, was shot at & narrowly missed, while a sentry pointed his rifle & threatened to shoot if Lord Shaw did not go back at once.

No steps whatsoever are possible. The streets around this hotel are far more unsafe today then yesterday.

Staff

I have with me in a temporary office hired in this hotel at the rate of 10/-[15] a day, Mr. Coonan, my senior Principal Clerk, who pluckily got here this morning. He was here also on Tuesday & Wednesday. I shall probably keep him here. Mr. MacMahon has been in bed at his house at Kingstown [Dun Laoghaire] with a heart attack for which rest is essential; otherwise his help would have been invaluable. Mr. MacDowell & Mr. Tipping were here in conference yesterday. Today the former has found it impossible to get here. Mr. Gomersall, the Superintending Engineer, is in constant communication with me, personally or by telephone. Many members of my staff are inaccessible.

Services

In Dublin
1. The Telephone service is intact.
   I was dissatisfied with the strength of the guard posted at the Central Exchange; & on application to the Under Secretary it has been strengthened.
2. The Superintending Engineer has managed (a) to assure himself that the rebels in the G.P.O. have no telegraphic communication with other parts of Ireland. This result was not attained without difficulty or danger – about which I shall have more to say later; (b) to open & maintain communications more exactly described in a note from him of which I annex a copy. Some alterations have occurred since yesterday morning, when the note was made – e.g. a wire is now open to London via Kingstown. But substantially the note is still correct.
   I am in full communication with the Postmasters of Cork & Belfast.

The state of things in Provincial Ireland is to some extent

described in the S.E.'s note already referred to. Galway is cut off this morning, apparently by interruption between that place & Athenry. Athenry-Limerick is also interrupted. Apparently there is trouble at Athenry.

The Under Sec. instructed me yesterday to suspend Telegraph & Telephone service (even local) all over Ireland, except for Military & Govt messages. This I did by means of instructions forwarded to central points – e.g. Cork, Waterford &c – for communication to all points which could be reached by whatever means. I am naturally unable to state positively that these instructions have been made universally effective, but I have reason to know they are effective over wide areas. In Ulster they are temporarily suspended at the express wish of Gen. Hacket Pain, the senior military officer in the Province. I do not know his reasons. I had mentioned to the Under Sec. the case of Belfast, as likely to present peculiar difficulties & on referring to him again I received his instructions to acquiesce, on condition that General Hacket Pain reported his reasons to Headquarters & obtained their concurrence. I instructed the Postmaster accordingly.

I annex copies of service messages from Belfast & Cork which will give the Secretary some useful information.[16] I am endeavouring to get similar information from Waterford, but it has not arrived.

I need hardly say that as soon as the Post Office is regained the whole staff will unitedly work unsparingly to restore the services. For the moment, I can think of nothing more which could be done in fulfilment of the responsibilities devolving on the Irish Post Office.

Since writing the above report I find the state of the City renders it quite impossible for Lord Shaw to leave Dublin today, it being at present put of the question to go outside this hotel. I therefore hold over the report.

Copy of Memorandum by Mr. E. Gomersall, Superintending Engineer, Ireland, dated 26 April 1916

The communications open are as follows:-

Cork & S.W. of Ireland

Things as normal. Cork has 1 line to London, and generally all lines are right. Little damage was done.

Waterford & S.E. Counties

West of Sallins on G.S.&W.R.[17] we are all right. Waterford is right. A little damage was done, but it has been remedied.

Dublin

I have opened a temporary telegraph office at Amiens St. Station. I have four working lines to London, and am arranging 7 more. I have also a circuit to Belfast. I have got a Trunk telephone circuit to the Curragh, and one to Maryborough.[18] Communications with places W. & S.W. of Maryborough may be obtained by calling upon the telephone. Two circuits are available to Belfast, and communication may be obtained via the Dublin Exchange with London and Great Britain generally.

Military H.Q. can get through to Arklow by telephone. I put them a call through at 5.30 this morning.[19]

I am endeavouring to get more circuits into Maryborough so as to give greater facilities to the S.W. of Ireland

As regards telegrams for the S.W. of Ireland I hope to open an office at Kingsbridge. In the meantime any urgent official messages may be handed to the Railway Telegraph office at Kingsbridge whose lines we have succeeded in maintaining.

Copy of Report from Postmaster, Belfast, dated 27 April 1916, received 11 a.m.

Have been able to maintain daily despatches across channel for both letters and parcels by Ardrossan service, by using Liverpool steamer when available, and by availing of offer of Rear Admiral, Larne Harbour, to convey mails to Stranraer by special Admiralty steamers, but no cross channel mails have reached Belfast since Tuesday morning. Route to west of Ireland via Clones being open correspondence for rest of Ireland is being forwarded to Mullingar, the powers there having intimated that they could dispose of it. Cross channel correspondence from west of Ireland is being received through Mullingar & disposed of at Belfast. Normal services to & from places in N. of Ireland generally are being maintained.

Arthur Norway to Sir Evelyn Murray (Secretary, GPO)

Royal Hibernian Hotel
Dublin
3 April 1916
8.30 a.m.

Dear Mr. Murray,

I hope you have now received the brief report which I sent by Lord Shaw, who must, I think, have been able to cross, though I am not sure of it. I have not been able yet to commence a full report, nor would it be of much use to do so until I have seen the ruins of the Post Office, & been able to form some sort of plan for the resumption of services. The surrender of the rebel leaders yesterday may make that possible this morning; & on the assumption that it might be so, I got the necessary passes last night, & am going down at 10 o'clock this morning with Gomersall, Tipping, Kenny & two of my principal clerks – if they all reach me, & satisfy all the sentries, of which one cannot be sure.

The position was made much worse last night by incendiaries, who fired the whole of the remainder of Sackville Street on both sides, including the Accountant's Office, which up to last evening was safe. The blaze was such on both sides that the Fire Brigade – which was out, as shooting has ceased at that spot – could do nothing. I appealed to Nathan to compel them with military aid to attempt to save the Accountant's Office, but he assured me nothing could be done.

Shooting is much less this morning, though a machine gun has been very busy close at hand, & a soldier in this street has just fired, I suppose at one of the snipers who are still on the roofs of many houses. He has just fired again. Big guns are quiet today.

I should like to suggest to you the expediency of coming over personally for a day or so. A big thing has happened here, to

which I know no parallel, and it has many aspects of importance, which cannot be discussed in correspondence. I doubt if
you can possibly understand without coming over how much
the service owes – to take only one point, and not the longest –
to the twenty girls who maintained the telephone service for six
days amid sounds of fighting which are very hard to describe,
and a certain indisputable personal danger, which has been met
with wonderful pluck. Had their courage given way, the all
important Telephone service must have collapsed, & with it all
Telegraph communications – which depended solely on it. Some
bullets came actually into the Switchroom, but the work went on
steadily.

Similar praise is due to the Telegraphists who maintained the
service at Amiens Street, & perhaps at Kingsbridge; and in an
especial degree to Gomersall & his staff, who took their lives in
their hands and did their work effectively & fearlessly. I have
distributed commendation from myself. But from you it would
be very highly appreciated. Probably more than commendation
is called for; but of this of course I have said nothing, & the
matter can be considered later.

Notwithstanding the surrender last night, some parties of
rebels still hold out. The machine gun close at hand fires almost
continuously. But the worst is over.

We got off a small mail to England last night from
 Rathgar
 Rathmines
 Balls Bridge

It would have been larger if the Castle could have given me its
concurrence in less than 4 hours. Perhaps we may send more
tonight. Central Dublin is still impossible, & as regards the
whole area, the difficulty is that roads & districts which are safe
one hour may be & often are most unhealthy when traversed an
hour later.

Broadly, I will take no responsibility for ordering resumption
of services unless & until the military authorities give me the
clear assurances of the <u>reasonable</u> – not absolute – safety of my
staff. Enough has been risked this week in Dublin by those
whose obligations were for the moment of essential importance
to the public safety. But I will not call on my staff to risk their
lives merely to get public correspondence into England a day or

two sooner. Therefore I will not move without the military assurance referred to.

All I got yesterday, after waiting 4 hours, was that the military authorities 'had no objection' to the despatch of the mails to Kingstown. That was not what I wanted; but I took it, & despatched whatever was possible.

Report by A. H. Norway, 22 June 1916[20]

With the exception of a report which I entrusted at an early stage of the outbreak to Lord Shaw of Dunfermline, I have not yet forwarded to the Secretary any connected statement on the subject of the circumstances connected with the work of the Post Office as affected by the recent rebellion in Ireland, the isolating character of the outbreak, and the extreme pressure on my time which it has since entailed making it impossible for me to approach the task at an earlier moment. And even now it seems to me that the Secretary will scarcely require any very elaborate account of the general circumstances which have been made known so widely through the medium of the Press, and especially as the results of the insurrection came under his personal notice in the course of his recent visit to Dublin.

I have already explained that after the taking of the Post Office by the rebels I rented for official purposes a room in the Royal Hibernian Hotel where I have been residing temporarily. A telephone was installed in it for my particular use, and by its means I was able to maintain communication with Dublin Castle, the Military Headquarters, the Police, and such members of my staff and the Public as it was necessary for me to confer with. It also enabled me to communicate by Telegraph with the Secretary and other parts of Ireland, the telephone being connected with temporary Telegraph Offices at Amiens Street and Knightsbridge which the Superintending Engineer had fortunately been able to provide. It was most fortunate that the Telephone Exchange did not fall into the hands of the rebels.

The most prominent feature of the first week of the outbreak was a pressing request on the part of the Lord Lieutenant and the Under Secretary that I should introduce some manner of Postal Service in Dublin; and some irritation was shown on my pointing out the impossibility of doing this. At the time the request was made the Rebellion was at its height, no trains were entering or leaving Dublin, vehicular traffic had entirely ceased, furious fighting was in progress in various parts of the City and its outskirts, sniping was almost universal, and the appearance of a Mail Car or any person in official uniform on the streets would in my opinion and that of any person whose views I sought have been simple madness. Moreover the great bulk of the Staff was impossible to reach; and, even if the officers could have been approached, access to the City was most difficult, if not indeed impossible. I succeeded in establishing my view of the suggestion, and it was, somewhat reluctantly, it seemed to me, dropped.

After the partial surrender of the insurgents on the 29th April, I visited, in company with the principal officers on the Dublin Establishment, the ruins of the General Post Office building, and on its being found that the premises were entirely destroyed and useless for any official purposes the question of future arrangements was taken into hand. But the insurrection proved to be by no means at an end, and, apart from the dangers incidental to the fighting and sporadic sniping which continued, there was great difficulty in moving into or out of the City owing to the severity of the Military restrictions which were very rigidly enforced. Ultimately however the Staff were collected and the Rotunda Rink in the immediate vicinity of the old General Post Office having been commandeered on the evening of the 2nd May sorting and delivery work was commenced on the morning of the 3rd. Temporary fittings were very kindly supplied by the Office of Works in England. At first only a partial service was given, but it has been gradually increased until at present it is almost normal. The Clerical Staff of the Dublin Postal District was housed in the Rotunda buildings proper pending a permanent arrangement being made. The Rotunda, it may be mentioned, is a structure containing a number of rooms of varying extent used for entertainments such as Cinemas, Concerts, Dances and such-like functions.

The best position for a temporary Instrument Room was found to be the top floor of the Parcel Depot at Amiens Street which fortunately escaped any damage. The necessary space was placed at the disposal of the Superintending Engineer on the afternoon of the 4th May and by the 9th May was in full working order and ready for the complete transaction of Public business as soon as the Military restrictions on the use of the Telegraphs had been withdrawn. This has since occurred and an unrestricted service has been in operation for some time. It may be mentioned that the varying requirements of the Military in respect of Telegraph and Telephone restrictions were very disturbing and caused infinite trouble. Accommodation was found in the same premises for the Telegraph clerical and delivery Staff, and the Trunk telephones were transferred to the Central Exchange.

The officers of my immediate office were distributed throughout the various other Post Office buildings in Dublin and remain so pending more suitable provision being made for them.

The consideration of future arrangements on all counts is in hand.

The distribution of money to Postmasters throughout the Country was conducted in accordance with arrangements devised and controlled by Sir Chas. King[21] through the Postmasters of Belfast and Cork, most valuable assistance being rendered in this connection by the Bank of Ireland and kindred institutions, and I have written to the authorities of the various Banks concerned expressing the high appreciation of the Department for the help so willingly and effectively rendered. No difficulty so far as I am aware arose in Ireland as regards the payment of separation allowances or Old Age Pensions except in Dublin where in addition to the physical obstruction caused by the outbreak the separation allowance records were burned in the General Post Office. But the difficulty was surmounted by the aid of particulars of preceding payments which were available in the Accountant's Office and the allowances commenced to be paid on the 3rd May, an armoured Motor Car being placed by the Military at the disposal of the Post Office for the distribution of funds to the various Branch and sub-Offices in Dublin. It was necessary to take temporary premises for the payment on the allowances normally paid from the Head Office.

The Military Authorities have written a flattering letter in respect of the measures taken by the Department to secure the earliest possible payment of these allowances and I attach it for the Secretary's information.[22] It has been seen by the Controller of the Dublin Postal District whom it concerns.

The conduct of the Staff generally throughout this most trying period was excellent. Admirable work was done by those

Officers in Dublin whom the outbreak found on duty, and by such outside the City as could render assistance. These observations apply especially to the Engineering Staff, the Telephonists at the Exchange, and the Sorting Clerks and Telegraphists at Amiens Street and Knightsbridge. In the three last-mentioned instances the officers concerned found it impossible to quit the official premises for many days. They obtained such rest and food as was possible under very trying conditions, and met the difficulties of the situation with commendable good spirit and devotion to duty. A letter was received from the General Commanding-in-Chief of Forces in Ireland expressing his high appreciation of the services rendered, and is attached to this report. A copy of the letter was sent after its receipt to the Heads of all the Departments in Dublin for exhibition in the various branches.

I send also some reports which have reached me bearing generally on this particular point. There is one from the Superintending Engineer, one from the Controller of Stores, one from the Surveyor of the Northern District dealing particularly with the measures taken at Mullingar which became temporarily a centre for Postal and Telegraph work, one from the Postmaster of New Ross which town threatened to become an important factor in the disturbance and special reports from the Controller of the Telegraph Office who encloses statements from the members of his Staff who intimately concerned with the circumstances following the seizure of the General Post Office by the Rebels.

I realise the difficulty of singling out officers for special commendation where the general level of service has been so high and the spirit in which great difficulties were met and overcome was one of conspicuous loyalty and devotion. But where all have done well, I feel some special mark of appreciation is due to those who served in Dublin during the actual hostilities, since they, besides sharing in the great example of loyal and zealous effort in a great emergency, submitted cheerfully during six or seven days at least to personal danger which was real and serious, and which was inseparable from their duties, since in fact it was the nature of these duties which exposed them to it.

I do not recommend pecuniary reward in any case. But I should be glad to see a week's additional leave given to those members of the Engineering Service, the Telegraph and Telephone Services and the Stores Department who were on actual duty during the insurrection; and if I am authorised to grant this in each case I purpose to ask the head of the Department to signify the officer concerned that the leave is granted as a mark of appreciation of unusually trying work done in circumstances of some personal danger.

The Secretary is aware that the prompt and effective restoration of the services after the insurrection was rendered possible only by the quite exceptional exertions on the part of all the Administrative Officers and the heads of Department. Mr. Gomersall, the Superintending Engineer, was indefatigable, and to the resourcefulness of himself and his Staff, and the courageous way in which they took their risks, the Post Office is deeply indebted. Mr. Tipping, the Controller of the Dublin Postal Service, and Mr. Kenny, the Controller of Telegraphs, both did admirable work, and bore a very heavy strain; as also did Mr. Reeves, in charge of the Stores at Aldborough House. If I do not mention officers of less standing in their different departments, it is merely because to specify some where all did their utmost would be invidious. The exertions of the Telephone Staff under Mr. Currall and Mr. Morgan, were acknowledged personally when Mr. Pease and Mr. Murray visited Dublin.

The services rendered by Mr. Forsythe, Postmaster of Belfast, and Mr. Hancock, Postmaster of Cork, in connection with the supply of cash and stamps to Postmasters throughout Ireland, were of the most valuable kind, and are well known to Sir Chas. King, who initiated the measures taken with their aid to avert the serious inconveniences resulting from the forced suspension of Accounting business in Dublin.

To Mr. Coonan, my senior Principal Clerk, I am indebted for constant & often very plucky help. Mr Coonan came to me at my hotel on each day of the insurrection, often at much personal risk, so that I at last insisted on his remaining, rather than expose his life to the considerable dangers of the streets. His work was invaluable to me, and I wish to put on record my high appreciation of it.

Mr. MacMahon, as the Secretary is aware, was suffering from illness at home but notwithstanding this he did much useful & valuable work at Kingstown. He draws my attention to the excellence of the service rendered by the Postmaster of

Kingstown, who worked assiduously & devotedly, under some well grounded apprehension of attack, & who showed tact and resource to an unusual degree in circumstances which were novel and bewildering. I hope ere long an opportunity may occur of offering him substantial promotion.

Notes

1. MS 24,894. Attempts to locate the original, and any other personal papers, through Norway's descendants have failed, and it now appears to be lost.
2. Report by Sir Warren Fisher, 12 May 1920, quoted in Keith Jeffery, *The British Army and the Crisis of Empire, 1918-22* (Manchester: Manchester University Press, 1984), p. 82.
3. A retired Indian civil servant.
4. The King's Own Scottish Borderers.
5. The Royal Commission on the Rebellion in Ireland.
6. Nathan was at the time Chairman of the Board of Inland Revenue, and had been Secretary to the Post Office, 1909–11.
7. Joint Second Secretary of the Post Office, 1914-19.
8. The headquarters of the Post Office was in St Martin's le Grand in the City of London, close to St Paul's Cathedral.
9. O'Connor, who was knighted in 1925, was at the time of the Rising Solicitor General for Ireland. He was not appointed Attorney General until December 1916.
10. A retired official whose career had spanned both the British and Indian civil services.
11. A barrister with a long record of public service. He was Under-Secretary to the Irish Office, 1916-18.
12. The report, and some other papers relating to Post Office employees, of the Wilson-Byrne Committee is in Chapter 8.
13. BPMA, POST 56/177
14. The letter is marked 'Rec[ieve]d 1/5 by post'.
15. Fifty pence.
16. Only that from Belfast is included.
17. Great Southern & Western Railway
18. Now Port Laoise.
19. The security of Kynoch's high explosives factory at Arklow was a particular concern for the military.
20. BPMA, POST 31/80, file VII.
21. Comptroller and Accountant-General of the Post Office, 1901–19.
22. None of the letters mentioned by Norway have been reproduced.

4 The Wife's Tale

In his memoir, 'Irish experiences in war', Arthur Norway remarked that his wife had 'herself told the story' of Easter Monday 'in the admirable letters published in a separate volume'. He had aimed, moreover, 'not to repeat' what she wrote 'but only to supplement it'. This chapter consists of the entire text of Mary Louisa Norway's little book, originally published by Smith, Elder & Co. of London in 1916. Mrs Norway is historically rather an elusive figure. She came from an impeccably respectable family of British imperial soldiers and civil servants. Her father, Frederick Gadsden, was a major-general in the Indian Army. Beginning in the Indian Police, her brother Edward ended up as Inspector-General of Prisons in Madras.[1] Mary was raised 'very well up in all the usages of polite society;...there was little', recalled her son, 'that she did not know about precedence, visiting cards, calling and "at home" days.'[2] In 1891 she married Arthur Hamilton Norway.

When they first moved to Ireland, the Norways leased an agreeable 'rambling country house' called South Hill at 91 Mount Merrion Avenue in the south Dublin suburb of Blackrock. For their two sons, Fred and Nevil, accustomed to life in the more urban London district of Ealing, the house 'opened up new country pleasures we had hardly dreamed of'.[3] When war broke out in August 1914, Fred was living at home and studying at Trinity College, Dublin, while his fifteen-year-old brother was a pupil at Shrewsbury School in England. Fred quickly secured a commission in the Duke of Cornwall's Light Infantry and soon after Easter 1915 was drafted to the Western Front where in June he was seriously wounded by German shell-fire and died after three weeks in hospital.[4] He was still only nineteen years old. The following autumn, his father gave up the lease of South Hill and the family moved into the Royal Hibernian Hotel in Dawson Street. Nevil speculated not only that the increasing cost of maintaining South Hill was a worry for his father, but also that 'the house held so many memories of Fred for my mother and myself that it would be better to get rid of it and start again'.[5] So it was that Mrs Hamilton Norway witnessed the 1916 Rising from the enviably central location of one of Dublin's leading hotels.

The most poignant feature of Mrs Norway's account concerns the fate of Fred's belongings, including his sword, which had been stored for safekeeping with other family valuables in Hamilton Norway's office safe and cupboard. Ironically Mrs Norway had thought it 'the safest place in Dublin'. Having inspected the burnt-out shell of the GPO two days after the Rising had ended, Mrs Norway sadly reflected that everything belonging to 'F.' had gone. Later, however, some precious little treasures were recovered. Mrs Norway concluded that other things had been taken by the insurgents, though it is as likely that their property was simply swallowed up in the conflagration.

Mrs Norway's account begins and ends with the GPO: from her own sight-seeing (with so many other Dubliners) in Sackville Street on the late afternoon of Easter Monday to the pathetic wreckage of the building following the Rising. But right at the end of her book she also provided a glimpse of events from inside the rebel headquarters by reproducing Pearse's moving final 'manifesto', issued on Friday 28 April, in which he declared that 'the soldiers of Irish Freedom', even if their fate was sealed by the advancing British forces, had 'already...won a great thing. They have redeemed Dublin from many shames, and made her name splendid among the names of cities'.

The Sinn Féin Rebellion as I Saw It
Mrs. Hamilton Norway
(Wife of the Secretary for the Post Office in Ireland)

For these letters I claim no literary merit: they were written during a period of extraordinary strain for family perusal only, and are a faithful record hour by hour of the Sinn Féin rebellion as I saw it. The wide interest the letters excited in the family circle and the little that seems to be known of a period of such intense interest is my reason for offering them to a wider public.

M. L. N.

July, 1916

Royal Hibernian Hotel,
Dawson Street, Dublin,

Tuesday, April 25th.

DEAREST G.,[6] – I am afraid by this time you will have seen a good deal in the papers to cause you alarm, and as it is impossible to get a letter or telegram through, I will write you a detailed account of what we are going through and post it to you at the first opportunity.

To begin at the beginning, the Sinn Féin movement, which is now frankly revolutionary and which must not be confounded with Redmond's Nationalist Party, has been in existence for years, but has always been looked on as a small body of cranks who were thirsting for notoriety. Redmond's policy has always been to treat them with utter contempt, and the Government adopted his view.

Since the outbreak of war this movement, encouraged no doubt by German intrigue and German money, has grown by leaps and bounds, and about eighteen months ago a large number broke away from Redmond's National Volunteers and formed a volunteer force which they called the Irish Volunteers. They are frankly and openly revolutionary, and when it became known some months ago that they were obtaining large quantities of arms and ammunition various persons did all they could to open the eyes of the authorities to the dangerous situation that was growing up. But as the explanation was always given that the force was for national defence only, the Government failed to take any steps to put down the movement.

During the past six months the body has grown enormously, as many as seven hundred recruits being enlisted on one night, and of course doing enormous harm to recruiting for the Army. On St. Patrick's Day they held a large review of several battalions, armed, and the trams were all held up for about an hour in College Green. Up to the last moment there was hope that this would be stopped, but protests were like a voice crying in the wilderness. Another time they held a full dress rehearsal of what has actually taken place when they 'took' the Castle, St. Stephen's Green, and various buildings. About a month ago one of their meetings in the country was broken up and the two leaders arrested and deported to England. A huge meeting of protest was held at the Mansion House, almost opposite this hotel, and attended by the Volunteers, all armed, who marched in procession. After the meeting they marched down Grafton Street, singing 'Die Wacht am Rhein' and revolutionary songs; a slight disturbance with the police took place and some shots were fired. People began to ask anxiously what next? but the Government looked on and smiled and H[amilton]. tore his hair.

On Saturday we were going to tea with friends at Bray, when just as we were starting H. got an 'official' from the Castle, so I went alone and he went to the Castle. News had come that a boat had been taken off the Kerry coast, landing ammunition, and a very important arrest had been made. Easter Sunday passed off in absolute calm, and yesterday (Easter Monday) morning H. said he had a lot of letters to write and he would go and write them at his club, almost next door to the Sackville Street G.P.O. He found he wanted to answer some letters that were in his desk at the G.P.O., so he walked over to his room and was just sitting down when his 'phone went, an urgent message to go at once to the Castle.

He had only just arrived there, and was in consultation with Sir M[atthew]. N[athan]., when suddenly a volley of shots rang out at the Castle gate, and it was found armed bodies of men were in possession of the City Hall and other houses that commanded the other gates to the Castle, and anyone attempting to leave the Castle was shot. All the officials in the Castle were prisoners.

News quickly came that the magazine in the Park had been taken, the G.P.O., two stations, and all the houses that commanded O'Connell Bridge had been stormed and taken, and the rebels had taken St. Stephen's Green, where they were entrenching themselves.

Meantime, knowing nothing of this, N[evil]. went for a country motor bike ride, and I did some sewing and wrote letters, etc., and when N. came in about 12.30 I said I wanted a walk before lunch and we would walk down to the club and meet H. The streets were quiet and deserted till we crossed O'Connell Bridge, when N. remarked there was a dense crowd round Nelson's Pillar, but we supposed it was a bank holiday crowd waiting for trams. We were close to the General Post Office when two or three shots were fired, followed by a volley, and the crowd began rushing down towards the bridge, the people calling out, 'Go back, go back; the Sinn Féiners are firing.' N. said, 'You'd better go back, Mother; there's going to be a row; I'll go on to the club and find Dad'; so I turned and fled with the crowd and got back safely to the hotel.

Here was excitement and consternation. Every moment people were coming in with tales of civilians being shot in the streets, and houses commanding wide thoroughfares and prominent positions being taken possession of by the Sinn Féiners, whose method was to go in detachments of four or six armed men, ring the bell, and demand to see the owners of the houses. In many instances they were away for the Easter holidays, when the frightened servants were just turned into the street to go where they would; but if the master or mistress were at home they were told with a revolver at their heads that the house was required by the Irish Republic for strategic purposes, and the owners were given the option of leaving the house or remaining as prisoners in the basement. A few elected to do this in preference to leaving all their household goods to the mercy of the rebels; but most thought 'discretion the better part of valour' and cleared out to friends, in some instances only to be hunted out from their house of refuge a second time. The windows of the houses were then barricaded with a reckless disregard to valuable furniture, which in many cases was turned into the street to form barricades.

You remember my nice housemaid Mary, gentle as a dove and timid as a hare. I had got her a very nice place with a lady who had taken a large house in Leeson Street close to the bridge and commanding Fitzwilliam Place. She went this morning by appointment to meet the lady at the house and found the Sinn Féiners on the steps, who pointed their revolvers at her and told her to clear out. She was so scared she nearly fell into the area, and came to the hotel looking like a ghost.

But to return to our own adventures. Directly I got back to the hotel I rang up the club and was told by old MacDermott, the hall-porter, that H. had left the club at 11.30 to go to the G.P.O., saying he would be back shortly; but he had not returned, and since then the Post Office had been stormed and the guard shot or overpowered, and the Sinn Féiners were in possession of the whole building, and firing volleys on the police from the windows! Imagine my feelings!

About 1.30 N. returned, having failed to find any trace of H., but he had seen some cavalry shot coming out of Talbot Street into Sackville Street. The first three or four were just picked off their horses and fell wounded or dead, and the horses were shot. He said the scene of excitement in Sackville Street was indescribable. We were just going in to lunch when a telephone message came through saying H. was at the Castle but could not leave.

This relieved our minds as to his fate, and after lunch I was kept busy at the telephone answering distracted messages from Post Office officials who were wandering about looking for H. At about 4 p.m. N. returned from a tour of inspection, and told me all was quiet in Sackville Street, and begged me to go out with him and see the G.P.O.

I quaked rather, but we set off and reached Sackville Street safely.

Over the fine building of the G.P.O. floated a great green flag with the words 'Irish Republic' on it in large white letters. Every window on the ground floor was smashed and barricaded with furniture, and a big placard announced 'The Headquarters of the Provisional Government of the Irish Republic'. At every window were two men with rifles, and on the roof the parapet was lined with men. H.'s room appeared not to have been touched, and there were no men at his windows.

We stood opposite and were gazing, when suddenly two shots were fired, and, seeing there was likely to be an ugly rush, I fled again, exhorting N. to take refuge at the club.

He never reached the club, but came back to the hotel, and we had tea, and he then went to inspect St. Stephen's Green.

He found all round the Green, just inside the railings among the shrubberies, the rebels had dug deep pits or holes, and in every hole were three men. They had barricaded the street opposite the Shelbourne Hotel, and there had been a lot of firing and several people killed, and shots had gone into the hotel, which is, as you know, a fine building facing the Green.

All the evening we heard firing in all directions of the city and rumours of troops having arrived from the Curragh. While at dinner another message came through from H. to say we were not to be alarmed; he was quite safe, but might not get home that night.

After dinner N. went out to see if he could get near the Castle, but he found awful fighting. The troops were storming the City Hall and using machine-guns, and it was too 'unhealthy' for him to get near, so he came back at 9 and went to bed.

I stayed up in case of being wanted on the 'phone, and at 11.30 p.m. went up to my room, and a few minutes later H. walked in, to my immense relief.

The troops had arrived from the Curragh at about 5 p.m. and had promptly stormed the City Hall, which commanded the main gate of the Castle, and had taken it after fierce fighting.

H. saw prisoners being brought into the Castle yard, and when all was quiet he and several other officials crept out and reached their various homes.

People are appalled at the utter unpreparedness of the Government. In the face of a huge body of trained and armed men, openly revolutionary, they had taken no precautions whatever for the defence of the city in the event of an outbreak. At the beginning of the war H. obtained a military guard, armed, for the G.P.O., and they have always been there. When the outbreak occurred yesterday the armed guard were there, but with no ammunition! The sergeant was wounded in two places and the rest overpowered.

All night the firing continued. Between 1 and 2 a.m. it was awful, and I lay and quaked. It was all in the direction of the Castle.

This morning we hear the military are pouring into the city, and are in the Shelbourne Hotel and Trinity College.

The rebels have barricaded Sackville Street, and it is expected to be very fierce fighting over the G.P.O. It is terrible!

All our valuables were stored in H.'s safe and cupboard when we gave up our house, and all our dear F[red].'s books, sword, and all his possessions, which we value more than anything else in the world. We would not trust them with the stored furniture.

Yesterday afternoon the mob broke all the windows in various streets and looted all the shops. The streets were strewn with clothes, boots, furniture, tram cushions, and everything you can imagine.

While I am writing now there is incessant firing in St. Stephen's Green, and we fear there may be street fighting in this street.

In case you have forgotten, I will put a little plan here [see p. 106].

Tuesday, 5 p.m.

This morning martial law was proclaimed (I will try and get a copy of the proclamation) at 11.30 and the rebels given four hours to surrender.

A cruiser and two transports are said to have arrived at Kingstown, with troops from England. At 3.30 p.m., as there had been no surrender, the troops started to clear St. Stephen's Green, and raked it with machine-guns from the top of the Shelbourne Hotel and the United Service Club. We hear there are many casualties. N. has just come in, and says a big fire is raging in Sackville Street in the shops opposite the G.P.O., supposed to have been caused by the mob finding fireworks in a toy shop. The fire brigade arrived almost at once and could easily have overcome the fire, but the brigade was fired on by the Sinn Féiners, making it impossible for them to bring the engines into action, and they had to beat a retreat and leave the shops to burn themselves out. N. says the troops are clearing the houses of rebels behind Dame Street and the region of the Castle, and there is a lot of firing. It has turned to rain, which has cleared the streets of people.

A telegram has just come from the Admiralty stopping the mail boat from crossing. No boat has gone to-day, and we are absolutely cut off.

All the roads leading out of Dublin are in the hands of the rebels.

H. and N. have just come in, having seen Dr. W[heeler]. (now Major W.), Surgeon to the Forces in Ireland.[7] He told them that so far we had had about 500 casualties, two-thirds of them being civilians, shot in the streets.

The first thing Dr. W. heard of the outbreak was a 'phone message telling him to go at once to the Shelbourne as a man had been shot. He supposed it was a case of suicide, so jumped into his car and went off, fortunately in mufti. In Nassau Street his car was stopped and he was ordered to get out by rebels. He attempted to argue, and was told if he did not obey instantly he would be shot. Had he been in uniform he would have been shot at sight. As a civilian doctor they allowed him to go, and he took his bag and ran. He found three men shot in the Shelbourne, and a boy was shot as he reached the door.

Wednesday, April 26th, 9.30 a.m.

Last evening was quiet till we went to bed at 10.30, when most immediately a furious machine-gun fire began. It seemed just at the back of the hotel, but was really at the top of Grafton Street and the street leading to Mercer's Hospital. It lasted about twenty minutes, and then almost immediately after we got into bed a 'phone came that H. was to go at once to the Vice-Regal Lodge in the Phoenix Park, so he dressed and tried every way to get a motor; but of course no motor would go out. After some delay he got the field ambulance of the fire brigade at Dr. W.'s suggestion; but when it came the men told H. they had been carrying wounded all day, and that they had been constantly stopped by pickets and the car searched, and if they went and the car was stopped and found to contain H. they would undoubtedly all be shot; so H. considered it too risky, and it had to be abandoned. Eventually his Excellency gave his instructions over the 'phone, first in French, but that particular 'phone either did not speak or did not understand French; so eventually he took the risk of the 'phone being tapped and gave them in English. At last H. got to bed about 1 a.m., to be at the 'phone again at 5 a.m.

While we were dressing a terrific bombardment with field guns began – the first we had heard – and gave me cold shivers. The sound seemed to come from the direction of the G.P.O., and we concluded they were bombarding it. It went on for a quarter of an hour – awful! big guns and machine-guns – and then ceased, but we hear they were bombarding Liberty Hall, the headquarters of Larkin and the strikers two years ago, and always a nest of sedition. It is now crammed with Sinn Féiners. The guns were on H.M.S. *Helga*, that came up the river and smashed it from within about three hundred yards. It made me feel quite sick.

We think that they are leaving the Post Office for a time with the hope that when other strongholds are taken the Republican Government will surrender. H. has just been summoned to the Castle, and there is no knowing when he will be back. All who go out carry their lives in their hands. I went out twice yesterday, but we were turned back by shots being fired from upper windows, and the Lord Lieutenant has issued a proclamation begging people to keep in their houses, so I must restrain my curiosity.

All the shops remain closed, and no papers are issued except the proclamation, and we know nothing of what is going on in other parts of Ireland. But there are wild rumours of insurrection in Cork and other places.

This morning there is firing again in St. Stephen's Green, so the rebels are still there.

N. did a very fine thing yesterday. After the Green had been raked by our machine-gun fire he strolled up, in his casual way, to see the result! In front of one of the side gates in the railings, which are seven feet high and spiked three ways, he saw a small group of men peering into the Green. He went to see what they were looking at. The rebels had barricaded the gate, which opened inwards, by putting one of the heavy garden seats against it *upside down* and on the top of it another *right side up*, and lying full length on the seat, face downwards, was a man, a civilian, with all his lower jaw blown away and bleeding profusely. N. immediately climbed the railings and dropped down on the Sinn Féin side and found that the man was still living; he then turned and fairly cursed the men who were looking on, and asked if there was not one man enough to come over the railings and help him. Whereupon three men climbed over and together they lifted down the seat with the poor creature on it, dragged away the other seat, when they were able to open the gate, and then brought out the seat and the man on it and carried him to the nearest hospital, where he died in about five minutes.

N.'s theory is he was probably one of the civilians taken prisoner by the Sinn Féin the previous day, and was trying to escape from the awful machine-gun fire when he was shot down and fell back on to the seat. It was a terrible case.

The rebels from St. Stephen's Green are now also in possession of the College of Surgeons and are firing across the Green at the troops in the Shelbourne Hotel.

Lord S[haw].[8] tells me that 30,000 troops were landed at Kingstown this morning, and we hear they are amazed at their reception, as they had been told that they were going to quell a rebellion in Ireland, and lo! on their arrival at Kingstown the whole population turned out to cheer them, giving them food, cigarettes, chocolate, and everything the hospitable inhabitants could provide, so that the puzzled troops asked plaintively: 'Who then are we going to fight, and where is the rebellion?'

However, they were quickly disillusioned, for in marching into Dublin, when they reached Ballsbridge they came within range of several houses occupied by Sinn Féiners, and without a word of warning the battalion of Sherwood Foresters came under terrible crossfire and were just shot down, unable to return a single shot. I have not heard how many casualties occurred, but two or three officers and many men were killed and a number wounded. So surely soon we must be relieved.

Thursday, April 27th

Last night the mail boat left carrying passengers, and if it goes this evening Lord S. may be crossing, and he will take this to you.

Yesterday afternoon and evening there was terrible fighting. The rebels hold all the bridges over the canal, one on the tram line between this and Blackrock, another at the end of Baggot Street, and the other at Leeson Street. The fighting was terrible, but in the end we took the Leeson Street bridge, and I hope still hold it, as this opens a road to Kingstown. We failed to take the other two.

At the end of Lower Mount Street the rebels held the schools, and there was fierce fighting: our troops failed to surround the schools, and in the end, when they at last took them by a frontal attack with the loss of eighteen men and one officer, only one rebel was taken, the rest having escaped by the back.

Yesterday, to our great indignation, the public-houses were allowed to be open from 2 till 5, though every shop, bank, and public building was closed – just to inflame the mob, it could not have been on any other grounds; and yet at 8 p.m., after being on duty from 5 a.m., H. could not get a whiskey and soda, or even a glass of cider with his dinner, as it was out of hours. I was *furious*!

I must close this, as Lord S. has come in and says he expects to go to-night and will take this and H.'s report, so I will start a fresh letter to-morrow.

Don't worry overmuch about us. We quite expect to come out of this, but if we don't N. is *yours*.

L.N.

SECOND LETTER

Friday, 10 *a.m.*

DEAREST G., – After all my letter did not get off last night, as the roads were too dangerous to admit of Dr. W. motoring Lord S. to Kingstown. He got a permit to pass our troops, but there were too many Sinn Féin positions and snipers to make it possible for them to pass through.

If the position improves, he will go tonight, so I may be able to send this too, if I can write enough to make it worth while, but I am still rather shaky from a fright I had last night.

Yesterday morning the Red Cross ambulance sent in to the hotel to ask for volunteer workers to act as stretcher-bearers and do all sorts of jobs connected with the Red Cross, and N. and several men staying in the hotel volunteered. I was glad he should, as he is of course safer attached to the Red Cross than roaming the streets making rescues on his own, and if he was killed or wounded we should at least hear of it. But the risks are many and great, as in this kind of street fighting, where all the firing is from windows or from housetops, the ambulance are frequently under fire.

However, N. having volunteered promptly went off, and we saw him no more. While we were having dinner Mr. O'B[rien].,[9] who had been out all day with the ambulance, was dining with us. H. was called to the telephone to receive this message: 'You must not expect to see or hear from me till this is over.'

H. asked who the message was from, and the answer came back: 'Your son,' in a voice that H. was sure was not N.'s. H. then asked where the message came from, and was told 'The Castle.'

He returned to us greatly perturbed, and we held a consultation. We all agreed there was only one interpretation to be put on it, viz., that N. had been taken prisoner by the rebels, and that someone who was well disposed to H. had taken this opportunity of letting him know, and that saying the message came from the Castle was just a blind. H. rang up the head of the Red Cross, and he told us only two of the Red Cross volunteers were missing who had been out that day, and both of them were known, and N. was not one of them, so we were still more mystified.

It then occurred to H. that it might be possible to trace back the message and find out where it really had been sent from, so he called up the exchange, and after a little delay he heard the message had actually been sent from the Castle and by N., who was there.

Imagine our relief! though still completely in the dark as to why the boy had not come back like other workers, and why we were not to expect to see him again.

Next morning in walked the truant, not best pleased that we had been inquiring for him. His explanation was quite simple. He had been attached to a branch of the ambulance that had its depot at the Castle, so worked from there and returned to the Castle at night. Hearing this, and not knowing in the least to what part of the city his work would take him, and the impossibility of sending any message or note to tell us where he was, and knowing how anxious I should be if he did not return, he asked the Castle authorities if he might send a message to relieve our minds! He was told he might do so, but it must only be one sentence, and he must have the censor in the box with him. This so flustered N. that he could think of nothing to say but the words I have quoted; they seemed to him to express the position exactly, and he never dreamt of the interpretation we should put on them. As it was I spent an hour I don't ever like to remember and which unnerved me more than I thought possible, and all I got was a trouncing from N. for being so 'nervy'. Surely much is expected from mothers these days!

The volunteer workers, among other things, enter houses where there are known to be wounded Sinn Féiners and bring them out and take them to hospitals.

This N. was doing yesterday. One of the most awful things in this terrible time is that there must be scores of dead and dying Sinn Féiners, many of them mere lads, that no one can get at in the houses, and where they will remain till after the rebellion; and in some cases the houses take fire and they are all burnt. However, whatever is possible is being done.

Yesterday was the worst day we have had, as there was desperate fighting in Grafton Street, just at our back, and the side streets; and several volleys in our street.

In the morning I was sitting on a settee near the window of the lounge, knitting and looking out and listening to the firing in Grafton Street, when shots were fired just outside our windows, and Mr. B[esson]., the manager, came in and said, 'We must shut all the shutters, Mrs. N., it is getting a bit too hot, and I am taking no risks.' So all the shutters were closed, and I moved to the drawing-room above, which also overlooks the street.

All the afternoon an awful battle raged in the neighbourhood of the river and quays, and the din of the great guns and machine-guns was tremendous. We now have 30,000 troops and plenty of artillery and machine-guns, so the result cannot be uncertain, though there is desperate work to be done before the end is in sight.

The troops are said to have formed a huge semi-circle with the G.P.O. as the centre, and, starting from the river, are driving the rebels back street by street, till eventually they will be in a small enclosure, when they will bombard it to pieces.

The G.P.O. has such valuable records, etc., and the contents of the safes are so precious, that they will not raze it to the ground if they can help it; but it has so much subterranean space, that would afford cover to thousands of Sinn Féiners, that we hear they are going to fire some 'gas' shells into it and then rush it!

Up to yesterday afternoon they had got to Abbey Street on the right, and no doubt were closing in equally on other sides. The shells had started several fires; nearly all the shops on the quay on the side of the Custom House were burning yesterday afternoon, and later in the evening many others broke out.

I cannot give you any idea of what it was like when I went to bed. I sent for Mrs. B., the manager's wife, such a splendid little woman, and together we watched it from my window, which is high up and looked in the right direction.

It was the most awe-inspiring sight I have ever seen. It seemed as if the whole city was on fire, the glow extending right across the heavens, and the red glare hundreds of feet high, while above the roar of the fires the whole air seemed vibrating with the noise of the great guns and machine-guns. It was an inferno! We remained spell-bound, and I can't tell you how I longed for you to see it. We had only just come down from the window – we had been standing on the window ledge leaning out – when H. came and told us no one was to look out of the windows as there was cross-firing from the United Service Club and another building, and Mr. O'B., who was watching the fires from his window, had a bullet a few inches from his head!!

About 2 a.m. I woke to find the room illuminated in spite of dark blinds and curtains, and I rushed to the window and saw an enormous fire; it seemed to be in the direction of the Four Courts, which is in the hands of the Sinn Féiners, and we hear this morning that a portion of the buildings was burnt last night.*

Yesterday Lord S. had a narrow escape from a sniper who has been worrying this street for two days and could not be located. He was picking off soldiers during the fighting in Grafton Street, but later turned his attention to the cross streets between this and Grafton Street, and there as nearly as possible got Lord S., who was coming back to us from the Castle.

The military thought the man was on *our* roof, which made us all bristle with indignation – the mere idea of the wretch being on our hotel; but a thorough search proved he was not here, though he evidently had access to some roof.

In this respect we are much better off than our friends the V[erschoyle].'s.[10] They came into their town house only about a month ago, and being in Upper Mount Street it was in one of the most active haunts of the snipers. They had several on their roof, and when they went up to bed at night they could hear the snipers walking about and talking on the roof. Does it not make one creep to think of it? Mr. V. had his bed put on the upper landing exactly under the trap-door on to the roof, so that had the rebels attempted to enter the house at night they would have come down 'plop' on to him in his bed. He surrounded himself with all the arms he could muster, and the wretched Mrs. V. lay in bed and quaked, expecting any minute to hear a battle royal raging outside her bedroom door. In this street an old lady of seventy-three was shot through the leg in her own room, and was taken to Dr. W.'s home, where she had to have her leg amputated; and in another house a servant flashed on her electric light when going to bed and was instantly shot through the head! Our friend Miss K. also had a narrow escape. She had only just left her drawing-room, when a bullet passed straight through the room and buried itself in a picture.

Yesterday afternoon, when the firing in Grafton Street was over, the mob appeared and looted the shops, clearing the great provision shops and others. From the back of this hotel you look down on an alley that connects with Grafton Street, – and at the corner, the shop front in Grafton Street, but with a side

---

*This was incorrect; it was the Linen Hall barracks that were burnt.

entrance into this lane, is a very large and high-class fruiterer. From the windows we watched the proceedings, and I never saw anything so brazen! The mob were chiefly women and children with a sprinkling of men. They swarmed in and out of the side door bearing huge consignments of bananas, the great bunches on the stalk, to which the children attached a cord and ran away dragging it along. Other boys had big orange boxes which they filled with tinned and bottled fruits. Women with their skirts held up received showers of apples and oranges and all kinds of fruit which were thrown from the upper windows by their pals; and ankle-deep on the ground lay all the pink and white and silver paper and paper shavings used for packing choice fruits. It was an amazing sight, and nothing daunted these people. Higher up at another shop we were told a woman was hanging out of a window dropping down loot to a friend, when she was shot through the head by a sniper, probably our man; the body dropped into the street and the mob cleared. In a few minutes a hand-cart appeared and gathered up the body, and instantly all the mob swarmed back to continue the joyful proceedings!

H. and Lord S. were sitting at the window for a few minutes yesterday when the fruit shop was being looted, and saw one of the funniest sights they had ever seen. A very fat, very blousy old woman emerged from the side street and staggered on to the pavement laden with far more loot than she could carry. In her arms she had an orange box full of fruit, and under her shawl she had a great bundle tied up which kept slipping down. Having reached the pavement, she put down her box and sat on it, and from her bundle rolled forth many tins of fruit. These she surveyed ruefully, calling on the Almighty and all the saints to help her!! From these she solemnly made her selection, which she bound up in her bundle and hoisted, with many groans and lamentations, on her back and made off with, casting back many longing looks at the pile of things left on the pavement, which were speedily disposed of by small boys.

On Wednesday when the looting was going on in Sackville Street a fine, large boot shop was receiving attention from swarms of looters. Ragged women and children were seen calmly sitting in the window trying on boots and shoes, and one old woman with an eye to future needs made up a bundle of assorted sizes and tied them up in her apron. She had only reached the pavement, when she bethought her to leave her bundle in a corner and return for a further consignment which she tied up in her shawl. On returning to the street great was her rage and indignation on finding the original bundle had disappeared. Then were there sore lamentations and violent abuse of the police, who could not even 'protect the property of a poor old woman'.

In Sackville Street was a very large shop called Clery's; for some reason the looters were afraid to start on it; and old women passed up and down gazing longingly at fur coats and silken raiment and saying sorrowfully, 'Isn't Clery's broke yet?' and 'Isn't it a great shame that Clery's is not broke!' Rumour and tragedy are so intermixed in this catastrophe. A very delicate elderly lady who is staying here said to me this morning, in answer to my inquiry as to how she had slept: 'I could not sleep at all. When the guns ceased the *awful silence* made me so nervous!' I know exactly what she meant. When the roar of the guns ceases you can *feel* the silence.

4 p.m.

When I had got so far this morning I got an urgent message from the Red Cross asking me to make more armlets for the workers. With two other ladies I had been making them yesterday, so I collected my helpers and we worked till lunch, when another request came that we would make four large Red Cross flags, as they were going to try to bury some of the dead and needed the flags for the protection of the parties. We have just finished them, and are wondering what will be the next call. It is such a good thing I have my sewing-machine here.

On Wednesday evening Lord S. was at Mercer's Hospital with a doctor when eleven dead were brought in, and a priest brought in a rifle he had taken from a dead Sinn Féiner. It had an inscription in German and the name of the factory in Berlin, which Lord S. copied. It is believed that nearly all the arms and ammunition are of German make, and it is said that the cruiser that was sunk on Saturday was bringing heavy guns and forty officers, but I don't know if there is any truth in that. The opinion is very strong that the Sinn Féiners were led to believe that they would have great German reinforcements, and that all they had to do was to hold the troops here for a couple of days while the

Germans landed a big force on the west coast of Ireland. We also hear that Sir R. Casement has been shot in London, but you probably know a great deal more about that than I do, as we see no papers and are completely cut off from all news.

On Wednesday three of the ringleaders were caught, and it is said they were shot immediately! It is also believed that Larkin was shot on the top of a house in St. Stephen's Green, but as the rebels still hold the house it has not been possible to identify him, but he is said to have been here on Monday.*

5 p.m.

Colonel C. has just come in, having been in the thick of it for forty-eight hours. He tells us the Post Office has been set on fire by the Sinn Féiners, who have left it. If this is true, and it probably is, I fear we have lost all our valuable possessions, including my diamond pendant, which was in my jewel-case in H.'s safe.

To-day about lunch-time a horrid machine-gun suddenly gave voice very near us. We thought it was in this street, but it may have been in Kildare Street; also the sniper reappeared on the roofs, and this afternoon was opposite my bedroom window judging from the sound. I pulled down my blinds. A man might hide for weeks on the roofs of these houses among the chimney stacks and never be found as long as he had access to some house for food. When we were working in my room this afternoon he fired some shots that could not have been more than twenty yards away.

The serious problem of food is looming rather near, as nothing has come into the city since Saturday. Boland's bakery, an enormous building, is in the hands of the rebels, who have barricaded all the windows with sacks of flour, and it is said it will have to be blown up. There is not a chance of getting them out in any other way. The rebels also have Jacob's biscuit factory, where there are still huge stores of flour. Every prominent building and every strategic position was taken before the authorities at the Castle woke to the fact that there was a rebellion!

I was almost forgetting to tell you how splendidly one of H.'s men behaved when the G.P.O. was taken. When the rebels took possession they demanded the keys from the man who had

---

*This was incorrect; it appears Larkin was not in Dublin.

them in charge. He quietly handed over the keys, having first abstracted the keys of H.'s room!

Imagine such self-possession at such a terrible moment.

A young man has come to stay in the hotel who saw the taking of the G.P.O. He was staying at the hotel exactly opposite the building and went into the G.P.O. to get some stamps. As he was leaving the office a detachment of about fifteen Irish Volunteers marched up and formed up in front of the great entrance. He looked at them with some curiosity, supposing they were going to hold a parade; two more detachments arrived, and immediately the word of command was given, and they rushed in through the door. Shots were fired inside the building, and, as the young man said, he 'hooked it' back to the hotel, which was one of those burnt a few days later. The whole thing occupied only a few moments, as, being Bank Holiday, there was only a small staff in the building.

6.30 p.m.

A party of soldiers and a young officer have just arrived to search the roof for the sniper. They say he is on the roof of the annexe, which is connected with the main building by covered-in bridges. They are now on the roof and shots are being fired, so I expect they have spotted him.

When N. was out last night another ambulance had a bad experience. They had fetched three wounded Sinn Féiners out of a house, and were taking them to hospital, when they came under heavy fire. The driver was killed, so the man beside him took the wheel and was promptly wounded in both legs. The car then ran away and wrecked itself on a lamp post. Another ambulance had to run the gauntlet and go to the rescue!

On the whole as far as possible the rebels have respected the Red Cross, but not the white flag. In house-to-house fighting there can be no connected action, and yesterday when a house was being stormed the rebels hung out a white flag, and when the troops advanced to take them prisoners they were shot down from a house a few doors higher up the street, so now no more white flag signals are to be recognised. If they want to surrender they must come out and take their own risks.

We asked N. if he knew what had happened to the ambulance that had two men missing yesterday, and he told us they were in the act of entering a Sinn Féin house to bring out wounded with two other men when the ambulance came under such heavy fire that, as it contained one or two other wounded men, it had to beat a retreat and moved off. Two of the volunteer helpers ran after it and succeeded in reaching it and climbed in, but the other two took refuge in the area, and N. did not know how or when they were rescued. This is an instance of the extreme danger that attends the ambulance work. The marvel is that the casualties are so few.

Guinness's Brewery have made three splendid armoured cars by putting great long boilers six feet in diameter on to their large motor lorries. Holes are bored down the sides to let in air, and they are painted grey. The driver sits inside too. They each carry twenty-two men or a ton of food in absolute security. N. saw them at the Castle being packed with men; nineteen got in packed like herrings, and three remained outside. Up came the sergeant: 'Now then, gentlemen, move up, move up: the car held twenty-two yesterday; it must hold twenty-two to-day'; and in the unfortunate three were stuffed. It must have been suffocating, but they were taken to their positions in absolute safety.

Saturday, 29th, 10 a.m.

Last night was an agitating one. The sniper was very active, and after dinner several shots struck the annexe, one or two coming through the windows, and one broke the glass roof of the bridge. Mr. B., who never loses his head, decided to get all the people out of the annexe, with staff (about forty people); and all we in the main building, whose rooms look out on the back, were forbidden to have lights in our rooms at all. There was such a strong feeling of uneasiness throughout the hotel, and always the danger of its being set on fire, that about 10 p.m. H. said we must be prepared at any moment to leave the hotel if necessary. So we went up to our room and in pitch darkness groped about and collected a few things (F.'s miniature and the presentation portrait of him, my despatch case with his letters, my fur coat, hat and boots), and we took them down to the sitting-room, which H. uses as an office, on the first floor. All the people in the hotel were collected in the lounge, which is very large and faces the street, and the whole of the back was in complete darkness. The firing quieted down, and about 11.30 we crept up to our room and lay down in our clothes. When dawn broke I got up and undressed and had two hours' sleep. All the rest of the guests spent the night in the lounge.

This morning we hear an officer has been to say that the shots fired into the hotel last night were fired by the military. People were constantly pulling up their blinds for a moment with the lights on to look at the city on fire, and the military have orders to fire on anything that resembles signalling without asking questions.

Reliable news has come in this morning that nothing remains of the G.P.O. but the four main walls and the great portico. It is absolutely burnt out. The fires last night were terrible, but we dared not look out. Eason's Library and all the shops and buildings between O'Connell Bridge and the G.P.O. on both sides of Sackville Street are gone.

It is difficult to think of the position without intense bitterness, though God knows it is the last thing one wishes for at such a time. In pandering to Sir E. Carson's fanaticism and allowing him to raise a body of 100,000 armed men for the sole purpose of rebellion and provisional government the Government tied their own hands and rendered it extremely difficult to stop the arming of another body of men, known to be disloyal, but whose *avowed* reason was the internal defence of Ireland! In Ulster the wind was sown, and, my God, we have reaped the whirl-wind!

We hear that many of our wounded are being sent to Belfast, as the hospitals here are crowded, and the food problem must soon become acute. Mr. O'B. told me his ambulance picked up four wounded, three men and a woman, and took them to the nearest hospital. The woman was dying, so they stopped at a church and picked up a priest; arrived at the hospital the authorities said they could not possibly take them in as they had not enough food for those they had already taken, but when they saw the condition of the woman they took her in to die, and the others had to be taken elsewhere.

If the main walls of the G.P.O. remain standing it may be we shall find the safe in H.'s room still intact. It was built into the wall, and my jewel-case was in it, but all our silver, old engravings, and other valuables were stored in the great mahogany cupboards when we gave up our house in the autumn, as being the safest place in Dublin.

4 p.m.

Sir M. N. has just rung up to say the rebels have surrendered unconditionally. We have no details, and the firing continues in various parts of the town. But if the leaders have surrendered it can only be a question of a few hours before peace is restored, and we can go forth and look on the wreck and desolation of this great city.

So ends, we hope, this appalling chapter in the history of Ireland – days of horror and slaughter comparable only to the Indian Mutiny. This seems a suitable place, dear G., to end this letter, and I hope to start a happier one to-morrow.

Yours,
L. N.

THIRD LETTER

Sunday, April 30th, 10 a.m.

DEAREST G., – When I closed my letter last night with the news that the rebel leaders had surrendered I hoped to start this new letter in a more cheerful strain; but while we were dining last night H. was rung up from the Castle to hear that the whole of Sackville Street north of the G.P.O. right up to the Rotunda was on fire and blazing so furiously that the fire brigade were powerless; nothing could go near such an inferno. There was nothing to be done but let the fire exhaust itself.

If this was true, it involved the loss of the Post Office Accountant's Office opposite the G.P.O., the Sackville Street Club, Gresham and Imperial Hotels, and other important buildings, and would have increased H.'s difficulties enormously, as it would have been necessary to build up the Post Office organisation again, with no records, registers, accounts, or documents of any kind – at best a stupendous task. However, fortunately this morning we hear the reports were exaggerated. The Imperial Hotel, Clery's great shop, and one or two others were burnt, but the upper part of the street escaped, and the Accountant's Office and the Sackville Street Club were not touched.

This morning Mr. C[oonan]., who has been H.'s great support all through this trying time (his second in command being away ill), and several other members of the staff are coming here, and with H. they are going down to see what remains of the G.P.O. It is being guarded from looters, as, from the enormous number of telegraph instruments destroyed, there must be a large quantity of copper and other metal, – a very valuable asset, – and also several thousand pounds in cash for payment of staff and soldiers' dependants, besides heaps of other valuable property.

Here I must tell you how absolutely heroic the telephone staff have been at the Exchange. It is in a building a considerable distance from the G.P.O., and the Sinn Féiners have made great efforts to capture it. The girls have been surrounded by firing; shots have several times come into the switch-room, where the men took down the boards from the back of the switch-boards and arranged them as shelters over the girls' heads to protect them from bullets and broken glass. Eight snipers have been shot on buildings commanding the Exchange, and one of the guard was killed yesterday; and these twenty girls have never failed. They have been on duty since Tuesday, sleeping when possible in a cellar and with indifferent food, and have cheerfully and devotedly stuck to their post, doing the work of forty. Only those on duty on the outbreak of the rebellion could remain; those in their homes could never get back, so with the aid of the men who take the night duty these girls have kept the whole service going. All telegrams have had to be sent by 'phone as far as the railway termini, and they have simply saved the situation. It has been magnificent!

The shooting is by no means over, as many of the Sinn Féin strongholds refuse to surrender. Jacob's biscuit factory is very strongly held, and when the rebels were called on to surrender they refused unless they were allowed to march out carrying their arms!

It is said that when Jacob was told that the military might have to blow up the factory he replied: 'They may blow it to blazes for all I care; I shall never make another biscuit in Ireland.' I don't know if this is true, but it very well may be, for he has been one of the model employers in Dublin, and almost gave up the factory at the time of the Larkin strike, and only continued it for the sake of his people; and so it will be with the few great industries in the city. Dublin is ruined.*

---

*As the book passes through the press, I learn on the one uninpeachable authority that the story about Messrs. Jacob & Co., however picturesque, is apocryphal. M.L.N.

Yesterday I made a joyful discovery. When we came back from Italy in March, H. brought back from the office my large despatch-case in which I keep all F.'s letters. I did not remember what else was in it, so I investigated and found my necklet with jewelled cross and the pink topaz set (both of these being in large cases would not go in the jewel-case), also the large old paste buckle; so I am not absolutely destitute of jewellery. But, best of all, there were the three little handkerchiefs F. sent me from Armentières with my initial worked on them; for these I was grieving more than for anything, and when I found them the relief was so great I sat with them in my hand and cried.

This week has been a wonderful week for N. Never before has a boy of just seventeen had such an experience. Yesterday morning he was at the Automobile Club filling cans of petrol from casks for the Red Cross ambulance. He came in to lunch reeking of petrol. In the afternoon he went round with the Lord Mayor in an ambulance collecting food for forty starving refugees from the burnt-out district housed in the Mansion House, and after tea went out for wounded and brought in an old man of seventy-eight shot through the body. He was quite cheery over it, and asked N. if he thought he would recover. 'Good Lord! yes; why not?' said N., and bucked the old man up!

Some of the staff who came here this morning had seen a copy of the *Daily Mail* yesterday, which devoted about six lines to the condition of things in Ireland and spoke of a Sinn Féin riot in which four soldiers and about six rebels had been killed. If that is all the English people are being told of a rebellion which 30,000 troops and many batteries of artillery are engaged in putting down, my letter will be rather a surprise to you; and as the news must come out, the English people will hardly be pleased at being kept in the dark. Such a rebellion cannot be suppressed like a Zeppelin raid. During the first three days our casualties were nearly 1,000; now we hear they are close on 2,000.*

The College of Surgeons in St. Stephen's Green is still held by the rebels, so the firing of machine-guns from the Shelbourne Hotel and the United Service Club goes on as before, and there is intermittent firing in all directions. I doubt if it will quite cease for some days, as these strongholds will not surrender. Also the incendiary fires will probably continue. The great fire in

---

*This was exaggerated, our total casualties being about 1,380.

Sackville Street last night was no doubt the work of incendiaries, as all the fires had died down. There was no wind, no shells were being fired, and no reason for the outbreak, but with all the relations and sympathisers of the rebels at large the fires may very well continue.

The staff have just returned. They are quite unnerved by what they have seen; they report nothing left of the G.P.O. but the four outside walls and portico, so we have lost everything. They say it is like a burned city in France.

May 1st, 11 a.m.

I had no time to continue this yesterday, but during the afternoon three of the rebel strongholds surrendered – Jacob's, Boland's, and the College of Surgeons on St. Stephen's Green. From this last building 160 men surrendered and were marched down Grafton Street. It is said that among them was Countess Markievicz, dressed in a man's uniform. It is also said that the military made her take down the green republican flag flying over the building herself and replace it by a white one: when she surrendered she took off her bandolier and kissed it and her revolver before handing them, to the officer. She has been one of the most dangerous of the leaders, and I hope will be treated with the same severity as the men. People who saw them marched down Grafton Street said they held themselves erect, and looked absolutely defiant!

2 p.m.

To-day for the first time since Easter Monday the *Irish Times* issued a paper with news of the rebellion. Very pluckily they had brought out a paper on Tuesday, but it contained only the proclamation and no reference to the rebellion, but a long account of Gilbert and Sullivan's operas which were to have been performed this week.

To-day's paper bears the dates 'Friday, Saturday, and Monday, April 28th, 29th, and May 1st' – an incident unique, I should think, in the history of the paper.

It contains the various proclamations in full, which I will cut out and send to you. Please keep them, as they will be of interest in the future.

The paper states that Sir R. Casement is a prisoner in the Tower. So he was not shot without trial, as we were told. It also gives a list of the large shops and business establishments that have been destroyed – a total of 146.

It really seemed delightful to hear the little paper boys calling their papers about the streets again, and they had a ready sale for their papers at three times their value. This so encouraged them that in the afternoon they were running about again calling 'Stop press.' Several people went out and bought papers, only to find they were the same papers they had paid 3*d*. for in the morning.

'But this is the same paper I bought this morning.'

'Sure, and it is, ma'am, but there's been a power of these papers printed, and they're not going to print any more till they're all sold.'

Another lady thought she would drive a lesson home, so she said: 'But you said it was a "Stop press", and you knew it was not.'

'It is, miss, but sure they hadn't time to print the "stop press" on it!!'

('Stop press' is the latest news, usually printed on the back of the paper.)

Anyway, so great was the relief at seeing a paper again that no one grudged the urchins their little harvest.

Yesterday H. visited the Telephone Exchange, and a point was cleared up that has mystified everyone; and that is why, when the rebels on Easter Monday took every building of importance and every strategic position, did they overlook the Telephone Exchange? Had they taken it we should have been absolutely powerless, unable to send messages or telegrams for troops. The exchange is situated in Crown Alley, off Dame Street, and the superintendent told H. an extraordinary story. It seems when the rebels had taken the G.P.O. they marched a detachment to take the exchange, when just as they were turning into Crown Alley an old woman rushed towards them with arms held up calling out, 'Go back, boys, go back; the place is crammed with military'; and supposing it to be in the hands of our troops they turned back. This was at noon. At 5 p.m. our troops arrived and took it over.

This saved the whole situation. Whether the woman was on our side or whether she thought she had seen soldiers will never be known.

When at the Castle yesterday H. got a copy of *The Times* for Saturday, the first paper we have seen since Monday, so you can imagine how eagerly we scanned the news about Ireland. More has got out than we expected, but still nothing like the true position. We rubbed our eyes when we read that 'two battalions' had been sent to Ireland, and wondered if it could possibly have been a printer's error for two divisions (40,000 men) which actually arrived on Wednesday. The people were in the streets of Kingstown for twenty hours watching the troops pass through. Since then many more troops and artillery have come in.

2 p.m.

I have just returned from walking round the G.P.O. and Sackville Street with H. and some of the officials. It passes all my powers of description, only one word describes it, 'Desolation.' If you look at pictures of Ypres or Louvain after the bombardment it will give you some idea of the scene.

We looked up through the windows of the G.P.O. and saw the safe that was in H.'s room still in the wall, and the door does not appear to have been opened or the safe touched, but the whole place has been such an inferno one would think the door must have been red-hot. Among all the *débris* the fire was still smouldering, and we could not penetrate inside. I picked up a great lump of molten metal, a fantastic shape with bits of glass embedded in it. It is bright like silver, but they tell me it is lead. It is quite curious. Do you realise, G., that out of all H.'s library he now does not possess a single book, except one volume of his Dante, and I not even a silver teaspoon!!

Everything belonging to F. has gone; as he gave his life in the war, so an act of war has robbed us of everything belonging to him – our most precious possession.

It has almost broken H. up; but he has no time to think, which is perhaps a good thing.

The old Morland and Smith mezzotints have also gone – things we can never replace.

Behind the G.P.O. was the Coliseum Theatre, now only a shell; and on the other side of the street was the office of the *Freeman's Journal*, with all the printing machinery lying among the *débris*, all twisted and distorted; but, worst of all, behind that was a great riding school, where all the horses were burnt to death.

If at all possible you ought to come over for Whitsuntide. You will see such a sight as you will never see in your life unless you go to Belgium.

When we came here H. was scandalised at the condition of the G.P.O. The whole frontage was given up to sorting offices, and the public office was in a side street, a miserable, dirty little place, that would have been a disgrace to a small country town.

H. found that plans had been drawn up and passed for the complete reconstruction of the interior, building in a portion of the courtyard an office for sorting purposes, leaving the frontage for the public office with entrance under the great portico.

So H. *hustled*, and the work was completed and opened to the public six weeks ago.

It was really beautiful. The roof was a large glass dome, with elaborate plaster work, beautiful white pillars, mosaic floor, counters all of red teak wood, and bright brass fittings every-where – a public building of which any great city might be proud; and in six weeks all that is left is a smoking heap of ashes!

N. had an extraordinary find inside one of the rooms. About six yards from the main wall he found, covered with ashes and a beam lying across it, a motor cycle. It was lying on its side. He got it out and found it perfect, tyres uninjured and petrol in the tank, and he rode it to the hotel, and has now taken it to the Castle to hand over to the police.

May 2nd, 10 a.m.

Last evening after tea I walked all round the ruined district with N. and two ladies from the hotel. The streets were thronged with people, and threading their way among the crowd were all sorts of vehicles: carts carrying the bodies of dead horses that had been shot the first day and lain in the streets ever since; fire brigade ambulances, followed by Irish cars bringing priests and driven by fire brigade men. Then motors with Red Cross emblems carrying white-jacketed doctors would dart along, followed by a trail of Red Cross nurses on bicycles, in their print dresses and white overalls, their white cap-ends floating behind them, all speeding on their errand of mercy to the stricken city.

From time to time we came across on the unwashed pave-ment the large dark stain telling its own grim story, and in one place the blood had flowed along the pavement for some yards and down into the gutter; but enough of horrors. We came sadly back, and on the steps we met Mr. O'B. returning from a similar walk. He could hardly speak of it, and said he stood in Sackville Street and cried, and many other men did the same.

Last night after dinner we were sitting in the room H. uses as a temporary office overlooking the street, when firing began just outside. They were evidently firing at the offices of the Sinn Féin Volunteers at the bottom of the road. It was probably the last stand of the rebels, and the firing was very sharp and quick. We thought bullets must come into the hotel. I was reading aloud some bits out of the *Daily Mail*, and the men were smoking. They moved my chair back to the wall between the windows out of the line of fire; but the firing became so violent we decided it was foolhardy to remain, so we deserted the room, took our papers, and went and sat on the stairs till it was over.

Since then we have not heard a shot fired; and it would seem that as we were present at the first shots fired in Sackville Street on Easter Monday so we have been present at the last fired eight days later in Dawson Street.

Out of all the novel experiences of the last eight days two things strike me very forcibly. The first is that, under circumstances that might well have tried the nerves of the strongest, there has been no trace of fear or panic among the people in the hotel, either among the guests or staff. Anxiety for absent friends of whom no tidings could be heard, though living only in the next square, one both felt and heard; but of fear for their own personal safety I have seen not one trace, and the noise of battle after the first two days seemed to produce nothing but boredom. The other is a total absence of thankfulness at our own escape.

It may come; I don't know. Others may feel it; I don't. I don't pretend to understand it; but so it is. Life as it has been lived for the last two years in the midst of death seems to have blunted one's desire for it, and completely changed one's feelings towards the Hereafter.

Now, G., I will end this long letter, and my next will probably deal with normal if less interesting matters, but intense interest must remain in the reconstruction of this great city.

Surely it must be possible to find men who will rule with firmness and understanding this fine people – so kindly, so emotional, so clever, so easily guided, and so magnificent when wisely led. One prays they may be found, and found quickly, and that we may live to see a Dublin restored to its former stateliness with a Government worthy of the nation.

Ever yours,
L. N.

FOURTH LETTER

Thursday, May 4th

DEAREST G., – I had not intended writing again so soon, but things are still happening that I think you will like to know, so I am going on with this series of letters, though I don't know when you will get them. But as by this time you will have seen N. you will have heard many details from him. How much he will have to tell his school-fellows when he returns to Shrewsbury to-morrow! I hoped to have sent my second and third letters by N., and in fact had actually packed them with his things. But when I told H. he said the rules were so stringent about letters that N. would certainly be questioned as to whether he was carrying any, and if he replied in the affirmative, which he certainly would have done, the letters would undoubtedly be confiscated and N. might get into serious trouble. So I had to unpack them again and must keep them till the censorship is removed, which will probably be in a few days. They have been written under much stress of circumstances, and are the only record we have of this most deeply interesting time, so I don't want to lose them altogether.

I am not too well, as they say here. The loss of eight nights' sleep seems to have robbed me of the power of sleeping for more than an hour or two at a stretch, and even that is attended often with horrid dreams and nightmares. But this is only the effect of over-strain, and no doubt will pass, though my head feels like a feather bed; so don't expect too much from these later letters.

Last night after dinner, when H. and I were sitting upstairs in attendance on the telephone, who should walk in but Dr. W. We had not met throughout the rebellion, so he had heaps to tell us.

His wife and children were down at Greystones, and the poor thing had had a terribly anxious time, hearing nothing reliable of her husband or of her father, Lord S. What she did hear was that Dr. W. had been killed and also that H. had been shot in the G.P.O. She became so anxious that her faithful Scotch nurse was determined to get into Dublin and get news or die in the attempt. I must tell you her adventures, not only to show you how impossible it was to get into the city, but also it is such an extraordinary story of endurance and devotion that it ought to be recorded.

The girl started from Greystones at 2.30 p.m. on the Thursday, I think it was, carrying for the officers' home 14 lbs. of beef and 4 lbs. of butter, as Mrs. W. feared supplies would have run short, since nothing could be got in Dublin except at exorbitant prices (7s. a dozen for eggs and 14s. for a pair of chickens); so the girl started carrying a dead weight of 18 lbs.

She walked to Bray (five miles) and took train to Kingstown; here she had to take to the road, as the line beyond Kingstown was wrecked. She walked to Merrion Gates along the tram line about four miles, when she was stopped by sentries. She retraced her steps as far as Merrion Avenue (one mile), went up Merrion Avenue, and tried the Stillorgan-Donnybrook route. Here she got as far as Leeson Street Bridge (six miles), when she was within 800 yards of her destination, Dr. W.'s house. Here again she was stopped by sentries and turned back. She walked back to Blackrock (seven miles), when she was again stopped by sentries. She then returned up Merrion Avenue and, seeing that all routes were impossible to Dublin, took the road to Killiney (five miles), where she arrived about 11.30 p.m., having done thirty miles. Here she got hospitality at a cottage and stayed the remainder of the night there, paying for her accommodation with the 4 lbs. of butter, but she stuck gamely to the beef.

Next day she walked five miles to Shankhill, when she met a cart going to Bray *viâ* Killiney, so she rode back to Killiney on it and from thence to Bray. She then walked the five miles from Bray back to Greystones, her starting point.

Arrived back, she reached home absolutely exhausted, having walked forty miles, and dropped down saying, 'There's your beef, and I never got there or heard anything.' Mrs. W. was greatly distressed at her having carried the meat back when so exhausted and asked her why she had not given it away. 'And

what for should I give it away when we'll be wanting it ourselves maybe?'

Next day Dr. W. managed to get a telephone message through
to his wife and relieved her anxiety.

He told us that on the first or second night of the rebellion –
he could not remember which – two ladies of the Vigilance
Committee patrolling the streets at night came on a soldier lying
wounded in an alley off Dawson Street, where he had crawled
on being wounded. They went to Mercer's Hospital and gave
information, and stretcher-bearers were sent out to bring in the
man, the ladies accompanying them. When he was on the
stretcher the two ladies walked up to the railings of St. Stephen's
Green and gave the Sinn Féiners inside a regular dressing down,
telling them they were skunks and cowards to shoot people
down from behind bushes and asking them why they did not
come out and fight in the open like men. Meanwhile the
stretcher-bearers had taken the man to the hospital, where Dr. W.
saw him.

'Well, my man; where are you hurt?'

'Divil a pellet, sorr, above the knee,' laughing.

'Does it pain you?'

'Not at all, sorr. Wait till I show you.' He pulled up his
trousers and showed five bullet shots below the knee.

'What regiment?'

'Royal Irish, sorr, like Michael Cassidy, of Irish nationality;
and I bear no ill-will to nobody.'

Cheery soul! His great pride was that about forty shots had
been fired at him and not one hit him above the knee.

Dr. W. must bear a charmed life. He told us of several escapes
he had. One, the most dramatic, I must tell you.

You know he is one of the surgeons to Mercer's Hospital, and
had to be perpetually operating there at all hours of the day and
night, besides having his own private hospital, in which he takes
wounded officers. It too was filled with rebellion victims, so his
work was tremendous.

One night he left Mercer's about 1 a.m., accompanied by
another doctor. When passing in front of the Shelbourne Hotel
they were challenged by our troops there. On explaining who
they were they were of course allowed to proceed, and they
stepped briskly out, wanting to get home. Suddenly, on the same
pavement, about twenty yards away as far as they could judge

in the black darkness, out flashed two little lights from small electric lamps, evidently Sinn Féin signals. Dr. W. stopped and said to his companion: 'Did you see that? it was a signal,' when almost before the words were out of his mouth two rifles blazed straight at them, almost blinding them with the flash, and they *felt* the bullets whiz past their heads. The two Sinn Féiners, having signalled, waited long enough to see if their signal was returned, and then fired straight at where by their footsteps they supposed Dr. W. and his friend to be, and missed them by an inch or two.

Dr. W. and his friend got into the shelter of a doorway and flattened themselves out, trying to look as if they were not there, and quite forgetting that they both had lighted cigarettes, whose red tips should have been a beacon light to a vital spot had the Sinn Féiners noticed them. But for some reason they did not proceed further, and Dr. W. heard their steps dying away in the distance. Meanwhile his companion had his finger on the electric bell of the doorway where they were hiding, and after a time which seemed like an eternity an upper window opened and a voice inquired who was there, whereupon the woman of the house came down and let them in, and they spent the remainder of the night there.

Yesterday the Post Office was able to pay the separation allowances to the soldiers' wives. Last week of course it was impossible, but as it would have been equally impossible for them to have bought anything it did not so much matter. The question was how to get so large a sum of money round to the outlying post offices in safety, for, though the city is now comparatively safe, there are still snipers in outlying districts, and any party of Post Office officials known to have possession of large sums of money would undoubtedly have been attacked. So H. bethought him to requisition for one of the boiler armoured cars with military guard, and it was at once granted him. We had heard of them from N., but had not seen one, and great was the excitement at the hotel when this huge monster arrived for H.'s instructions. We all went out and examined it.

It was not one of Guinness's, but one that had been rigged up by one of the railway companies, with an engine boiler fixed on to a huge motor trolley, all painted light grey; and all down each side were black dots in an elegant design ...

One of the armoured cars manufactured by Guinnesses's Brewery
(from *The Sinn Fein Rebellion As I Saw It*)

Here and there one of these squares was cut out and acted as an
air-hole, but they all looked exactly alike, so a sniper on a roof or
from a window aiming at one of these squares probably found
his bullet struck iron and bounded off to the accompaniment of
derisive jeers from the 'Tommies' inside. From the hotel the car
proceeded to the Bank of Ireland, and took over £10,000 in silver,
and started on its round to all the post offices, delivering the
money in perfect safety. I will try and send you a photograph of
one of these most ingenious conveyances.

After it had started on its round I went with H. to see the
temporary sorting offices. H. had secured an enormous skating
rink at the back of the Rotunda, and here all the sorting of letters
was going on, with no apparatus whatever except what the men
had contrived for themselves out of seats, benches and old
scenery. They were all hard at work – a regular hive of bees. We
think it is greatly to the credit of the Post Office staff that in twelve
days from the *outbreak* of the rebellion and three days after the
actual cessation of hostilities the whole service was reorganised,
with two deliveries a day in Dublin, besides the ordinary country

and mail deliveries. The engineers and telegraphists were no less wonderful. Indeed the staff from top to bottom of the office have worked splendidly, and H. is very proud of them. We looked in at the poor G.P.O. on our way back. It is still smouldering, and it will be quite a fortnight before any excavations can be begun, but H. hopes to get the safe that contains many of our treasures out of the wall and opened in a few days.

To-day a Dr. C. who is staying in the hotel told me of an extra-ordinary escape he had had during one of the days of the rebellion. He was walking through one of the squares, which he had been told was clear of snipers, with an old friend of about eighty, when suddenly a bullet struck the pavement at the feet of his friend and ricochetted off. It was within an inch of the old gentleman's feet, and he was greatly interested, wanting to find the bullet to keep as a memento. While they were looking about for it a man who had been walking just behind them passed them on the pavement, and had only gone a few yards when they heard a second rifle shot, and the man dropped like a stone, shot through the heart. Dr. C. ran up to him, but he was quite dead. There was absolutely no safety anywhere from the snipers; man, woman, or child, nothing came amiss to them. It was dastardly fighting, if it could be called fighting at all.

A few days after St. Stephen's Green was supposed to have been cleared of rebels, we were told of a young woman whose husband was home from the war wounded and in one of the hospitals. She was going to see him, so took a short cut through the Green, when she was shot through the thigh; it is supposed by a rebel, in hiding in the shrubberies.

Sunday, 7th

I am sending off my other letters to you to-morrow, as we hear the censorship is no longer so strict, and as from the papers the position here seems now to be known in England private letters are not likely to be stopped. I will keep this till the safe is opened and tell you the result.

15th

To-day Mr. O'B. brought his wife to see me, and they have offered us their lovely house, Celbridge Abbey, about ten miles from

Dublin, for five or six weeks from June 1st as they are going abroad again, and they thought we should like it for a change. We are more than grateful, as all our plans for going to Greystones for June and July are knocked on the head; but to Celbridge there is a good train service, and H. can come into Dublin every day, while I can revel in the lovely garden and grounds and recover in the peace and quiet my lost powers of sleep. What a kind thought it is, and how welcome at such a time! Celbridge Abbey was the home of Swift's 'Vanessa', and later of Grattan, Ireland's greatest orator, so is a most interesting and historical place.

17th

To-day the safe was opened, and contained nothing of any value, only a few official papers!

With this has gone our last hope of any salvage from the wreck of our property. Dillon's 'perfect gentlemen,' of whom he expressed himself so proud in the House the other night,[11] had evidently broken open H.'s great official desk, and found the key of the safe and abstracted my jewel-case, F.'s field-glasses and several other of his much-prized possessions, and then locked the safe again. The only document they stole from among the official documents was F.'s commission. Why, we cannot imagine, unless the fact that it bore the King's signature made it worthy of special insult and desecration.

H. was very sad when he told me, but I think I am past caring about any possessions now. F. and all his precious things are gone. Nothing else seems worth considering. Perhaps some day we may pluck up heart to collect things again around us, but at present one can only feel, 'Let the dead bury the dead.'

20th

To-day they are beginning on the excavations of H.'s room; the fire burnt with such ferocity that there is much less rubble in it than one would imagine. As you probably remember, H.'s room was on the first floor, with a storey above it. When the whole place fell in, H.'s room fell through into the room below, and a portion of that had fallen through to the cellars. The men are removing everything of the nature of bricks and iron and stone coping of the roof, and then four extra-careful men are to be put on to shovel up the rest of the *débris*, which is burnt to powder, and Noblett, H.'s confidential messenger, is going to be there to receive anything of ours that may be found.

23rd

Yesterday morning and this morning I have been down watching the excavations of H.'s room. It is quite like the excavations at Pompeii. Every shovelful is most carefully overlooked, and several of our things have turned up, though so far nothing of any intrinsic value. When I went there yesterday morning Noblett produced a great lump of molten glass of no shape or form with one or two metal nobs [*sic*] sticking up at odd angles. He thought it was the remains of a cruet, but we had none; and on further examination it flashed across my mind that it was the cut-glass bottles in the large rosewood and brass-bound dressing-case in which I had packed all my jewellery – family miniatures, four gold watches and chains; diamond pendant, etc. It had been stolen out of the safe, and evidently the looters had not been able to get it away. Noblett was thrilled, and the men redoubled their carefulness, hoping to find some of the jewellery. When I went down again in the afternoon Noblett produced three little brooches that F. had given me on various birthdays when a wee boy. He always went out with his own sixpence, and nearly always returned with a brooch, which I used to wear with great pride. One, a Swastika brooch, he gave me when he was at Margate after that terrible illness, and he used to go on the pier in his bath-chair. The blue enamel on it was intact in several places; the other two were intact in form, but charred and black, with the pins burnt off. But how glad I was to see them again! During the afternoon two or three more brooches turned up, but nothing of any value whatever. So we came to the conclusion the rebels had broken open the box and taken out everything of value and thrown away the rest. The few burnt bits of jewellery that were found all came from one spot.

This morning when I went Noblett had nearly a sackful of curiosities, which I sorted over. Evidently these were the whole contents of the canteen of plated things we used to take with us when we took a furnished house and put the silver in a bank, quantities of spoons and forks, black, and looking like old iron, many twisted into weird shapes, and the knives, which were

new when we came here, without a scrap of ivory handle, and
the blades burnt and twisted in the most extraordinary way. A
most miserable-looking collection, fit only for the dust-heap.

25th

They are nearing the end of the excavations, and nothing of any
value has been found. This morning when I went I found them
cutting into a mound of what looked like solid white chalk. I
could not imagine what it could be, but the men told me it was
the books that had been stored in one of the great mahogany
presses; not a trace of burnt wood was found. I could not believe
that books could be reduced to such a substance. I had expected
to find quantities of charred black paper, with possibly some
fragments of binding, and was quite incredulous. However, on
examining it I found the substance was in layers like the leaves
of a book, but when I picked some up it felt like silk between my
fingers, and you could blow it away like thistle-down. Had I not
seen it myself I should never have believed such a thing
possible. Besides H.'s and F.'s books there were a number of
great official books in leather bindings half an inch thick, but all
was reduced to the same substance.

  Noblett gave me to-day one of Princess Mary's gift boxes that
had been sent to me by a soldier at the front; except for being
black instead of bright brass, it was absolutely uninjured – the
medallion in the centre, and the inscription, date, etc., perfect.
The Christmas card inside and the Queen's letter were just black
charred paper, but you could see the M. and the crown above it
on the card. Also an antique brass snuff-box inlaid with mother-
of-pearl turned up but little injured.

26th

To-day the men finished their work on H.'s room. At the last
about eight fragments of silver forks and two tablespoons were
taken out and a foot of a silver sugar-bowl with a bit of something that looked like burnt tissue paper attached to it; and that
was all that was found of all our silver. The half of a copper base
of one of our beautiful Sheffield plate candelabra came out of
one of the last shovelfuls, – and there was an end of all our
property.

So that page is turned, and it seems a good place to end this over-long letter. On Thursday we go down to Celbridge, where with memories of Swift and the wretched and foolish Vanessa and in company with a beautiful swan and swaness, which bring their babies to the lawn to be admired and duly fed, I am going to rest and recuperate for the next five weeks and try to remember out of this awful time only the kindness and sympathy that has been shown to us by so many Irish friends. I shall not write any more of these diary letters unless there are further acute developments, which God forbid.

Ever yours,
L. N.

PROCLAMATION DECLARING MARTIAL LAW

WHEREAS, in different parts of Ireland certain evilly disposed persons and associations, with the intent to subvert the Supremacy of the Crown in Ireland, have committed divers acts of violence, and have with deadly weapons attacked the Forces of the Crown, and have resisted by armed forces the lawful authority of His Majesty's Police and Military Forces:

And, WHEREAS, by reason thereof, several of His Majesty's liege subjects have been killed, and many others severely injured, and much damage to property has been caused:

And, WHEREAS, such armed resistance to His Majesty's authority still continues,

Now I, IVOR CHURCHILL BARON WIMBORNE, Lord Lieutenant General and General Governor of Ireland, by virtue of all the powers thereunto me enabling,

DO HEREBY PROCLAIM that, from and after the date of this Proclamation, and for the period of one month thereafter (unless otherwise ordered), that part of the United Kingdom called Ireland is under and subject to Martial Law.

AND I DO HEREBY call on all loyal and well-affected subjects of the Crown to aid in upholding and maintaining the peace of this Realm and the Supremacy and authority of the Crown, and to obey and conform to all Orders and

Regulations of the Military Authority. And I warn all peaceable and law-abiding subjects in Ireland of the danger of frequenting, or being in, any place in or in the vicinity of which His Majesty's Forces are engaged in the suppression of disorder.

AND I DO DECLARE that all persons found carrying arms, without lawful authority, are liable to be dealt with by virtue of this Proclamation.

GIVEN AT DUBLIN
This 29th Day of April 1916.
(Signed) WIMBORNE.
GOD SAVE THE KING.

PROCLAMATION POSTED OUTSIDE THE GENERAL POST OFFICE.

POBLAGHT NA H EIREANN
The Provisional Government
of the
IRISH REPUBLIC
To the People of Ireland.

IRISHMEN AND IRISHWOMEN: In the name of God and of the dead generations from which she receives her old tradition of Nationhood, IRELAND, through us, summons her Children to her flag and strikes for her freedom.

Having organised and trained her manhood through her secret revolutionary organisation, the Irish Republican Brotherhood, and through her open military organisations, the Irish Volunteers and the Irish Citizen Army, having patiently perfected her discipline, having resolutely waited for the right moment to reveal itself, she now seizes that moment, and, supported by her exiled Children in America and by gallant Allies in Europe, but relying in the first on her own strength, she strikes in full confidence of victory.

WE DECLARE the right of the people of Ireland to the ownership of Ireland, and to the unfettered control of Irish destinies, to be sovereign and indefeasible. The long usurpation of that right by a foreign people and Government has not extinguished the right, nor can it ever be extinguished except by the destruction of the Irish people. In every generation the Irish people have asserted their right to national freedom and sovereignty; six times during the past three hundred years they have asserted it in arms. Standing on that fundamental right and again asserting it in arms in the face of the world, we hereby proclaim the Irish Republic as a Sovereign Independent State, and we pledge our lives and the lives of our comrades-in-arms to the cause of its freedom, of its welfare, and of its exaltation among the nations.

THE IRISH REPUBLIC is entitled to, and HEREBY CLAIMS, the allegiance of every Irishman and Irishwoman. The Republic guarantees religious and civil liberty, equal rights and equal opportunities to all its citizens, and declares its resolve to pursue the happiness and prosperity of the whole nation and of all its parts, cherishing all the children of the Nation equally, and oblivious of the differences carefully fostered by an Alien Government, which have divided a minority from the majority in the past.

Until our arms have brought the opportune moment for the establishment of a permanent National Government, representative of the whole people of Ireland and elected by the suffrage of all her men and women, the Provisional Government, hereby constituted, will administer the civil and military affairs of the Republic in trust for the people.

We place the cause of the Irish Republic under the protection of the Most High God, Whose blessing we invoke upon our arms, and we pray that no one who serves that cause will dishonour it by cowardice, inhumanity, or rapine. In this supreme hour the Irish Nation must, by its valour and discipline and by the readiness of its children to sacrifice themselves for the common good, prove itself worthy of the august destiny to which it is called.

Signed on behalf of the Provisional Government,

THOMAS CLARKE.

SEAN MACDIARMADA.	THOMAS MACDONACH.
P. H. PEARSE.	EAMONN CEANNT.
JAMES CONNOLLY.	JOSEPH PLUNKETT.

MANIFESTO ISSUED FROM THE REBEL HEADQUARTERS, GENERAL POST OFFICE.

HEADQUARTERS ARMY OF THE IRISH REPUBLIC.
General Post Office, Dublin.
28th April 1916 – 9.30 a.m.

The Forces of the Irish Republic, which was proclaimed in Dublin on Easter Monday 24th April, have been in possession of the central part of the Capital since 12 noon on that day. Up to yesterday afternoon Headquarters was in touch with all the main outlying positions, and despite furious and almost continuous assaults by the British Forces all those positions were then still being held, and the Commandants in charge were confident of their ability to hold them for a long time.

During the course of yesterday afternoon and evening the enemy succeeded in cutting our communications with our other positions in the city, and Headquarters is to-day isolated.

The enemy has burnt down whole blocks of houses, apparently with the object of giving themselves a clear field for the play of artillery and field guns against us.

We have been bombarded during the evening and night by shrapnel and machine-gun fire, but without material damage to our position, which is of great strength.

We are busy completing arrangements for the final defence of Headquarters and are determined to hold it while the buildings last.

I desire now, lest I may not have an opportunity later; to pay homage to the gallantry of the soldiers of Irish Freedom who have during the past four days been writing with fire and steel the most glorious chapter in the later history of Ireland. Justice can never be done to their heroism, to their discipline, to their gay and unconquerable spirit in the midst of peril and death.

Let me, who have led them into this, speak in my own, and in my fellow Commanders' names, and in the name of

Ireland present and to come, their praises, and ask those who come after them to remember them.

For four days they have fought and toiled, almost without cessation, almost without sleep; and in the intervals of fighting they have sung songs of the freedom of Ireland.

No man has complained, no man has asked 'Why?' Each individual has spent himself, happy to pour out his strength for Ireland and for freedom. If they do not win this fight, they will at least have deserved to win it. But win it they will, although they may win it in death. Already they have won a great thing. They have redeemed Dublin from many shames, and made her name splendid among the names of cities.

If I were to mention names of individuals my list would be a long one. I will name only that of Commandant General James Connolly, commanding the Dublin division. He is wounded, but is still the guiding brain of our resistance.

If we accomplish no more than we have accomplished, I am satisfied. I am satisfied that we have saved Ireland's honour. I am satisfied that we should have accomplished more, that we should have accomplished the task of enthroning, as well as proclaiming the Irish Republic as a Sovereign State, had our arrangements for a simultaneous rising of the whole country, with a combined plan as sound as the Dublin plan has been proved to be, been allowed to go through on Easter Sunday. Of the fatal countermanding order which prevented those plans from being carried out, I shall not speak further. Both Eoin MacNeill and we have acted in the best interests of Ireland.

For my part, as to anything I have done in this, I am not afraid to face either the judgment of God, or the judgment of posterity.

(Signed) P. H. PEARSE,
Commandant General,
Commanding-in-Chief the Army of the Irish Republic
and President of
the Provisional Government.

The day following this proclamation the rebels surrendered unconditionally.

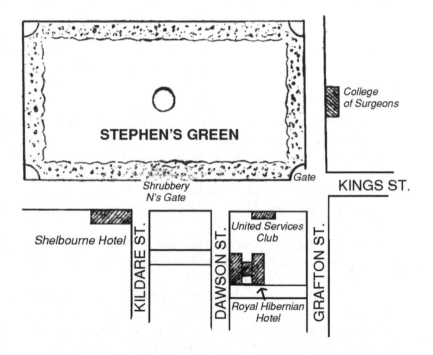

Mrs Hamilton Norway's sketch map of St Stephen's Green
(from *The Sinn Fein Rebellion As I Saw It*)

View of Royal Hibernian Hotel from Molesworth Street, 1946
(Hope Collection) Courtesy of the National Library of Ireland

The Shelbourne Hotel from St Stephens Green (Lawrence
Collection) Courtesy of the National Library of Ireland

Notes

1 Obituary of Maj.-Gen. Gadsden, *The Times*, 28 Feb. 1899; entry for Edward Holroyd Gadsden (1859–1920) in *Who Was Who 1916-28*.
2 Nevil Shute, *Slide Rule*, p. 14.
3 Ibid. Addresses, and various other details, have been extracted from contemporary issues of *Thom's Directory*.
4 He died on 4 July 1915. See Everard Wyrall, *The History of the Duke of Cornwall's Light Infantry, 1914-1919* (London: Methuen, 1932), pp. 130, 479.
5 Shute, *Slide Rule*, p. 22.
6 Mrs Norway's sister, Grace.
7 William Ireland de Courcy Wheeler. Wheeler's brother, Major Henry de Courcy Wheeler, was present when Patrick Pearse formally surrendered at the end of the Rising.
8 Lord Shaw of Dunfirmline, father of William Wheeler's wife, Elsie. Shaw was a law lord and former Liberal M.P., who when he retired from the bench in 1929 became Lord Craigmyle.
9 Edmond O'Brien, a wealthy and well-connected Catholic landowner.
10 William Henry Foster Verschoyle and his wife, who lived at 36 Mount Street Upper. He was a chartered surveyor and land agent.
11 On 11 May, John Dillon, the veteran Irish Nationalist MP, had passionately declared that the insurgents had 'fought a clean fight, a brave fight, however misguided' (see F. S. L. Lyons, *John Dillon: A Biography* (London: Rouledge & Kegan Paul, 1968), pp. 380–2).

5 The Civil Servants' Tales

The documents in this chapter comprise the immediate 'after action' reports of the main technical staff in charge of the telegraph service, Samuel Guthrie, the Superintendent of Telegraphs, his deputy, W. A. Pemberton, and J. H. Reeves, who was in charge of the Post Office Stores Department at Aldborough House in Portland Row,[1] a few hundred metres from Amiens Street Station. Some of the timings in Guthrie's report do not quite match those recorded on the messages reproduced in chapter one, but his account confirms the essential sequence of events, and reveals that apparently secure military communications between Ireland and Great Britain were established by just after five o'clock on the Monday evening.

Pemberton's rather Pooterish narrative takes us into County Wicklow where he was sent to secure the telegraph cables to Nevin (Nefyn) in North Wales, as well as the Irish lines south to Waterford. The journey out of Dublin was accompanied by many vicissitudes and the problem of getting both a car and a driver has a mildly comic air which belies the seriousness of the situation. He also ran up expenses of over ten pounds, a considerable sum bearing in mind that his superior Mr J. J. Kenny's annual salary was approximately five hundred pounds a year.[2]

J. H. Reeves's report of how the Post Office Stores Depot at Aldborough House was kept going also reflects the extent to which ordinary life in Dublin was not completely interrupted by the events of Easter Monday. Having managed (with some difficulty) to get back home on Monday evening to Sutton, six miles out of town, he got an early train back in the next morning to return to work, which evidently a fair number of other Post Office staff did as well. It was only during Easter Tuesday morning that the situation became so perilous that he suspended normal working. In his account, Reeves (who had been at home in Sutton on Easter Monday morning) mentions that he had been told of the events in central Dublin from a motor cyclist sent by a friend. The friend (unnamed in Reeves' account) was a man called Best, a fellow-member of the 'Howth and Sutton Volunteer Training Corps'. Best afterwards wrote a letter (reproduced below) telling his side of the story in terms which show him clearly keen to curry favour and also suggest that he might have been angling for some sort of reward. There is also a series diary notes made by J. J. Fogarty which give us a picture of what Easter Week was like for the Post Office employees in Dublin Castle, as well as a dramatic narrative of the abortive rebel assault on the Castle which reveals that some four Volunteers actually penetrated as far as the middle of the Lower Castle Yard. The chapter concludes with eyewitness accounts by Post Office staff, both at the GPO and in the Dublin Telephone Exchange, which were published in the Post Office 'house magazine'. One of these, 'by a lady telegraphist', gives a rare female perspective of the events.

Samuel Guthrie (Superintendent of Telegraphs) to the Central Telegraph Office Controller, GPO[3]

Telegraph Office
Amiens St. Railway Station
Dublin

6 May 1916

With reference to the seizure of the G.P.O. on Easter Monday the 24th. ult by the Sinn Féin Volunteers I beg to report as follows:-

At 12 noon (I)[4] a great many of the wires – including all the cross channel wires – became disconnected, apparently close up. At 12.10 pm. I was informed that the Sinn Féin Volunteers were taking possession of the Public Counter and after a short time I heard the breaking of glass in the lower storey. On looking out of a window in the Telephone Room I saw that the windows of the Public Office and other windows looking into Sackville Street were being smashed, the fragments of glass falling on to and covering the pavement, and several members of the Sinn Féin party stood round the public entrance with rifles and revolvers. I at once got Mr P. I. Kelly to 'phone the Headquarters of the Army Command, the Police Office in the Castle, and also to Marlboro' Barracks asking for assistance. At 12.30 pm I was informed by the Sergt. of the Guard that the Rebels were forcing the stairs leading from Henry Street to the Instrument Room and he asked me to obtain assistance for him. I explained to him what we had already done to obtain assistance. The guard consisted of a Sergeant and 4 men. The passage leading from the head of the stairs to the Instrument Room was then barricaded from the inside by filling it with chairs, wastepaper boxes etc. in order to delay the entry of attackers as much as possible, the guard of 1 Sergeant and 4 men standing inside the Instrument Room prepared to receive the rebels if they broke through the obstructions. Several volleys were fired by the rebels through the passage into the Instrument Room but entrance here had not been effected when a short time before 1 pm. a party of the Rebels gained an entrance to the Instrument Room by the Southern Corridor after having passed through the Dining Room. As there was only one sentry on that corridor he was easily overpowered.

When it was quite evident that an attack on the Instrument Room was intended through the Northern Corridor I instructed the Female operators at that end of the Instrument Room to clear away down to the Southern end, and as time progressed and matters became worse I told the Females to go into their Retiring Room and put on their outdoor apparel in case they would have to leave the building. Before the Rebels made their appearance at the Southern end of the room I was told that an officer of the besieging force wished to see me on the Southern landing to arrange for the withdrawal of the Staff. I sent word to him that I would not hold any parley with him as I did not recognise he had any right to be where he was. A few minutes later the officer – whom I now believe was The O'Rahilly – accompanied by a few supporters entered the Instrument Room each carrying a revolver and told all the officials in the Room to clear out at once at the same time questioning each one of them as to whether he carried arms. At this time all the Females had left the Instrument Room.

By 1 o'clock (I) the last of the Staff had left the building and were in Princes Street. I stood in Sackville Street for a short time and then walked towards Abbey Street where I met Mr Doak of the Engineering Branch. After conversing with him for some time we proceeded to Amiens Street Rail Office to see if we could pick up London or other wires there. On arriving at the Amiens Street Office I found that Mr Pemberton (Asst Supt) and a few operators were already there, and we were able to get London on two wires. At 2 pm. (I) spoke to the Superintendent London on one of the wires and explained to him the state of affairs and asked him to advise all Irish offices with which he had communication and also the principal English centres. About 2.20 pm. I thought it advisable to try and reach Mr Norway in order that he might be acquainted with the position of affairs, and accordingly I went to the Hibernian Hotel Dawson Street but I was informed that Mr Norway was, it was thought, in the Castle.

As the Castle was at the time invested by the Rebels I returned to Amiens Street Office and explained to the London Superintendent what I had done and told him that Mr Norway could not be reached for the present. The Superintendent London then said he wanted a man to be sent to Newcastle Hut to make some wire changes in conjunction with Nevin (the Relay Station). As Westland Row and Harcourt Street Stations were both in the hands of the Rebels I instructed Mr Pemberton to try to get a motor car at Thompsons or some other garage and proceed to Newcastle, and I also instructed Mr Boyle, a Telegraphist, to accompany him in case it was necessary that an officer remain at Newcastle Hut. Mr Doak (Engineer) succeeded in raising the Military Adjutant on the Amiens Street Station Parcel Office telephone about 4.20 pm. And informed him we had a wire to London working from Amiens Street Station if he wished to communicate with London. At 5.5 pm. a cypher message was received by Special Messenger from Commandeth Dublin (Military Headquarters) to 'Troops London' and duly dispatched. This was the beginning of the Military Telegraph Service between London and Dublin in connection with the disturbances.

During the evening one of the two London wires was put through to the Irish Office in London. As no length was available between the Castle and Amiens Street Mr Doak proceeded to the Castle to try and arrange an extension but he returned at 8.30 pm. having failed to get into the Castle. We therefore transmitted the work between the Irish Office London and the Irish Office Dublin Castle by means of a telephone wire through Crown Alley Exchange. The Telephone Exchange wires did not appear to have been interfered with by the Rebels. As the ordinary Telegraph Office premises at Amiens Street Railway

Station occupied a very exposed position it was deemed advisable to seek other more safe and larger premises, and Mr Doak arranged with Mr Campion, the Engineer of the Great Northern Railway Company, the use of the Drawing Room, a large apartment about 50ft x 30ft and as this room already contained large broad benches used for dealing with maps & plans the change was most satisfactory as the benches suited admirably for the fixing of Telegraph apparatus. The wires were run into the new office on the evening of the 25th ult. by an emergency cable, and all was in readiness for work there on the morning of the 26th ult.

On Monday and Tuesday nights it was possible for me to return to my home at 9 pm and 7.30 pm respectively for rest. On the morning of the 27th (Wednesday) it was with difficulty I reached the office at 10 am. owing to street fighting in a portion of the district through which I had to pass; as the day progressed matters in this respect became worse with the result that both Mr Sweeney, Acting Evening Supt, and Mr Doyle, Assistant Superintendent, could not get into the city for duty in the evening. I accordingly remained on duty that night and as the whole City became involved in the disturbances all travelling through the street was practically suspended and remained so up to Sunday the 30th when a portion of the City reopened for foot traffic. I remained on duty until 12 noon on Monday the 1st inst. The Staff was practically shut up in the Amiens Street premises from Wednesday morning until the following Sunday and Monday.

At 1pm on the 25th ult. (Tuesday) two additional wires were provided, one for London and one for Liverpool and each was fitted with a transmitter for wheatstone working, and as a precautionary measure about 2.30 pm. all the wires in the Amiens Street Testbox, other than those we were working, were disconnected by Mr Doak – a barricade of sandbags was subsequently erected in the ordinary Telegraph Office to protect the Testbox. On the same day a confidential service from the Secretary Telegraphs London to the Controller Dublin was received to stop all private and press telegrams passing between the United Kingdom and Ireland and to hold until further instructed. I replied that the Service had attention so far as Dublin only was concerned as we were at present isolated from other offices in Ireland.

The wires available on the 26th (Wednesday) ult. were as follows:-

One to Liverpool   (BM BE wire) Wheatstone
"   London   (LV DN1 wire) Wheatstone
"   I. O. [Irish Office] London (DN GW 1. wire) Sounder
"   Horse Guards London (DN MR 1. wire) Sounder
"   London   (LV CK to LKV then via NV) Sounder
"   Belfast   (DN BE 2 wire) Sounder.
Three Telephone circuits to Crown Alley Exchange.

These latter were taken on loan out of different Railway Offices on the premises.

On the morning of the 28th ult. the Horse Guards wire was extended to Headquarters Dublin (Parkgate Street) and we became right on a wire to Howth Summit (DN Howth 2).

On the afternoon of the 29th ult. we got through to Dundalk Junction on the usual Railway wire, and as we were pressed to Belfast with Constabulary priority work a second outlet to Belfast was obtained at 7.50 pm. on TS BE 5.

At 8.15 pm. on the 29th ult. a second circuit from Horse Guards to Headquarters Dublin was asked for but there was no Dublin Headquarters length available at the time. A length was however subsequently provided which gave Horse Guards 2 circuits to Headquarters Dublin.

On the 30th ult., in reply to a query as regards the disposal of a message for Balbriggan, the Telephone Exchange reported that the Balbriggan and Belfast Trunks had been cut near Swords.

The wires available on this date (30th) were as follows:-

One wire to   Liverpool (BM-BE wire) Wheatstone
"   London (LV1. extended)   "
"   I. O. London (DN-GW 1) Sounder
"   Belfast (DN) BE 2)   "
Two wires to Horse Guards and H(DN-MR 1 & LV-CK &
             Nevin extension) Sounder
One wire to   Howth Summit (DN-HPV 2)   Sounder
"   Dundalk Junction (Usual rly. wire) Sounder
Three Telephone circuits to Crown Alley Exchange.

The work dealt with from the 24th ult. to the present time was purely on Military and Constabulary Service, no public messages being accepted for transmission, and all work was disposed of by key and phone.

The Staff responded most willingly to the demands made on their service and endurance. I enclose a statement showing the names of the officers who voluntarily attended at the office from the 24th ult. to the 1st inst.[5] The Constabulary messages were without exception lengthy and being principally in cypher were intricate to deal with.

I have pleasure in testifying to the able and courteous manner in which Messrs Doak and Dawson of the Engineering Branch fulfilled the onerous duties imposed on them in connection with the providing of the different circuits during the period under review.

W. A. Pemberton to Controller, GPO, 6 May 1916[6]

Easter Monday 24th April 1916 12.23 pm. (G)[7] Miss Brennan reported that all the stations on Switch 1 were disconnected. Mr Doak (Sectional Engineer) was speaking to me with reference to the Showyard Special wire[8] which was also disconnected. On hearing Miss Brennan's report we thought the main batteries might be gone but having proved these right several of the lines were found to be disconnected including the cross-channel circuits. I got the key of the Secondary Cell Room and with Mr Doak proceeded to the basement and examined the heat coil frame which appeared to be all right. I returned to the Instrument Room and proved some of the circuits right to the Heat Coil frame and suggested that ex Sergeant Connell should accompany Mr Doak to the basement to make further examination beyond the Heat Coil Frame.

In the meantime the rebels had attacked the building and were firing through a barricade at the Sergt. and a Private of the Guard who were standing at each side of the Southern entrance door of the Instrument Room with fixed bayonets. I saw the Sergt. stagger as if wounded and then looking to the Northern end of the room found the rebels with revolvers in their hands. A rebel ordered us out of the building with the remark 'sorry to disturb you Gentlemen' and made some additional remark like 'this is the first and last act'.

We left the Instrument Room at 1.31 pm. (G) and were let out of the main gate in Princess Street by the rebel Guard.

I went to Brunswick Street Police Station and reported the

matter but was told to make the report in Store Street Police Station. I made the report in Store Street and went on to Amiens Street Railway Station Telegraph Office where I found the North of Ireland route stopped but the LKV cable route right. I got through to TS (Telegraph Service] and Mr Guthrie arriving he reported the matter to the Supt. TS. Mr Doak also came to Amiens Street and we jointly proved the lines to LKV, Mr J. F. Connell and Mr P. I. Kelly came with me to Amiens Street.

Mr Guthrie left me in charge of Amiens Street while he went to report the matter to Mr Norway and during his absence I made some Staff arrangements and spoke to TS answering the questions asked as well as I could to establish my genuineness. TS decided to wait for Mr Guthrie's return before communicating further.

When Mr Guthrie returned TS asked for some one to prove the Newcastle [County Wickow] route. I volunteered to go to Newcastle if possible and Mr Boyle volunteered to come with me.

In the meantime it was reported that bombs with long fuses were being laid in Earl Street, we did not then know that the Telephone Exchange was free from rebels, so we thought it better to make a personal report of the barricade to the Police authorities. I took £1 from the stock in Amiens Street and accompanied by Mr Boyle we went to Brunswick Street to obtain a motor car at Thompson's Garage but could not get one as all the cars were out at Fairyhouse Race Meeting. We then went to the Police at Brunswick Street to ask them to get a car for us and to report the barricade and bomb in Earl Street and asked them to ask the Adjutant General to send forces sufficient to guard the communication between Amiens Street and London. The Police were unable to send a messenger to the Castle but sent a message over their private telephone. The Police informed us that persons in plain clothes might get into the Castle at the Palace Street entrance but their men, even in plain clothes, would be recognised and probably shot. We regarded the possibility worth the risk and accompanied by Mr Boyle I went to the Lower Castle Yard and explained matters to the Adjutant-General who offered me a motor car which was outside his office but neither Mr Boyle or I could drive a car.

Col. Johnston, the Chief Commissioner D. M. P. [Dublin Metropolitan Police] gave me a note to Mr Chaytor Secretary Automobile Club asking him to give us a car if possible and timed the note 4.15 pm. When passing through the Lower Castle Yard I saw Mr Norway and reported the condition of affairs at Amiens Street when I left, and told him I was going to get a motor to Newcastle if possible.

I presented my note to the Automobile Club and was offered the use of a Ford Car but could not get a driver. A Lady volunteered to drive the car if either of us would turn the starting handle for her but we decided that this would be unsafe and left to get a driver. We succeeded in getting Mr Manthorpe of Gt. Brunswick Street to agree to drive us and returned to the Club where the car was prepared for the journey but Mr Manthorpe did not arrive at the appointed time and we had arranged with a Lady to take us to Bray in her motor when Mr Manthorpe arrived. The Lady left and then the Porter at the Club refused us the Car till Mr Chaytor returned. Mr Chaytor returned and questioned the genuineness of Col. Johnston's signature and failing to get through to Col. Johnston or the Adjt-General on the Telephone refused the car. There appeared little prospect then of getting through on the telephone, it was getting dark, I gave Mr Chaytor fifteen minutes to make up his mind and told him that if he doubted Col. Johnston's signature he had let 3 hours elapse before attempting to verify it and that if he had expressed his doubts when we presented the note we could have had the signature verified by now. We left the Automobile Club and proceeded to Thompson's Garage but could not hire a car. I saw a Mr Keogh of Enniscorthy had a car hired to take him home and I asked him would he take me as far as Bray. He agreed and I drove to my home getting some warm clothing for Mr Keogh, Mr Boyle and myself and proceeded to Bray Railway Station where I picked up lineman Kennedy and found the line stopped between Bray Rail and Nevin. Mr Boyle and I then had some food and went to the District Inspector Bray for authority to enter the Cable Hut. When we satisfied the D.I. as to our genuineness, by obtaining a letter from the Postmistress, the D.I. gave us the permit to be handed to the Sergt in charge.

We hired a motor car in Bray, took instruments and batteries to the hut, and proved the wires to Nevin. There was a telephone in the Hut which worked to Wicklow who could extend to Wexford and Waterford. I made up a TS circuit and left Mr Boyle in the Hut to take any messages TS might have for Wicklow or Wexford.

I arrived home in Sandymount at 4 am. Tuesday 25th April and after a few hours rest reported myself to Mr Kenny.

Mr Kenny communicated my report by telephone to Mr Gomersall, it was agreed I should return to Bray if possible and restore communication between Bray and England. I hired a motor car and took Messrs J. Coloe, J. J. Pakenham and G. Kean with me to Bray Rail. We were stopped by armed Police at Cabinteely and had some difficulty of satisfying them of our identity. At Bray Rail I found MR DN 2 right to Nevin. I left Mr Pakenham and Mr G. Kean at Bray Rail and took Mr Coloe with me to Newcastle to relieve Mr Boyle.

At Newcastle I got into communication with Mr Ray of Waterford by telephone. He informed me that he was arranging to give me Waterford on the Enniscorthy wire, and that he would send me men and apparatus to restore communication between Newcastle and Bray.

I took Mr Boyle and Mr Coloe back from the hut as I saw no further need for them there and put the speaking set in circuit on a through wire (I think it was Manchester Racing[9]) so that the land side of the wires stopped n the cable could be proved by the lineman when communication was restored. I sent the motor and staff back to Dublin and remained in Bray on Tuesday night.

Early on Wednesday morning I got a certificate from Head Constable Bray in order to make necessary repairs on the line and proceeded to Greystones. I found that damage to the lines had been repaired by the gang. I went to Greystones Post Office and proved Dublin-Enniscorthy right to Waterford and returned to Bray Rail to make up a TS-WT circuit. I thought it safer not to make any record of the various changes I made on this day and asked Nevin to record them for me. I advised the Engineer-in-Chief, London, Mr Gomersall and Mr Kenny of the various changes as I made them.

Having wires to TS I decided to put them through to Kingstown if possible, and knowing that the Bray and Rathdrum wires passed through Kingstown I proposed to prove them to Kingstown. Mr O'Dowda had arrived at Bray Rail at this time. I told him my intention, he volunteered to go to Kingstown I hired a motor to take Mr O'Dowda and men to Kingstown and told him to join the Bray side of Dublin-Bray to the Kingstown-Dublin circuit and look out for me. We got this circuit through to London and I then arranged with Mr O'Dowda to look out for

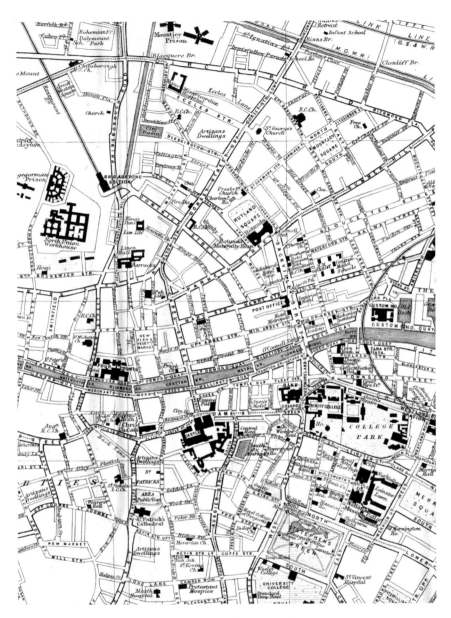

1. Map of Central Dublin in 1916, showing the GPO, Amiens Street
   Station, Aldborough House, Dublin Castle and St Stephen's Green
   (from Ward Lock & Co.'s *A Pictorial and Descriptive Guide to Dublin*,
   London, 1917)

Supt DW

2.50.

from Mr. S.S. Guthrie
Supt. Tel. Office. Dublin

I am spkg for Amiens St RO The GPO has been taken possession of by the Irish Volunteers who have turned out everyone. I am afraid they are bent on demolishing the inst room. I tell you in case you may have wondered why you did not get DW call, you please advise Seaday + anyone else that it may concern + also advise any Irish Stns u may be in ght to

2.50 pm.

Message sent from Amiens St. Ry. Station Dublin to the Supt. on Duty, C.T.O. (Mr. H.T. Phillips)

War Office & Admiralty informed.

Yes I will take good work + will do best to deliver it. The streets are not safe

2. Note of the first telephone message from Dublin, Easter Monday 1916, as preserved in the British Postal Museum and Archive (BPMA, POST 56/177)

give the matter special attention. Having settled these
at about 6 pm
matters and the necessary staff having arrived, I tried to
get home on a bicycle. About a mile from the Depot I ran
into a patrol of Sinn Feiners actually in action with the
military. One young gentleman pointed his rifle at me but
"don't shoot me; you'll get into awful trouble"
when I bellowed at him not to fire he lowered his rifle and
told me to turn back. This I did and remained at the Depot
for some hours longer. One or two small demands for Amiens
Street were executed during the evening . It was a curious
on the ground floor
and somewhat exciting experience to sit in my room and see
parties of armed Volunteers escorting wagon loads of
ammunition and supplies to various pre-appointed destinations.
If the small military guard had been in evidence at the Depot
on this evening the place would certainly have been taken but
I had had the gates locked; no lights were showing and the few
of the staff that were present were inside the building.
close by
At 8 p.m. there was rifle fire at various points. At 8.30
I went to Amiens Street and saw Mr Doak. He said that I
could do nothing more. Indeed it was evident that little
more could be done until the Military Authorities became
masters of the situation. I came back to the Depot till
bicycled
10. 15 p.m. and then rode home to Sutton after arranging for
a small portion of the labour staff to come on in relays.
I passed through two lines of outposts of the Volunteers with
the aid of a Dublin accent and a certain amount of "old-soldier"
sense, *acquired in the South African Campaign.*

3. Extract from J. H. Reeve's report of 6 May 1916 (BPMA, POST
31/80, file VI)

4. The ... from Nelson's Pillar (BPMA, POST 56/179)

5. O'Connell Bridge and Eden Quay after the Rising (BPMA, POST 56/179)

6. 'Separation women' waiting to collect their British army allowances at Aungier Street Post Office (BPMA, POST 56/179)

7. Dubliners waiting outside the Dublin Savings Bank in Lower Abbey Street; note the notice: 'Will open when law & order is fully restored' (BPMA, POST 56/179)

8. 25th anniversary stamp commemorating the Rising, designed by Victor Brown (courtesy of An Post)

me on Rathdrum and got this circuit through to London thus giving Kingstown two wires to London.

I received instructions to return to Headquarters and was going to get a meal when I was told the District Inspector was looking for me to try to get through a message to the County Inspector, Wicklow. I returned to Bray Rail and went in on the Rathdrum side of Dublin-Rathdrum, got off the District Inspector's message and joined Bray P.O. through to Rathdrum P.O. I then went to Bray Post Office where I reversed the battery connection on the Dublin Instrument and left Bray through to Wicklow P.O.. and Rathdrum. I informed the Postmistress and the District Inspector that Police messages could be got off between Bray and Wicklow and Rathdrum.

I returned to Bray Rail and found Mr O'Dowda back from Kingstown when I handed over to him, and through the courtesy of Mr Collier, Bray, who sold sufficient petrol to the lineman was enabled to get a motor car home.

I submit the following bills for payment:-

		£	s.	d.
Royal Hotel, Bray		1	8	1
Mackey Motor, 24th-25th April, Bray to Newcastle				
	Newcastle to Sydney Parade	2	14	0
	26th April, Kingstown to Bray,			
	Bray to 4, Clyde Terrace	2	10	0
Fitzgerald	Ranelagh to Newcastle and back			
	(25th April 1916)	4	4	0
		£10	16	1

Report by J. H. Reeves (1st Class Clerk in charge of Stores Department), 6 May 191610

Sinn Féin Rising, Easter Monday, April 24th 1916

About 2.45 p.m. on Monday April 24th a friend sent a motor cyclist to my residence at Sutton to say that the G.P.O. and other Government buildings were in possession of the Sinn Féiners and that there was a riot in town. A similar message was conveyed about half an hour afterwards by Mr Brown, 3rd Class Storeman (Mr Brown rode out to Sutton at some risk), but I was already on my way to the Depot being very fortunate in catching a special (Easter Excursion) train at 3 p.m. I met Mr Doak 'Sectional Engineer' at Aldborough House and he confirmed the news. The Post Office was being wrecked and many shops were already being looted; wires were cut and tramway and train services stopped, some of the tramway cars being placed across streets, as barricades. Mr Doak told me that fortunately he had effected communication with England from a little telegraph office at Amiens Street and that he was giving his attention to the development of this channel of communication. I told him that I would stay at the Depot or would keep in touch with him otherwise and that his demands would receive special and personal attention. I then brought on duty a few of the Stores Staff to 'stand by'. I accompanied Mr Doak to Amiens Street and from there we spoke (telegraphed) to Sir William Slingo[11] and I was able to give some information off hand in general terms of what Wheatstone Apparatus, flame-proof wire and aerial cables we held. I afterwards made out a list of stock balances and handed it to Mr Doak.

Amiens Street Station at this time was in a state of siege and I was exceptionally fortunate, after some delay, in being able to get through on the telephone, from the Parcel Office, to the Garrison Adjutant at the Castle to ask for military protection for Aldborough House. I explained to him the paramount import-ance of amply safeguarding our Stores Depot. He quite agreed and said that he would give the matter special attention. Having settled these matters and the necessary staff having arrived, I tried at about 6 p.m. to get home on a bicycle. About a mile from the Depot I ran into a patrol of Sinn Féiners actually in action with the military.[12] One young gentleman pointed his rifle at me but when I bellowed at him not to fire ('Don't shoot me: you'll get into awful trouble!') he lowered his rifle and told me to turn back. This I did and remained at the Depot for some hours longer. One or two small demands for Amiens Street were executed during the evening. It was a curious and somewhat exciting experience to sit in my room on the ground floor and see parties of armed Volunteers escorting wagon loads of ammu-nition and supplies to various pre-appointed destinations. If the small military guard (which, on an intimation from the Controller that it was considered as no longer desirable, had been withdrawn by the military authorities for some two or three weeks) had been in evidence at the Depot on this evening the place would certainly have been taken (a sentry would have attracted the attention of the rebels) but I had the gates locked & by my express directions no lights were showing and the few of the staff that were present were inside the building. At 8 p.m. there was rifle fire at various points close by. At 8.30 I went to Amiens Street and saw Mr Doak. He said that I could do nothing more. Indeed it was evident that little more could be done until the Military Authorities became masters of the situation. I came back to the Depot till 10.15 p.m. and then bicycled home to Sutton (passing the spot at which I was formerly turned back) after arranging for a small portion of the labour staff to come in on relays. I passed through two lines of outposts of the Volunteers with the aid of a Dublin accent and a certain amount of 'old-soldier' sense, acquired in the South African campaign.

On the next morning the 25th I got to the Depot very early and as it happened by the only available train that day. Some demands for Amiens Street were prepared and executed as far as possible (the trouble was to procure a lorry). At 10.10 a.m. ['practically' crossed out] the whole of the Engineering clerical staff left the building en bloc and this had rather an unnerving effect on my staff. I received almost immediately deputations begging me to shut down but I refused. I gave instructions to Mr Jeffries, 2nd Class Clerk (who, in the absence of Mr Mahon, on loan to the Ministry of Munitions in London, is the senior clerical officer under Mr Reeves) for the clerical staff and to Mr Phelan, 2nd Class Storeman, for the stores staff that those men who were particularly nervous or had a long way to go might go home but that I earnestly desired that all officers should stick to their posts even at some risk. I took special steps to release the ladies.

I was very anxious at this time about the safety of the building and went across to Amiens Street railway station, by this time a fort, and with some difficulty got through again to the Garrison Adjutant. He told me that he had not overlooked my previous request and that he was making the necessary arrangements for the protection of the building but that it might be some time before the troops could get to the Depot. I next saw Major Carter, the officer who appeared to be in charge of the fighting unit at the station and asked him to give me an escort for some stores already packed up at the Depot and waiting to be delivered to the Engineers in Amiens Street Parcel Office. He said that he could not do much with the few men at his disposal as the sniping was now getting rather severe. Some of the stores were, however, got over in small parcels by our own men, and more were brought across by linemen, and at 2 p.m. I ascertained that the Engineers had all that they really needed for the present. Firing was now pretty general but up to this I had not run much personal risk as civilians were not being fired upon. At about 3.30 p.m. I allowed several members of the staff to go home. At 5 p.m. I tried to get home encouraged by my success on the previous evening but I was stopped by the Volunteers again at Annesley Bridge. They were by no means so polite and accommodating as on the previous evening and although I tried all forms of argument that I could muster I was unsuccessful and had to return to the Depot and stop for the night. At 6 p.m. the firing became heavier for a short time. The business appeared to me to be like hundreds of the celebrated 'Sydney Street' affair.[13]

At 8.30 p.m. I got a verbal message from Mr Doak for some small pieces of apparatus and these were sent. At 9 a.m. the next morning (Wednesday 26th) I ventured out and had my foot cauterised. I had poisoned it in some way a few days previously and the running about of the previous two days made it in a wretched state. Several of the staff could not get to the Depot. With difficulty I rode home on a bicycle at about 10 a.m. and returned to the Depot at 2 p.m. after many exciting experiences with which I need not burthen this report. I felt much relieved to find that the military guard – and it was a strong one of about 100 men (4th Royal Dublin Fusiliers and Royal Irish Rifles) – had arrived. These troops attacked the snipers in all directions from the roof of Aldborough House and in showing the officer in charge of the soldiers the way to the roof Mr Brennan 3rd Class Clerk had a narrow escape. The whole of the evening and during the night sniping and collected fore was very heavy. The whole of the clerical staff had gone home as well as the stores staff with the exception of a few individuals who lived at Blackrock and who could not possibly get home. These men I made as comfortable as possible and I selected Mr E. W. Mann (unestablished packer) to wait upon the officers and myself. Sleep was impossible during this night for the firing was particularly heavy. On Thursday April 27th the same sniping and return of compliments continued. I was alone with Mr Mann, a few marooned depot hands – and the military. It was impossible now to communicate at all with

Amiens Street. If one walked from the hall door to the gate at about 12 noon on this day one stood an excellent chance of being sniped. None of the clerical staff came on duty and, needless to say, such of the stores staff as had got home on the Wednesday remained at home. The Watchmen, too, had not come. For the few marooned in the building I made out passes and also got the passes signed by military officers and left it to themselves to venture out of the building. None of them took the risk.

This Thursday afternoon was the most trying experience of all. The Dublin Fusilliers had been at the Depot in force and I have nothing but admiration for the way they kept down the sniping. They were replaced early in the afternoon by a small body of Lancers (about 20 only) and in a very short time the snipers got the upper hand. I came upstairs with Lieutenant Davis – the Officer in Charge of the Lancers – to show him from what houses the sniping proceeded. He had a corporal with him and both got to work at one of the windows of a room appropriated to the Engineering Staff. I was half way down the stairs in response to a call to do something for a man (another corporal) who was shot (wounded) at the gate, when Lieutenant Davis came out of the top room in a frightful state of distress to say that the corporal there was shot dead. The bullet had also cut the cloth of Lieutenant Davis' cuff. I asked Lieutenant Davis if there was any hope for this corporal and he said no. I then rushed downstairs to the waiting room where I found the other corporal of the Lancers with a ghastly-looking wound in the centre of his forehead. The bullet had, however, I found not penetrated the brain and after I had bandaged this man's head from an ambulance case kept in my room he pluckily remained on duty. The Lieutenant was now terribly anxious about the safety of the building. I took him into my room and he wrote an urgent despatch for immediate reinforcements. We got this despatch to Amiens Street by what strictly speaking was a questionable subterfuge. When the (Corporation) ambulance called to take away the corporal from upstairs I suggested that they might deliver the message. It was really our only way because no single man in khaki could at that time have got to Amiens Street. We had a very anxious time then for about half-an-hour until in response to our message about 100 men (Royal Irish Fusiliers) doubled into the Depot and took shelter with an alacrity that one does not usually see at Territorial manoeuvres.

I should like here to pay a tribute if I may be allowed to do so to the courage of Lieutenant Davis. He kept as hot a fire up as he possibly could until he got reinforcements and from that time the sniping died away – I rather fancy the snipers were being attended to by the military elsewhere. I should like also to say how much I am indebted to Mann. He is a little Londoner with absolutely no sense of fear. All through the piece the Officers and myself are personally indebted to him for many attentions. He procured food from nobody knows where and on this particularly trying afternoon when the few storemen who were marooned in the building huddled together under the stairs Mann followed Lieutenant Davis and myself wherever we went like a dog.

When the sniping had died down as I thought, I told Lieutenant Davis that I was very anxious about my wife and children living in a lonely house in the country and that I would try to get to them. I made out a pass, got Lieutenant Davis to sign it and told Mann to keep in touch with the Depot as it was possible the military would be withdrawn in a day or two. (The military were withdrawn on Sunday morning 30th April.) These instructions he carried out very faithfully.

Some time after 6 p.m. I set out to walk to Sutton – about 6 miles – with a very cheap right foot. I was sniped for a distance of 40 yards to Seville place where a sentry hurriedly looked at my pass from the shelter of a doorway and let me go on. I was the only civilian in the street. I was passed by the next sentry at the canal bridge but further on (Newcomen Bridge) was refused a passage. I came back to the canal Bridge and the sentry who let me through would not let me back. I passed backwards and forwards without success either way and then by what I can only say was a special mercy of providence I noticed a side street named Nottingham St. and I remembered that one of my staff lived there. The sniping in this street was particularly brisk and was drawing the fire from the soldiers on the Great Northern Railway line. I knocked at door after door and had these doors banged in my face, as the people were in a state of terror, until at last Mrs. Brown the wife of a 3rd Class Storeman opened her door. She put me up in the parlour for the night – a night of incessant sniping down the street – and in the morning about 10 o'clock after very many trying experiences I managed to reach the country on Brown's bicycle getting home by a circuitous route. My wife was in a state of collapse particularly on account of a foolish rumour that had gained credence in the district to the effect that Aldborough House had been burnt down.

I rested at home till Monday except for the journeyings I had to make for food for the household. On Monday and Tuesday I tried without success to ride back to the Depot but the Military were now complete masters of the situation and their cordon was too tight to get through. I wrote myself out a pass on Official note paper stating who I was[14] and this pass got me through on Wednesday.

Since that date the staff have been gradually coming back to duty and to-day (Saturday May 6th) there are only 3 absentees amongst the male staff, viz., Messrs. Cremen, O'Doherty and MacSorley (resumed on 8th).[15] These cases are being specially inquired into and I shall submit further reports.

Since my return I have been in close touch with the chiefs of the various Post Office Departments and up to the present I am happy to be able to state that the Staff is coping well with the exceptionally heavy demands that are being made on the Depot. Mr. Jeffries managed to get to the Depot on Tuesday 2nd May. He, Mr. Reynolds, Mr. Clarke, and Mr. Cummins are doing a great deal of good work and the situation is well in hand. I am making special demands upon a great many of the staff both stores and clerical, and extra efforts are being ungrudgingly made by all concerned. There was perhaps – as I anticipated – a kind of panic rush on the Depot after the trouble was over and I have had to take a somewhat strong line to ensure that the work should be carried out in an orderly and regular manner. The steps I have taken have had most beneficial results and I am sure the work of supplying stores of all sorts for the restoration of facilities Postal and Telegraph will be carried out with the utmost expedition and without any confusion.

I should like to close my report with a further reference to Unestablished Porter Mann. He lives a few doors from the Depot and he kept a watchful eye on the place after the military had left on Sunday 30th ult.

My first consideration was to do all I possibly could to ensure the safety of the building not only from the Sinn Féiners but also from the particularly virulent tribe of looters that were sacking the city unmolested, a really serious menace – more serious, according to many eye-witnesses, than the actual fighting.

Secondly I did not want it to be said that if the Engineering Department wanted material the Stores Department Staff had decamped.

I was a little exercised in my mind at some periods by the thought that I might be criticised for exposing the staff to undue risk but risks have to be taken in times like these. The Superintending Engineers and his Engineers and Linemen took risks and it would have been a pity if the Stores Department Staff could not say that they took their share. It is a great thing for our Department to have it to say that we carried on Post Office business as long as there was business at all to be done.

Letter from Mr R. Best of Sutton, County Dublin, to Commanding Officer, Main Supply Depot No. 5, Dublin, 28 April 1916[16]

I beg to report that on Monday 24th instant, I came to Dublin for medicine, leaving Sutton at 11.04 a.m. and arriving at the G.P.O. about 11.30 a.m., where I saw the rebels enter, pull down the blinds, and take possession without any resistance.

I at once concluded that they would stop all communications by cutting the cable and smashing the instruments, and seeing them swarming about in all directions, with loaded revolvers, rifles, etc., I rushed off to Amiens Street Station to raise the alarm there, and secure the 50 odd rifles lent by the Government to our Volunteer Corps,[17] and to secure, if possible, the line of communications through Howth before the rebels could reach it. I gave the alarm and warning the Sergt. of the Railway Transport on duty there, had word sent out to warn the Commandant of our Corps, who was out on a route march with the men and rifles, but minus ammunition. This was successful, as they were attacked coming home. They, however, reached Beggars Bush Barracks with rifles intact, and only one casualty (Platoon Commander W. J. Home, with eight bullets in him).[18] I then caught a train to Sutton, and commandeering a friendly motor-cyclist, sent off a message to J. Reeves, Esq. Superintendent of the Engineering Stores G.P.O., who was in charge of the Aldborough House, and resides some two miles from Sutton. He started at once for Dublin, caught a special train, got a loop cable across from Aldborough House to Amiens St. Station, got through to London, and saved the situation. I next warned all the Loyalists in my district, and started to walk in to the Main Supply Depot (10 miles) and reported myself to Major Haycock at 4.20 p.m., where I remained on duty till relieved on Tuesday.

The roads to the city being closed, I had to remain at Sutton till Friday, but I was not idle in the mean time, as I assisted to convey provisions etc. to friends in Dublin who had exhausted their stocks in feeding the troops guarding the line from Amiens Street to Clontarf.

I enclose a note from Mr. Reeves for your kind perusal,[19] and will hand up some receipts for some small items of expenditure so soon as I can get them vouched.

I am glad to be able to render you some small service in return for your invariable kindness to me since I joined the Depot, and to prove my loyalty on all future occasions, you have only to command.

Diary Notes of Work Performed by Postal Telegraphists at Dublin Castle During the Insurrection, compiled by J. J. Fogarty, 3 May 1916[20]

Easter Monday

Arrived Office 9.35 a.m. Very busy morning. Large number of Police messages. Reports received stating Railway lines cut in several places by Irish Volunteers.

10.45 a.m. Sent for by Under Secretary who enquired if Irish Office open. Handed long message for Chief Secretary to be despatched immediately & if possible direct to London as Irish Office not open. Dublin asked for use of direct wire to London and cipher forwarded.

11.30 a.m. At this time there were in the building Under Secy., Clerk in Waiting, Typist, one Messenger, policeman and ourselves (secret Telegraphists, Galbally & Fogarty). Local wire continued busy and our phone also constantly engaged.

About 12.10 p.m. we heard several shots in the Street just outside our office & on looking out the gate, policeman could be seen lying on the ground. Five or six Irish Volunteers in green uniform could be seen firing from Castle Street at the Guard who withdrew inside the Guard Room, one of the sentries half shutting the large gate. The Volunteers then advanced through the gate and 2 or 3 endeavoured to enter the Guard Room; the others came right into the middle of the Castle yard. I left the Office to seek instructions from the Under Secretary, and as I crossed the hall the policeman on duty shut the door with a loud bang the report of which startled the Volunteers (about 4 in number) who quickly withdrew from the Castle and joined by others entered the City Hall. I could not find the Under Secretary, and policeman said he had gone to Police Office when the first shots were fired. Returning to the Office I immediately phoned to Head Quarters Parkgate[21] & asking for General Officer Commanding was put through to Major Owen Lewis to whom I reported the attack on the Castle & managed to convince him of my identity & the genuineness of my report. I then phoned Ship Street Barracks, Police, and Portobello. Both Military Barracks said they had been attacked too. We were unable to get through to Marlboro', Beggars Bush or the Royal Bks. From this on we were expecting the Volunteers to return any minute and several shots shattered windows in the adjoining rooms.

At 12.30 p.m. Dublin [i.e. the GPO] asked us to report attack on Post Office to authorities. We informed Police, but they had already received the news & we were unable to get through to Head Quarters, all lines being engaged. Many calls from various places (Four Courts, Jacobs, Distillery & Railway Stations) reporting attacks by Sinn Féiners.

About 12.40 we observed several Volunteers making their way along roof of City Hall and some could also be seen in the Municipal Buildings on other side of the Street (this was exactly in front of our room), thus commanding entrance to the Castle.

About 12.45 a motor car with (I think it was) Sir Thos Myles[22] drove up and stopping outside the gate picked up the policeman and brought him into Hospital. From this on things remained stationary outside as far as could be seen until 3 p.m.

About 12.50 p.m. (I) we lost communication with Dublin for good and though wire looked O.K. could not get attention. Shortly after 1 p.m. a motor drove up to the side entrance of the City Hall with 4 or 5 Volunteers and 1 woman dressed in green in it. They handed out many rifles & ammunition to those already in City Hall & were about to hand out more when Major Price came up from R.I.C. Office and fired a revolver at them. He appeared to hit one man who fell forward in car which was then rapidly driven away. Nothing further occurred save several shots until 2.30 when 50 or 60 soldiers arrived from Portobello (R.I.R. and Dublin Fusiliers). They got through fairly easily once Camden Street was passed, but another half company which arrived at 3.30 had to fight all the way down. We breathed more freely now we had at least some defensive force.

About 1.20 p.m. 6 of our 9 Exchange lines were cut. The other three only worked with difficulty – heavy overhearing and only able to gain attention of Exchange after many efforts. Spoke Supervisor who promised to allot Operator specially to Castle lines. Owing to the faults on lines our generator did not drop Exchange indicator and it was only by getting the Operator to keep cutting in so as to see if lines clear that calls could be effected. (This was the only method of working during whole period 24th April to 2nd May). Our three lines were the only ones working from Upper and Lower Castle Yards (except Military), the R.I.C., D.M.P. and Castle Hospital[23] lines having been cut.

From 3 p.m. on there was a constant exchange of shots between Volunteers & Military; the latter however were too small in numbers to venture an attack as all the surrounding buildings in Dame Street, Cork Hill, Parliament Street, Lord Edward Street & Castle Street were in the hands of the rebels who had snipers on every roof.

3.30 asked local chemist to inform my wife not to expect me for a long time. Switch now very quiet, only occasional calls; shooting continued all round, the Soldiers firing whenever a Volunteer appeared.

5.30 Feeling rather hungry. Not had anything since 8.30 a.m.

6.30 Managed to get tea from Resident Messenger who had barely enough to go round for us all, including some officers.

7 p.m. Large numbers of Military now began to arrive from the Curragh & other places, and soon a machine gun was placed in the room immediately over ours.

About 9 p.m. it opened fire on the City Hall and after demolishing most of the lower windows of the City Hall a storming party advanced & effected an entrance & shortly after 10 p.m. had completely cleared the building of rebels. Later on the machine gun played on the Municipal Building, but it was not entered until the morning. Heavy firing continued all round, but most of the soldiers that arrived made ready for resting on the ground for the night. We had great difficulty in working as we could not switch on lights. We could not approach the window to lower the blind and even if we had it was not provided with shutters. On one occasion we flickered the light for a second and a shot entered the room next ours. However, we managed to obscure the light over the switch board with brown paper and removing the bulbs from the other lamps managed with the aid of a heavy draught screen to arrange enough light to discern switch board.

Shortly after 11 p.m. Amiens Street came through & we were delighted to know all communication was not cut off. Received a few messages on one of the extensions (43). This room is on the other side of building, and being provided with shutters & the light shaded on the reverse we had no difficulty in working. Tried to sleep on floor, but every time we settled down some one called, mostly with military messages. Gave up the attempt to sleep. Shot firing inter-mittently all night.

Tuesday. Soldiers started moving early & many more arrived. Feeling very hungry & not able to get anything to eat. Hospital had no bread or milk or we might have got some. About 9.30 a.m. we got some biscuits & 2 tins of beef from the military which we found very acceptable. Earlier the troops had occupied the Municipal Buildings & were firing at the Volunteers on the Mail Offices and Parliament Street, but a machine gun on the roof of Henry & James gave them a lot of trouble. Round the Lower Yard bullets came from every direction, snipers being on the roof of Pims & the houses in Stephen Street & Ship Street. Some also came from further off, probably Jacobs, and others from Dame Lane and Dame St. I crossed this yard about 10.30 to see Under Secretary who was now stopping with Capt. Kelly in the Master of the Horse's House. He enquired about communicating with London & later on sent some wires. From this on one of our telephone lines was continuously occupied with telegrams, leaving us only 2 junction lines for the whole Castle – an almost impossible job. The telegram work too was exceedingly difficult owing to heavy overhearing & an earth fault which caused cutting off owing to the Exchange Operator mistaking it for a clearing signal. The number of telegrams increased during the day, and we were kept busy right on into the night. We had two more meals of biscuit & beef, and in the evening Tea. In turn we each had about 2 hours rest. Shots were fired throughout the night, but not so heavily as the previous night.

Wednesday. Arrangements practically same as previous day. We, however, were supplied with food from Police stores (they commandeered some during the previous evening) & it was arranged to do so regularly, the Resident Messenger very kindly cooking for us. Things much quieter in Upper Yard, but Lower Yard if anything worse. As on previous day had no Messenger, and whenever I had messages for Under Secretary had in nearly every case to cross Lower Yard and deliver them myself. (Constabulary of course called for theirs). We were kept very busy all day & could scarcely manage time to eat our meals. We worked on right through the night & got practically no rest. Sniping all round from early evening.

Thursday. Very much the same as the previous day, only things quieter outside. Many more telegrams especially on Trunks from and to Maryboro', Kilkenny, Carlow, Naas & Dunlavin. Telephone lines engaged all the time. Mr. E. Smyth S.C. & T.[24] arrived at 11 a.m. but was not prepared to remain as no provisions at home. He tried to leave about Noon, but had to wait some time as a heavy fusillade was kept up on the Castle from a distance and it was unsafe to go out. He got away later, but was unable to return. Large number of officers looking for Phone calls, but unable to accommodate all. Got about 1? hours rest between 1 and 3 a.m.

Friday. Much as previous day, only number of messages shews further increase over 120 each way. Feeling very tired and doing what we could to keep things going. Mr. Quinn S.C. & T. spoke from Head Quarters about 6.30 p.m. and said he hoped to come to us. He could not, however, get through much to our disappointment, as we were very fatigued and we could have had sleep in turn if he had arrived. Managed to snatch 2 half-hour rests during night.

Saturday. One of the telephone wires commandeered by Food Supply Committee in order to make arrangements for supplying food to citizens. This left us only one wire for Military & other official calls, which caused great delay. Many callers asking to get through and great difficulty experiences in explaining matters to them. So busy was it that we had scarcely a chance of eating, & in order to dispose of some very urgent telephone calls had several times to ask Amiens Street to wait for long intervals. Spoke to Controller about 2.30 who promised assistance as soon as possible & kindly communicated home. Heard of surrender of rebels, but country work greater than ever. Busy as before all evening and night & until 5 a.m. when we rested until nearly 7 when we started again.

Sunday. Very much the same as Saturday. Officers constantly waiting to get through military calls, & large number of telegrams. Snatched 1? hours sleep.

Monday. Not quite so busy earlier, but as busy as ever later. Spoke to Controller who said Messrs. J. Smyth & Fitzgerald would arrive shortly. 10.30 Mr. E. Smyth arrived, but as he said he was not prepared to stay right on but would go home to dinner & arrange with his wife to stay all night neither of us left office. We had plenty for all three to do, especially as it enabled us to work 2 lines at times to Amiens Street. 1.30 pm. Mr. E. Smyth left for home. 3 o'c. Mr. J. Smyth & Mr. A. Fitzgerald arrived. Spent over an hour shewing them working arrangements. 4.10 left office, feeling almost too tired to walk. Reached Leeson Street Bridge & found could not even approach sentries to show Pass, and had to go via Charlemont Street & home at last. Had a very exciting time, strenuous work & fatigue, but would not have been away for worlds. Everybody in Castle, from Under Secretary down, exceedingly kind and doing all they could (which was not indeed very much) to help us and make things easier.

The General Post Office, Dublin.[25]

About noon on last Easter Monday some fifty rebels dashed into the public office of the General Post Office, half proceeding at once to smash the street windows under the portico while the remainder, armed with revolvers, jumped across the counter and shouted 'hands up'. The staff were not allowed to get their hats and coats except any that were at hand under the counter, and were threatened with death if they attempted to touch anything else. One of the counter-men relates that the rebel who confronted him had a bayonet in his left hand and an automatic pistol in his right. The brave rebel's hands were trembling so much that there was every fear he would let off the pistol unintentionally.

The following personal statements will be read with interest:-

The seizure of the G.P.O. Dublin by the Sinn Féin Volunteers on Easter Monday, 1916.

A Few Notes by One Who Was There

Looking back on the events that happened on Easter Monday, 1916, when the Sinn Féin Volunteers rose in armed rebellion and proclaimed an Irish Republic under the portico of the G.P.O., Dublin, the whole proceedings appear to have been more like a dream than reality. The dream is rudely dispelled, however, by paying a visit to Sackville Street, where the ruin and desolation caused by the gigantic fires that raged during Easter week is only too pronounced. The weather on Easter Monday was ideal for outdoor amusements, and the thought of one at least in the Instrument Room on that forenoon was that it was fortunate for the holiday makers that the sun shone so brightly. This train of thought, however, was roughly interrupted at 12 noon by the announcement from our Chief Technical Officer on duty that the majority of the lines running into the Instrument Room, including our cross channel wires, had become stopped, due to the fact that the leading in cables in the basement had been cut.

Almost simultaneous with the receipt of this information the news was brought that the Sinn Féin Volunteers had entered the public counter – the new office only recently opened to the public – had taken possession and had turned everybody else out into Sackville Street. Credence could not at first be given to this story, but the noise of breaking glass in the front of the building partly verified it, and on looking out over the top part of the window into Sackville Street it was only too evident that the story was true, as all the windows in the lower storey were being smashed from the inside, the broken glass being thickly strewn over the pavement. It was also seen that a number of the rebels guarded the entrance to the public counter with rifles and revolvers, whilst others were distributing to a crowd large poster sheets which proved to be copies of the Proclamation of the Irish Republic.

Since the beginning of the war we have had a military guard of a sergeant and half a dozen men to provide a sentry at each of the two entrances to the Instrument Room. About 12.30 p.m. the sergeant of the guard reported that the rebels were forcing the stairs leading up to the northern entrance. The corridor leading from the top of the Northern stairs to the Instrument Room – about 10 yards long – was then hastily filled with chairs, waste paper boxes and other portable articles that could be laid hold of in order to impede the entrance of the besiegers as long as possible in the hope that help would arrive in time to prevent them gaining possession. The sergeant and the guard could only stand inside the Instrument Room door ready to receive the attackers if they broke through the obstructions in the passage. The rebels then commenced to fire through the passage into the Instrument Room, and the noise thus made in a confined space greatly alarmed the female members of staff. When the corridor had been barricaded all the female staff were cleared down to the southern end of the room, and as matters became worse they were instructed to proceed to their Retiring Room on the southern landing and put on their outdoor apparel in case it became necessary that they should leave the building. About 10 minutes to 1 o'clock a message was brought to the Superintendent from an officer of the Sinn Féiners who was stated to be on the southern landing to go out to him to make arrangements for the staff to leave the building. The Superintendent declined to go, sending word that he would not hold any parlay with the officer as he (the Superintendent) did not recognize the right of the officer to be where he was. (By this time all the females had left had left the Instrument Room.) A minute or two afterwards the officer in question, with a few supporters, came into the Instrument Room each being armed with a revolver and ordered everyone to clear out, at the same time ascertaining that no one was in possession of arms. This officer it was subsequently ascertained was The O'Rahilly.

By 1 o'clock the last of the male staff had left the G.P.O. building. The guards were made prisoners and detained. The officer and his party had gained access to the southern corridor through the dinning-room by means of a flight of stairs leading from the Sorting Office to that room, and as there was only one sentry guarding the southern corridor he was easily over-powered.

About 1.20 p.m. the Lancers arrived from Marlboro' Barracks and rode down the street from the Rotunda. About a dozen of them had passed the Nelson Pillar Monument towards Clery's shop when the fusillade was opened on them from the windows of the G.P.O. Several saddles were emptied and the horses stampeded, some of the later being badly wounded, two ultimately died, and their carcasses lay in the streets for some days. I was subsequently informed that four of the Lancers were killed and some wounded. The rest of the party retired down the side streets to shelter. When the firing had ceased several street urchins rushed out from where they had been sheltering in the adjoining houses, and helped to capture the riderless horses and led them away. One of these horses was badly wounded in the shoulder, and as it limped along a bare-footed urchin managed to withdraw the trooper's carbine from its case and at once made all speed with it to the G.P.O. building and thrust it through one of the barricaded windows to a member of the *garrison*. It showed in a small way that the invaders of the G.P.O. had some sympathisers amongst the crowd outside.

All the windows of the G.P.O. in each storey were broken by the rebels and then barricaded with mail bags, tables, chairs and such like, in order that they could fire out at any relieving force that might make its appearance. A machine gun was subsequently erected by rebels on the roof of the G.P.O., and another on Clery's roof on opposite side of street. I think it was on Friday in Easter week that the G.P.O. was burned. The rebel garrison sought to make their escape through Moor Lane – opposite the Henry Street entrance to the G.P.O. – but were met by military machine guns and very few got away. The O'Rahilly was killed in this way. He was of gentlemanly appearance and good manner, and it must be said that he behaved most court-eously in the matter of clearing out the staff in the Instrument Room.

It would appear that the rebels had prepared postage stamps for use under the *Republic*. They had seized a lot of British stamps in the public office and used them for sticking up on the walls near the G.P.O. the notices or proclamations of the Irish Republic.

By a Lady Telegraphist

I went on duty at 8 a.m. Easter Monday. At about 12.20 p.m. I was relieved for luncheon. I went into the dining-room and shortly afterwards one of our girls came in saying the Volunteers had taken the Sorting Office. Several other clerks then came in looking very frightened, and told us that the Volunteers were proceeding up to the Instrument Room. By this time we were all beginning to realise that matters were serious, and just as I was going back to the Instrument Room one of the male clerks entered the dining-room and said something to the waitress, whereupon they all ran towards the door.

I then made enquiries and was told that the Volunteers were coming up the stairs, and that the best thing to do was to remain at the end of the Instrument Room. I went to the Instrument Room and found that all the clerks had left their circuits and were mostly in groups looking for the most part very pale.

I looked out of the windows onto Sackville Street and saw crowds of people looking up at the G.P.O.

We were all anxious at this time to get out of the office, but we were told that no one could leave the building as the entrances were barricaded. The report of a revolver at the Henry Street end of the Instrument Room was next heard, and the Superintendent ordered all ladies into the retiring-room. We hurried in and put on our outdoor garments so as to be in readiness to leave, although we did not know what might happen next. The room was rather congested but everyone was cool and there was no unnecessary excitement. We stayed in this room for about a quarter of an hour when we were told that ladies could leave the building. We were conducted by one of the Volunteers through the dining-room into the yard, and after some little delay in opening the gate we passed out feeling greatly relieved, but fully aware that we were still in danger from stray shots. One of our lady Supervisors bravely refused to leave the building. The sergeant of the guard having been wounded in the head our lady Supervisor rendered First Aid, but as the wound was rather serious she was permitted to bring him to Jervis Street Hospital and have it dressed. She returned with the sergeant and remained in the G.P.O. until about 5 p.m.

(N.B.- This permission was only given on their word of honour to return which they bravely fulfilled although the Jervis Street authorities tried to persuade the sergeant to stay.)

The Dublin Telephone Exchange is, as stated earlier in this article, situated at Crown Alley, near Dame Street, and the devotion of the Telephonists to their duty during a most trying week has been referred to in the local press as worthy of special comment. It was to be expected that the courteous and able District Manager and his male staff would stick to their posts, but one would not have wondered if the nerves of the ladies had proved unequal to the strain. Such, however, was not the case even when the operators were at intervals told to lie on the floor during the rattle of rifles and machine guns. They wept but carried on the work notwithstanding the fact that the switch-board and ceiling were scarred with bullets.

For the first two days groups of operators relieved each other impelled to make the perilous journeys to and from their homes by a sense of duty, but by Wednesday morning conditions had become so bad that they had to settle down in the Exchange for the rest of the week. Expeditions for food were made at great risk by the male staff, and beds and bedding for about forty persons were secured.

The military defence of the Exchange had been undertaken by a body of the Royal Irish Rifles, and barricades had been constructed of stationary presses, pads of tickets and sand from the fire buckets.

More than once members of the Engineering Staff risked their lives in repairing lines wilfully damaged by the rebels.[26]

Notes

1. The 'grandiose yet remarkably dull' Aldborough House in Portland Row, completed in 1799, was 'the last grand free-standing aristocratic house to be built in Dublin' (Casey, *Dublin*, pp. 170–2). By 1916 it had for many

years been used as a Post Office depot.

2. Information from *Whitaker's Almanack*.

3. BPMA, POST 31/80B, file III.

4. This is twelve noon 'Irish time'. Up to October 1917 Irish time, or 'Dublin Mean Time', was 25 minutes behind Greenwich Mean Time.

5. This is not reproduced.

6. BPMA, POST 31/80B, file III.

7. Greenwich time.

8. This was for the Royal Dublin Society Spring Show at their Ballsbridge grounds.

9. The Post Office had a whole department devoted to the telegraph service for race meetings.

10. BPMA, POST 31/80, file VI.

11. Engineer-in-Chief to the Post Office, 1912–19.

12. These were most likely some of the Volunteers commanded by Frank Henderson in the Fairview area and at the Tolka Bridge at Ballybough. See the account in Michael Hopkinson (ed.), *Frank Henderson's Easter Rising: Recollections of a Dublin Volunteer* (Cork: Cork University Press, 1998), pp. 44–51.

13. The 'siege of Sidney Street' in the East End of London, in January 1911, had involved a sustained gun-battle between a gang of burglars and armed police and military.

14. Appended to this remark is a note from Reeves: 'I attach it with every apology. On this and other occasions I had to assume myself a much higher official than what I am. Particularly was this so when getting thro' to & talking with the Garrison Adjutant.' A further minute from George Morgan (Controller of the Post Office Stores Department) reads: 'I agree all's fair in love and war'.

15. A minute appended to the file from George Morgan to Sir Evelyn Murray (1 June 1916) notes that O'Doherty and Cremen had both been arrested and transferred to Stafford Detention Barracks in England on 30 April. O'Doherty was released in late May, 'having been arrested & deported under a misapprehension'. Cremen had been warned in January to sever all links with the Irish Volunteers. See below in chapter 8 for further mention of Cremen (named in one document as 'Michael Crimmins') and O'Doherty, among the civil servants 'suspected of complicity in the Sinn Féin Rebellion'.

16. BPMA, POST 31/80B, file XII.

17. Best was a member of the Howth and Sutton Volunteer Training Corps, of which J. H. Reeves was also a member.

18. 'W. J. Horne', platoon commander in the 1st (Dublin) Battalion Associated Volunteer Training Corps, is listed in the Weekly Irish Times, *1916 Rebellion Handbook* (Dublin: Mourne River Press edn, 1998), p. 56, as having been severely wounded.

19. Not reproduced.

20. BPMA, POST 31/80B, file III.

21. Army headquarters.

22. Myles was medical head of the Richmond Hospital. He was an active

nationalist, and not unsympathetic to the rebel cause, but also a 'Consulting Surgeon' to the British forces with the honorary rank of lieutenant colonel.

23. Part of the Castle was used as a wartime military hospital. A vivid account of the Rising by one of the hospital nurses, Vivienne Smyly, was published anonymously as 'Experiences of a V.A.D.', in *Blackwoods Magazine*, 200 (July-Dec. 1916), pp. 814–40.
24. Letters presumably designating Smyth as a 'Secret Telegraphist' like Fogarty.
25. From *St Martin's-le-Grand Magazine*, vol. xxvi, no. 103 (July 1916), pp. 263–5, and no. 104 (Oct. 1916), pp. 356–60.
26. The article is signed 'John Stuttard', who appears merely to have compiled it from other people's recollections.

6 A Rebel's Tale

The narrative reproduced in this chapter, although written in a self-consciously 'literary' style, gives an especially vivid account of what it was like inside the GPO. According to a hand-written note (apparently by the author himself) on the 26-page typescript preserved in the National Library of Ireland, the account was 'compiled from notes written in Wakefield Prison (England) during the first few weeks in May 1916 while in solitary confinement'. It was, furthermore, 'written incidentally on toilet papers as we were allowed no books or writing material, until sometime later when John Dillon M.P. protested on our behalf in the House of Commons'.

Dick Humphreys had just turned 20 when the Rising started,[1] and had been brought up in a fervently republican family. He was educated at Patrick Pearse's school, St Enda's, and became an Irish Volunteer while still a schoolboy. A major figure in the narrative is Humphrey's uncle, The O'Rahilly, a larger-than-life figure whom the younger man hero-worshipped. O'Rahilly, having spent the weekend trying to stop the Rising taking place, joined the rebels on Easter Monday, famously remarking 'I have helped to wind up the clock, and must be there to hear it strike'.[2]

In sharp contrast to the detailed and atmospheric description of the fighting, the situation inside the GPO and the great fires which devastated it and surrounding buildings, Humphreys says nothing at all about the surrender. Perhaps the memory of defeat was too bitter to be recalled, and his narrative jumps to the imprisonment of the rebels, both in Dublin and England.

EASTER WEEK IN THE G.P.O.
Dick Humphreys[3]

Easter Monday, 1916, Noon.

Suddenly through the lovely summer-like air of that fatal bank holiday two shots ring out reverberatingly. Then follows a machine-gun-like succession of reports, and finally an immense explosion. People stop on the footpaths and look questionably at one another. A very few straightaway realise what has happened, and become the centres of chattering crowds. All at once one notices that a great silence, terrible in its unnaturalness, has fallen on the city. Then again come those foreboding shots, seven or eight whipping out viciously the imperial summons of the god Mars. Two policemen run up from the Stephen's Green direction and scurry into Lad Lane. Some queer feeling in the air prevents one from wholly realising the utter ridiculousness of their action. At the moment one seems capable of unmovably watching the most grotesque thing. A valiant sergeant suddenly makes his appearance, and proceeds to stop all inward-bound cars. One motor driver remonstrates indignantly, disdainfully daring anyone to stop him. Later on his car was seen picturesquely placed at one end of the Shelbourne barricade.

At Stephen's Green (East) a large and ever-increasing crowd had collected. rumours of Hun-like atrocities abound on all sides. Nevertheless the self-same crowd seems to have a strange confidence in those 'Huns', considering that barely the width of a street separates them. Save for the complete absence of holiday-makers, and the barred gates, indeed, one would notice nothing unusual on glancing inside the Park.

* * *

Tension grows throughout the afternoon. Crowds throng around the different positions. Everyone is waiting for the supposed coming advance of the military. Then suddenly rumour has it that the Germans have been seen on the North side. One old lady informs me gratuitously in Westmoreland Street that a 'corpse of Germans' has landed in the Park, whether from warships or Zeppelins not stated. Likewise she adds that the Sinn Féiners have set up a courthouse in the G.P.O. At O'Connell Street I finally learn that Ireland has been proclaimed a Republic.

Slates of broken glass lying on the Pavement outside attract gruesome crowds. They look just like pools of crimson blood. The numbers of onlookers in O'Connell Street and around the G.P.O. is truly stupendous. It takes me fully twenty minutes to get as far as the Metropole Hotel.

Here a strange sight confronts me. Swaying gently in the evening breeze from flagstaff is the tricolour Republican flag. In the building itself all the lower storey windows have been barricaded with bags of mails, boxes of sand, ironwork, chairs, tables, etc. Through roughly-formed loopholes one catches sight of glistening, exultant faces, shining gun barrels and well-stocked bandoliers. From all sides resounds the nerve-shattering jar of breaking glass, and occasionally the hoarse orders of unseen officers. Here and there posted along the walls are copies of the famous Proclamation. In the street outside the temper of the crowd is fairly mixed. A few soldiers' wives create a scene by attempting to enter, but happily they are overborne by friends in the crowd, and forcibly dragged away.

Inside the central postal hall, round the three sides of which run the newly-built letter counters, all is bustle. Every inch of space between the counters and windows is occupied with uniformed men, boxes of ammunition, pikes, blankets, mess-tins, bandoliers, knapsacks, and all the paraphernalia of warfare. The central portion of the hall is set apart for headquarters use, and at a table P. Pearse, W. Pearse and T. Clarke are conversing together. Farther over J. Connolly is dictating something from a piece of paper. He looks very stern and care-worn. Behind him a lady typist is calmly click-clacking away, as though accustomed to working in this martial atmosphere all her life. Ammunition of every description overflows counters, tables and chairs, while revolvers and automatic pistols of all shapes and sizes are scattered among them. The O'Rahilly and Joe Plunkett come in from tour of the defences. The former, as usual, is relating some joke at which they both laugh heartily.

Later on in the evening I come face to face with my old schoolmaster, Commandant Patrick Pearse. I haven't met him since the time when I descended on my old Alma Mater like a poor relation after a three day, intensely cold, and equally lonely bivouac in the Dublin Mountains. I had run away from a new boarding school to which I was being sent. My aim was to get back to Sgoil Eanna from which I had been removed at the behest of certain rather pro-British friends of my mother who believed in a more 'practical' form of education than that offered by the Pearse family. My hopes were dashed, however, when Pearse pointed out that parental wishes were the vital ones in cases like this. He remembers that incident and goes on to say that he is glad to see me back with the Sgoil Eanna contingent in their hour of need. I then learn that the majority of the school has marched into the G.P.O. from Rathfarnham earlier in the day. He has a roll of papers in his hands, and asks me if I had seen, and read the Easter Week Proclamation. His eyes light up with intense joy when I say that these posters were attracting great attention, and excitement, where I had seen them posted on the walls in O'Connell Street and Henry Street on my way into the building.

It is now eight o'clock and already getting dark. Manfield's boot shop, at the corner of Abbey Street, is looted by the unruly element in the crowd, and for the next hour or so a steady stream of people flows past the windows, their arms piled high with boots and shoes of all shapes and sizes. Soon a brisk trade in footwear line is going on, for those lucky enough to secure the boots immediately trade them to covetous late-comers. A shop right opposite us either goes, or is set on fire, but the prompt arrival of the Brigade soon quells it. More shop windows are smashed and wholesale looting commences. Other fires break out, and the Brigade is kept busy up till twelve. After this hour the crowds gradually decrease, and by 2 a.m. the streets are bare.

* * *

Tuesday

The sun rises about 4 a.m. It is a beautiful summer-like morning. Firing has ceased and everything is silent save for the soughing of a slight breeze through the glassless sashes of countless windows. O'Connell Street presents a strange aspect. The cobbles as far down as the Monument are snow-white with sheets of paper and cardboard boxes. Not a living thing is in sight. Even the birds shun the district. On a house-top near the D.B.C.[4] two slender poles rise up high above the chimneys. Silver-like aerials stretch between them. It is the wireless station, our only method of communication with the outside world.

Some distant clock booms five times. The sound seems terribly pregnant in this unnerving silence. Scarcely have the last vibrations died away in tiny pulsations when a volley of shots rings out with startling distinctness away up in 'The Green' direction. For some minutes an irregular fusillade goes on. One can clearly distinguish the heavy boom of the 'Howth' rifle[5] from the sharper crack of the Lee-Enfield. Eye-weary men rise up anxiously from their sleepless couches. Then it stops as suddenly, and the stillness becomes more intensified.

* * *

Upstairs on the top storey of the building the P.O. restaurant has been turned into the Volunteer mess-quarters. Desmond FitzGerald, at the head of a busy ration party, is preparing breakfast for the few hundred defenders of the G.P.O.[6] Five or six captured 'Tommies' have also been requisitioned. By this time everyone has been allotted to his different station, and the building no longer presents the appearance of an overturned anthill, as was the case the evening before. All street-facing windows have been barricaded and manned by single, double or treble guards of Volunteers, as the case may demand. An ambulance department and hospital have been prepared. Armourers have collected all the loose and spare ammunition, rifles, revolvers, pikes, etc., into one central depot. Another room has been set apart for hand and fuse grenades. Chemical fire extinguishers are distributed at the different danger points, while in the yard outside other parties are busy filling sand-bags.

The O'Rahilly gets in touch with me on Tuesday morning, and tells me to see Desmond FitzGerald who is in charge of the commissariat department and find out what supplies he may require. My uncle has driven his De Dion car into the G.P.O. on Monday, and it now rests down in the yard after being emptied of its initial load of rifles, revolvers, and ammunition. Desmond FitzGerald gives me a long list of items which he considers he needs and I set off with two volunteers through the Princes Street gate. We call at various addresses in the vicinity of O'Connell Street, Pearse Street,[7] and Ringsend, and encounter mixed receptions from the amazing number of citizens who still throng the streets in this area. As the majority of shops are either closed up completely, or pretty empty when broken into by looters, we become expert house-breakers in our efforts to fill the car with the required foodstuffs. I become quite proud of one particular exploit where my assistants lift me up to a trap door high in the wall. I experience a most exciting moment where I more or less dive head-first, and in compete darkness, into a stack of cardboard and wooden boxes. This place proves to be Anne Lynch's depot in Westland Row. We remove sufficient supplies in our two trips to this address to withstand a year's siege.

My greatest difficulty, indeed, is to prevent my good body-guards from utterly overloading the poor car. Our first trip proves to be very nearly our last one as the sadly overloaded vehicle creeps along on completely flat springs, and with both rear mudguards scrapping the tyres.

* * *

Wednesday morning finds things beginning to get lively. Bullets are pattering on the walls and windows of the Imperial, Reis's, the D.B.C., Hopkins,[8] etc., all of which are held by us. An ever-inquisitive crowd is standing in D'Olier Street and O'Connell Bridge, right between the two firing parties. They appear quite unconcerned. Indeed, one would think from their appearance that the whole thing was merely a sham battle got up for their amuse-ment. Towards ten o'clock, however, they gradually disappear, and half an hour later the streets shine bare in the sunlight.

For the next few hours we work hard, rendering our section of the defences (the east room) as bullet-proof as possible. Stationary presses are raided, and a wall of notebooks six or seven feet deep is built inside the window. Then follows a line of sacks full of coal, all the sand having been utilised in the lower storeys. To prevent these rather inflammable materials caching fire the whole place is drenched by means of one of the large firing hoses. Four loopholes have been left in the barricade, through which we place our rifles. There follows an unexciting vigil during which we watch the empty streets unceasingly. Our window commands O'Connell Street from the Imperial Hotel to Carlisle Building and the fire station on the opposite side of the Liffey. Intermittent fire is going on on all [sides], but, save for the occasional spent bullet, our building is not touched as yet.

About 2 o'clock p.m. a gigantic boom shakes the edifice to its foundations, and everyone looks up with startled eye. From all

sides come questioning words. Some say that a bomb has explo-
ded in the lower room. Others that it is a dynamite explosion,
but a second and third in quick succession prove the correctness
of those who proclaimed it heavy artillery. The detonations are
truly tremendous, and were we not absolutely certain that the
gun was situated on the opposite side of the river, one could
have sworn that it was at least in Abbey Street. For a time the
men are uneasy at this their first experience of heavy gun-fire,
but soon they become quite accustomed to the sound, and take
no more notice of it than of the ordinary rifle fire. About 4 o'clock
we learn that Kelly's shop[9] has been shelled and its defenders
forced to retire. A machine-gun has meantime been placed on the
Brunswick St. Fire Station, and a hail of bullets begins to speckle
the walls of the Imperial. Another one situated somewhere near
Trinity College raises little rippling clouds of mortar from the
front facade of the D.B.C. No. 1 is then turned on the G.P.O. It
sounds like a sudden burst of hail against the ceiling. Our roof-
snipers can command practically every point within range of the
building, and they soon silence the machine-guns. Firing is still
brisk on the west side, where the military are shooting from the
Rotunda direction. Towards six o'clock, however, the uproar
gradually subsides, and for a few hours there is a local silence.

About ten o'clock we suddenly noticed a well-dressed,
middle-aged man coming up to O'Connell Bridge from the
direction of Butt Bridge. The light of the electric arc lamps shine
on his carefully-brushed tall hat. Both sides shout to him to get
away. He seems dazed, and walks uncertainly for a few minutes.
Suddenly a volley rings out from D'Olier Street, and he jumps
about four feet into the air. Then with another bound he reaches
the corner of the bridge and rushes down Eden Quay at racing
pace. There seems something unreal about the thing. Seen in the
unnatural light from the street standards, one cannot imagine it
to be real live drama. Suddenly an officer enters the room. He
orders three or four crack shots to smash the arc lamps. A few
seconds later O'Connell street is plunged into darkness. Only
the stars shed a mystic glare over the house-tops.

Sleeping accommodation, as far as the rank and file are
concerned, is pretty nonexistent. When our 'off-duty' turn
arrives we hunt around for a reasonably quiet spot where we
might snatch a short sleep. But despite its huge size the G.P.O.
seems to possess no amenities of this kind and the best most of

us can do is to bed down under a table, or desk, with a top cover thrown over us in lieu of the normal sheet or blanket. Needless to say no-one gets much sleep. The short intervals of silence outside are even more ominous in their eerie intensity than the shots, explosions, strange whistling and odd bursts of patriotic song which punctuate the night.

* * *

Thursday, April 27th, 6 A.M.

It is a glorious day again with a burning sun glowing in a cloudless blue sky. A sullen rumble of heavy shooting from 'Jacob's'[10] direction vibrates on the cool breeze like the rattle of a deadly snake. At the O'Rahilly's orders we spend the morning constructing imitation barricades in every window which opens outwards This work necessitates the breaking in of numerous locked doors. The building seems immense. The number of separate rooms in the place is unbelievable. Meantime the bombardment has recommenced. Hopkins', the D.B.C., and the Imperial being under continuous fire, while the G.P.O. is subject to much sniping. The everlasting wait for the unexpected is terribly nerve-racking. Machine-guns stutter irregularly from all sides and add to the growing uproar.

Towards 3 o'clock we learn that there is going to be an attack from the North-west side. All the available men, therefore, are withdrawn from the eastern posts, and take up positions at the western windows. The excitement grows intense. Everyone is waiting. Suddenly rumour has it that an armoured car is approaching up Henry Street. Men show themselves insanely a the window to obtain a view. Then comes a tremendous explosion rising high above the rattle of rifle and machine-gun fire. The shooting dies down all at once, and there is a lull.

Pearse takes this opportunity of speaking to the men. His words consist of a short resume of events since the Monday morning. He commences by saying that K. has succeeded in overturning the armoured car with a bomb. 'All our principal positions,' he continues, 'are still intact. Commandant Daly has captured the Linenhall Barracks, taken two officers and twenty-three men prisoners, and set fire to he building. The country is steadily rising, and a large band of Volunteers is marching from

Dundalk on Dublin. A successful engagement between a large
body of police and an inferior number of Volunteers has taken
place near Lusk, between thirty or forty police being captured.
Barracks have been raided throughout the country, and
especially in the Counties Dublin and Meath Wexford has risen
and a relief column, to be marched on Dublin, is being formed.
A large store of food supplies has been discovered in the building which will enable us to hold out till reinforcements from the
country arrive and release us.'

He concludes by saying that we have now successfully held
out as a Republic against the might of England for three full
days. Wherefore, according to International law, we are legally
entitled to the status of Republicanists and the presence of a
delegate in that Peace Conference which must inevitably follow
the war.

His words are answered by a deafening outburst of cheering
which spreads throughout the whole building. Needless to say,
this account puts new vitality into the men which three days'
uncertainty and suspense had rather dispersed.

3.45 P.M.

The military commence shelling us in real earnest, and shrapnel
shells begin to drop on the roof in quick succession. Two
howitzers have been mounted near Findlater's Church.[11] For ten
or fifteen minutes our roof-snipers stand the fire, but begin to
suffer heavily, three being wounded severely. Word to evacuate
this position is accordingly given, and a minute later they come
tumbling down through the safety man-holes into the telegraph
room. These man-holes are just rough spaces torn in the slates
and mortar through which a rope stretches down to the floor.
Some of the men in their hurry fail to catch the rope altogether,
and take the eighteen foot drop as though it were an everyday
occurrence. The wounded are lowered safely by means of two
ropes. This cannonade continues for about two and a half hours,
but the shells, the majority of which seem to be shrapnel, fail to
do any serious damage to our position. Snipers on the Gresham
[Hotel], however, are sending a fusillade of bullets in through
the western windows, and we are ordered to keep under cover
as much as possible. We allow them to continue firing till, mystified at our silence, they grow bolder, and incautiously show

themselves over the top of the parapet. Immediately a single volley rings out. There is no more sniping that evening from the Gresham.

The continuous 'boom' of the Howth guns echoing from all sides of the building show that the military are at length beginning to show themselves, but towards seven o'clock the cannonade slackens, and finally subsides to an occasional report now and again. The G.P.O., Imperial, Reis's, and all our minor posts are still intact.

7.30 P.M.

The surplus men return to their former positions in the eastern rooms, where the single guards have spent a most uninteresting and nerve-shattering evening listening to the firing all round them, but seeing nothing tangible. Hopkins is just beginning to blaze, while somewhere down in Abbey Street a thin column of smoke is rising into the still evening air. Not realising that this is the commencement of that huge conflagration which is to devastate O'Connell Street, we watch the leaping flame while gradually night darkens over the city.

On returning to our posts after tea we are appalled at the stupendous increase the fire has made. The interior of our room is as bright as day with the lurid glow of the flames. Reis's jewellery shop is a mass of leaping scarlet tongues of light. Behind it huge mountains of billowing jet black smoke are rolling up into the heavens. A roaring as of a gigantic waterfall re-echoes from the walls. Hopkins is completely hidden from view by a curtain of skimmering, hissings sparks. Up through the ever-changing haze of smoke and flame, lifting itself proudly like one who scorns to notice the taunts of an enemy, rises the tower of the D.B.C. Ringed round with fire it stands undaunted while overhead the very sky quivers with the simmering heat. It seems symbolical of Ireland. Suddenly some oil works near Abbey Street is singed by the conflagration, and immediately a solid sheet of blinding, death-white flame rushes hundreds of feet into the air with a thunderous explosion that shakes the walls. It is followed by a heavy bombardment as hundreds of drums of oil explode. The intense light compels one to close the eyes. Even here the light is so terrible that it strikes one like a solid thing as blasts of scorching air come in through the glassless windows.

Millions of sparks are floating in impenetrable masses for hundreds of yards around O'Connell Street, and as a precaution we are ordered to drench the barricades with water again. The whole thing seems too terrible to be real. Crimson-tinged men moved around dazedly. Above it all the sharp crackle of rifle fire predominates, while the deadly rattle of the machine-gun sounds like the coughing laughter of jeering spirits.

Gradually the fire spreads along O'Connell Street, and from a hissing murmur the sound grows to a thunderous booming, like the song of a great dynamo. Awe-stricken, the men gather together at the different posts and discuss the outbreak in hoarse whispers. 'How will it end?' 'Will it reach the Imperial?' 'Will the Post Office catch fire?' 'Is the whole city doomed?' Such are some of the questions that pass from lip to lip.

Suddenly an armoured car appears in Westmoreland Street. It moves towards us, and seems about to advance, but reverses instead, and disappears in the direction of Dame St. A shout rings out from the Imperial Hotel, and we see a figure standing at one of the windows. He makes a trumpet of his hands, and in clear tones informs us that the building has caught fire at the rear. He asks for further orders, and is told to get his men across to the G.P.O. if possible. Five minutes later four Volunteers are seen at the door of the Hotel. They signal to open the main door downstairs, and rush across the street in turns. From their windows we watch their passage breathlessly.

Ten minutes later the Imperial, together with the buildings on either side, is well ablaze, while over in the Henry Street direction another fire has broken out. We seem to be situated in the midst of a circle of flame. Inside the central telegraph room, which runs along the whole length of the G.P.O., the men standing silently at their posts, black and bronze statues against the terrible glare of the sky. Unawed and undaunted, their gaze ever fixed on the glistening cobbles and shadowed lanes whence all attacks must be directed, they wait expectantly. Now and again the flames beat upwards in a flesh of light that reveals every detail behind the barriers, then they subside as suddenly, and lines of black shadows, rays of darkness, as it were, creep over us. Fortunately the wind is blowing seawards, and the myriads of blazing fragments are carried away from the G.P.O. Glowing sparks, however, now begin to shower down with a pattering like soft rain, and threaten to set everything on fire. All bombs and hand grenades are taken to the centre of the building, and again we drench barricades, walls and floors. Even in the midst of this inferno we are sniped at by the enemy, and occasional bullets com in through the windows. Clouds of dirty grey smoke prevent us fro replying.

At about 12.30 the two Pearses, The O'Rahilly and some other officers make a tour of our defences. They seem quite satisfied as to the progress of things.

* * *

Friday, April 28th, The Fifth Day of the Irish Republic.

The weather is sunny and fine as usual. On the opposite side of O'Connell Street nothing is left of the buildings save the bare walls. Clouds of grey smoke are wreathing around everywhere, and it is difficult to see as far as the Bridge. Occasionally some side wall or roof falls in with a terrific crash. The heat is stupefying, and a heavy odour of burning cloth permeates the air. All the barbaric splendour that night had lent the scene has now faded away, and the pitiless sun illuminates the squalidness and horror of the destruction. The morning is fairly quiet, but occasional shots ring out from the direction of the Four Courts.

After breakfast we again take up our positions at the windows. The morning passes uneventfully in our area. We hear that Maxwell has arrived in Dublin. Towards twelve o'clock the smoke clears away from Hopkin's corner, and a machine-gun opens fire on our windows. From then on till 3 o'clock the shooting increases on all sides, the report of the Howth guns sounding more like artillery than rifles. About 3.30 p.m. a differently-noted fusillade rings out from the Gresham Hotel direction, and, to our astonishment, the side of the walls where the bullets lodge seem to flash into flame. Finding no hold, however, they became immediately extinguished. A minute or so later someone discovers that the roof is on fire, and immediately commences a perfect babble of shouting, order-giving and talking. The two main lines of hose are quickly brought to the spot, and two streams of water are thrown against the lower part of the roof. Lines of buckets are also organised, and after a quarter of an hour's hard work the outbreak seems to be practically under control. Suddenly another part of the roof is set on fire by the incendiary bullets, and half the available water supply has to be turned upon it. Heavy firing is meantime going on in all directions, and adds to the confusion. Pearse and J. Plunkett hold a short conversation at the doorway. They both appear very excited. Finally a large number of men are selected for extinguishing work, and the remainder are ordered to the windows. Everyone seems to consider it his duty to give orders at the top of his voice. The noise is terrific. The fire is gaining ground like lightning.

The O'Rahilly comes into the room. He is as cool as ever, [one of the very few officers at this moment who really keeps his head[12]]. We are ordered to bring all bombs, spare rifles and loose ammunition down to the yard of the G.P.O. This done, we return to the windows again.

From our posts we can see right down along the telegraph room. It presents a most extraordinary spectacle. In one part the fire has eaten right through the roof, and slates and mortar are commencing to fall on the floor. The two hoses are brought to bear on this spot. They are held six feet above the ground (to enable a better head of water to be obtained) by lines of men. Here and there the water spurts out through small holes in the rubber, drenching the men completely. In one place a huge leak from a faulty connection runs down the uniform of an officer. In a few seconds he is wet to the skin, but stands as unconcernedly as though on parade. Further over a line of buckets extending down to the second floor is working with incredible rapidity. After a few minutes, however, we see that all is useless. The fire is gaining ground in all directions. Huge masses of the roof commence to fall inwards with terrific noise. The floor on which the men are working threatens to give way with each blow. Clouds of smoke from the burning debris writhe around the corridors and passages. It gets into our eyes and noses, and compels fits of coughing. The floors are covered to a depth of three inches with grimy water.

From the yard below comes a noise of shouting, pulling about of bales and packages, and the thunderous report of the Howth rifles. We are warned to be ready for an attack at any moment. A thick pall of smoke has come down over O'Connell Street again, and we are unable to see beyond the corners of the Imperial Hotel. Ten or twelve minutes pass anxiously. The noise below increases in intensity.

The fire has practically demolished the whole telegraphic room, and is threatening every moment to cut off our retreat. O'Rahilly again appears, comes over, and tells me to join Desmond FitzGerald down in the restaurant. The G.P.O. is about to be evacuated. With a cheerful wave of his hand, and a smile, he steps quickly down the smoke-filed stairs. Little did I know that this would be the last time I would ever see him alive. Suddenly we hear a great cheer from somewhere beneath, followed by the quick beat of doubling footsteps. A sudden fusillade seems to burst out on all sides. Two or three machine-guns cough threateningly. The first party has left the G.P.O.

* * *

The further history of the defence of the G.P.O. area is a tragic one. An attempt is made to reach Williams and Woods' Factory,[13] in order to use it as a base. It is soon discovered, however, that the military are massed in far too great a force along the Parnell Street district to render this plan possible. A body of select rifle men are, nevertheless, picked out, and with The O'Rahilly at their head a gallant charge is made at the barricades. On reaching the corner of the lane they come under the point-blank fire of a hidden machine gun. Practically every member of the little band is hit, The O'Rahilly and two others being wounded mortally.

Sniping continues all through the night. Though the men are scattered between the various buildings between Parnell Street and Henry Street, the military are still afraid to advance in force. All night long the fire gains ground. The G.P.O. is now nothing but an empty shell. The Coliseum [Theatre] and the Metropole are rapidly being reduced to ruins. Arnott's [shop] is already licked by the devouring flames. Overhead the quivering sky reflects the angry crimson of this furnace. It looks like a pall of blood. The ever-changing roaring sounds like the shrieks of a thousand demons. So our last night of freedom passes. Everyone seems to realise that our chances at length are hopeless. Without a central base, and completely isolated from our other strong-points and garrisons, how is it possible to hold out longer?

* * *

Saturday, April 29th.

Saturday morning finds desultory shooting still going on. Headquarters' staff holds a long consultation in the office of a small shop. A <u>conditional</u> surrender is decided upon. Negotiations and an armistice go on from one till four o'clock. Then comes the fateful surrender. We are convinced, however, than an <u>absolutely</u> unconditional surrender was not agreed to.

[Arms are given up near the Rotunda and the men examined. A section is made of the wounded and marched to the Castle at the point of the bayonet. The remainder lie on the grass inside the Rotunda railings. No covering or food whatsoever is given them throughout the night.[14]]

On Sunday morning we are paraded in the Castle Yard, while all around crowds of jeering soldiers threaten us with the most Hunnish atrocities. After being numbered off individually we are marched off to Kilmainham Gaol. Here the majority are confined in couples in separate cells, with the exception of a number of us who are placed in a separate building known as the Hospital. Between thirty and forty men are squashed into this room, which measures roughly eight yards by five. One blanket apiece is served out on Sunday evening. An old campaigner teaches us how to use our shoes, our boots, as pillows and it is amazing what a difference they make in enabling one to get to sleep. Later in the week we hear the ominous shootings at dawn. Tommy tells us that our leaders are being executed but most of us refuse to believe that the British could be so brutal. However one thing does strike us as rather ominous. Every day we all paraded for identification followed always by the removal of three or four of our members to an 'unknown destination'.

On Friday, May 5th, we are marched in pouring rain up to Richmond Barracks[15] where our finger-prints are taken. We are left standing in the open yard for about five hours and then examined. Towards five o'clock the strangest rumours are floating around. Some say that we are to be court-martialled, others that internment in England is our fate, while a pessimistic few are firmly convinced that the military are but waiting the cessation of the rain to shoot the 700 or so odd prisoners.

Finally at 6 p.m. we are again set on foot, and marched down along the pouring quays to the docks. By nine o'clock we are all on board a L.N.W.R.[16] cattle boat. It is a frightful night. A half gale is blowing, and the sea is running very high. Down in the cattle stalls we have no shelter whatsoever, and every big wave sends tons of water and spray into the decks. The rain has drenched us to the skin long before this, however, so it does not matter much. The boat rolls and pitches, and as the majority of men have never undertaken a sea voyage before, they do not relish the sensation. Someone suggests the Rosary, and a Volunteers recites the Mysteries in a voice that rings high above the shriek of the wind and the beat of the lashing waters. The responses come in a sonorous murmur from all points of the vessel. Afterwards 'A Soldier's Song' and 'God Save Ireland' are sung, and the men take heart and courage at the sound of the undaunted voices. The shivering soldiers look on obviously nonplussed at the demeanour of their prisoners.

Holyhead is reached at about 2 a.m., and we are entrained by special to Wakefield.

We reach Wakefield Station, in Yorkshire, at 7.30 a.m. on Saturday, May 6th. A large crowd throngs the streets outside, and watches us phlegmatically as we are lined up and counted. The order is given to march, and a few minutes later we reach a grim, embattled group of tall buildings. It is Wakefield Military Detention Prison. On entering we are searched for the third time since arrest – everything except our Rosary beads being taken.

We have come to the end of the road. England has triumphed once again, but the very fact that she has had to transport hundreds of Irishmen hundreds of miles from their native shore proves that this fight has shaken her as she has never been shaken before. Next time the whole country, and not Dublin alone will join the fray. Unity of purpose, and plan must be the National aim! This is surely the lesson that to be learnt from our tragic, but gloriously uplifting, Easter week Rising.

Notes

1. He was born on 19 April 1896. Biographical information from the files of the Dictionary of Irish Biography.
2. Desmond Ryan, *The Rising*, p. 124. F. X. Martin observed that 'there is no reliable evidence that O'Rahilly spoke these words' (Martin, '1916', p. 36).
3. National Library of Ireland, MS 18,829.
4. The six-storey building housing the Dublin Bread Company (a restaurant)

was situated between Lower Abbey Street and Eden Quay.

5. These were some of the 1,500 'elderly but serviceable Mauser rifles' landed at Howth by Erskine and Molly Childers' yacht *Asgard* in July 1914 (see Jim Ring, *Erskine Childers* (London: John Murray, 1996), pp. 140–8).

6. According to Charles Townshend, the 'most careful subsequent calculation' (by Diarmuid Lynch) of the size of the GPO garrison put it at 408 (Townshend, *Easter 1916*, p. 175).

7. Called Great Brunswick Street in 1916.

8. Reis's Chambers was on the corner of Lower Abbey Street and O'Connell Street. Hopkins and Hopkins, Jewellers, was on the corner of Eden Quay by O'Connell Bridge.

9. Kelly's gunpowder store was on the Bachelor's Walk corner opposite Hopkins and Hopkins.

10. Jacob's Biscuit Factory in Bride Street was another of the rebel strong-points.

11. The Presbyterian Church on Parnell Square.

12. The words in square brackets are crossed out in the typescript.

13. A jam factory in Parnell Street.

14. Passage crossed out in the typescript.

15. Richmond Barracks (now demolished) was west-south-west of Kilmainham Gaol, between Emmet Road and the Grand Canal.

16. London North Western Railway.

7 A Priest's Tale

This narrative is one of a series of accounts of the Rising which were published in the monthly *Catholic Bulletin* under the general title 'Events of Easter Week'. Edited by J. J. O'Kelly ('Sceilig'), who was returned as a Sinn Féin MP for County Louth in the 1918 general election, the *Bulletin* took a very pro-rebel line, and the articles about Easter Week were clearly intended to support and glorify the republican cause. They include some dramatic and compelling stories, including that of Father John Flanagan reproduced in this chapter. Based at the pro-Cathedral in Marlborough Street, Flanagan became 'unofficial chaplain to the garrison' in the GPO.[1] He was in the GPO for a time on Easter Monday evening, and then on Thursday and Friday, finishing up with a hair-raising journey escorting women and wounded volunteers from the GPO to Jervis Street Hospital.

Events of Easter Week: The General Post Office Area[2]

A Dublin priest has favoured us with the following interesting narrative: My first visit to the G.P.O. was paid on a Monday night at nine o'clock in a response to a request from Patrick Pearse. I went into an office at the back of the Central Hall and was there engaged hearing confessions until half past eleven. During the ensuing two days I attended several men shot in the streets. The military began to close in, on Tuesday evening, and machine gun and rifle fire made it unsafe to be about. On Wednesday morning at eight I said Mass at the pro-Cathedral to a congregation consisting of a few women and the server. The bombardment of Liberty Hall and of other Volunteer positions began as if I had given the signal at the beginning of Mass. I have never discovered what objective the artillery had beside Liberty Hall that morning, but the passage of the shells over the church was a rude accompaniment to the Holy Sacrifice. Marlboro' Street was swept from end to end by machine guns posted on the roof of the Theatre Royal,[3] and Abbey Street from the Custom House. Immediately after Mass, while on my way to attend two boys shot at 6 Lower Marlboro' Street, I had some difficulty in persuading a crowd of people that I would be safer alone, and that they would be safer at home. One poor man was so far from realising the seriousness of the situation that when I turned him back he objected and said he wanted to get to his work 'across the water' – somewhere in Grantham Street!

Subsequently I got down to Jervis Street and with several other priests had a busy day attending the wounded – both soldiers and civilians. Coming home by Parnell Street I noticed some soldiers home on leave, standing about hallways with their friends. Though in khaki, and well within the danger zone, they did not seem to fear being shot at by the Volunteers. On my return I found the church and sacristy pretty full of refugees from neighbouring houses, and as the night fell, the fire which had been smouldering in Lawrence's at the corner of the Cathedral and O'Connell Streets blazed out afresh. A steady west wind swept the sparks across the church roof. The Brigade, we were told, in a response to a call, would not be allowed out, and further fires might be expected before the week closed! We therefore spent the night preparing for the removal of books, registers, and sacred vessels, feeling that if the fire spread along Cathedral Street nothing would have saved the church. Luckily the wind died down towards daybreak.

On Thursday morning I said Mass at eight o'clock – again to the accompaniment of the guns – but, as we had closed the church, without any congregation. Two of my colleagues were on duty in Jervis Street Hospital, two away on holidays, and three of us remained in the Pro-Cathedral. About half past ten we were astonished to hear the hall-door bell ring. Responding, I admitted a young lady who had come from the G.P.O. with an urgent request for a priest to attend a dying Volunteer. It did not seem a very responsible request, considering that the way from the Post Office to Jervis Street Hospital was comparatively safe, and that we had stationed two of our priests there specifically to meet such a contingency. However, I accompanied the messenger back to the G.P.O. by a very circuitous route – *via*

Thomas's Lane, Marlboro' Street, Parnell Street, and Moore Street. We experienced more than one thrill in Marlboro' Street, and while crossing by the Parnell Statue. In Moore Street an old friend was shot down just beside me, and I anointed him where he lay. Some brave boys, procuring a handcart, bore him to Jervis Street Hospital where, after a couple of days, he died. Proceeding on our errand, my guide and I ran across Henry Street, into Randall's hall-way, upstairs, and, through gaps in the walls of intervening houses the G.P.O.

On my arrival at the Volunteers' Headquarters, I looked among the wounded for the patient to whom I had been called, and received a hearty welcome from as gay and debonair an army as ever took up arms. They evidently had felt their organisation incomplete without a Chaplain! and I immediately entered on the duties of my new position, which kept me pretty busy all day. My services were also in request for the soldier prisoners, one of whom was mentally affected by the unexpected events of the week. We had our first serious casualty about one o'clock, when James Connolly was brought in with a nasty bullet or shrapnel wound in the leg. He endured what must have been agony in grim fortitude. Soon I had another to anoint; and, though we had many minor wounds to attend to, these were the only two serious cases. As night fell, the fires along the other side of O'Connell Street – from Eden Quay to Earl Street- were a sublime and appalling spectacle. Truly might it be said that Dublin 'showed another sight, when the drums beat at the dead of night, commanding fires of death to light the darkness of her scenery.'

Friday dawned to the increasing rattle of rifle and machine gun. Early in the day I succeeded in getting through the *Freeman* office[4] into a house in Middle Abbey Street where I prepared for death a poor bedridden man whose house soon became his funeral pyre. In the afternoon – about four o'clock – the first incendiary shell landed on the roof of the parapet of the G.P.O. A large hose was at once turned on, but the effect seemed to be rather to spread the flames. All hands were then summoned to the front hall and I asked what could be done for the wounded of whom we had by that time fifteen or sixteen. Earlier in the day a good number of the ladies who had volunteered to help the wounded and see after the commissariat had been sent away under a white flag and reached their homes in safety. Some, however, remained. We were told we should be quite safe at the back of the building, which was newly built of ferro concrete, or in the crypt. But it soon became clear that we should have to find safety in flight. While the wounded were being prepared for the perilous journey now before them, I stood for a moment discussing the situation with the O'Rahilly. When the word of command came for the charge into Henry Street, he turned to me, and, kneeling down, asked me for a Last Absolution and my blessing. 'Father.' said he, 'we shall never meet again in this world.' Then he calmly and courage-ously took his place at the head of his men. The stretcher cases were then taken in blankets through the walls of intervening houses, across a roof, up a ladder, and into the bar of the Coliseum Theatre.[5] I am glad to be able to testify here that though that last element of the Volunteer Army which would correspond to the 'Rough Riders' had been in possession of the Coliseum Theatre for nearly a week – a trying and nerve-wracking week – not a single bottle of liquor had been disturbed or taken when we arrived on Friday night. There on the fine deep carpet our wounded were laid about 7 p.m. Meanwhile the Volunteers had rushed from the central hall into Henry Place – whence they fought their way into houses in Main Street. The military had set up two barricades – one at the end of Moore Lane and the other at the end of Moore Street – both in Parnell Street. They had, besides, an armoured car from which they poured machine gunfire up Sackville Lane and Moore Street. Passing these streets in the front rooms of the Henry Street houses we had to creep on hands and knees beneath the windows to escape the bullets. That no one of our Red Cross party was hit and that the wounded were got safely into the theatre was really remarkable.

Our first idea was to hang a Red Cross flag out of the roof of the theatre; but the storm of bullets and shrapnel that rained round the doomed building made it impossible to venture on the roof. The G.P.O. was already ablaze and it seemed quite certain that the theatre would soon catch fire too. We searched round for an exit – but all the doors were securely padlocked save one – the last we tried – which gave access to a passage. We pulled the bolts of this door with a sigh of relief and got, by the passage, to the collapsible gate leading into Prince's Street. Having again secured a pickaxe previously left in the post office yard, we broke the lock of the collapsible gate and, still carrying our flag made for the narrow passage leading from the end of Prince's Street into Middle Abbey Street. The entrance hereto was, however, blocked by a barricade of paper on fire, so we found that there was nothing left us but to select the lowest spot and jump across it. One of our stretcher cases, the boy I anointed the previous day, was unconscious all this time. At the other end of the passage we encountered a further barricade before emerging into the battle zone of Middle Abbey Street, just then the scene of a warm exchange of rifle fire between the Volunteers in the houses and a military barricade down at the Dispensary entrance to Jervis Street Hospital.

In the fierce glare of the burning houses in O'Connell Street our Red Cross flag was plainly distinguishable and the firing on both sides ceased as our little procession made its way to the corner of Liffey Street. There we were halted by a command from the officer in charge of the barricade, who evidently feared a stratagem. After five or six interminable minutes, he shouted down the street that the bearer of the flag and one other might advance for a parlay. I at once went forward, accompanied by a British officer in khaki, who had been taken prisoner and had humanely given his services to our wounded. Twenty paces or so from the barricade we were halted again and covered by the rifles of the men behind it, we were examined by the officer. He refused point blank to let us pass the barricade; but I explained that our objective was the hospital, which we could enter by the side door without crossing his men or upsetting his sandbags. After a long conversation with a monocled Major, he fetched two of the students from the front of the hospital in Jervis Street. Their recognition of me quite satisfied him, and, after asking who and how many I had in the party, he allowed me to call the rest up from Liffey St. It was within an hour of midnight when the good Nuns and Nurses in the hospital received us all—weary and well-nigh exhausted.

Next day, Saturday, the male members of our Red Cross party were marched off to the Castle, the ladies being permitted to return home. The wounded all recovered, and neither they nor anyone concerned are likely to forget the experiences of that terrible night.

Notes

1. Caulfield, *The Easter Rebellion*, p. 182.
2. From the *Catholic Bulletin*, vol. 8 no. 8 (Aug. 1918), pp. 405–8.
3. In Hawkins Street, which runs from Burgh Quay to D'Olier Street.
4. The offices of the *Freeman's Journal* were in Middle Abbey Street.
5. In Henry Street. It was later destroyed by fire.

8 An Onlooker's Tale

The Belfast-born St John Greer Ervine was a critic, playwright and novelist who in 1916 was manager of the Abbey Theatre in Dublin. On Easter Monday morning he was in the theatre, in Middle Abbey Street, just round the corner from the GPO. Although he does not specifically mention it, Ervine resided in the United Arts Club, which had premises in Stephen's Green. On one of the early days of the Rising, Maurice Headlam, an English civil servant posted to Dublin, found that Ervine 'had been marooned in the Club since the outbreak of the rebellion'.[1] But the location gave Ervine a grandstand view of the happenings in the Green which he made good use of in his narrative. Ervine also wove his experiences during the Rising into a semi-autobiographical novel, *Changing Winds*, which was published in 1917, and some of the descriptive passages in the book clearly draw on the account reproduced below. The central character in the novel, Henry Quinn, is a Protestant from the north of Ireland who, reflecting Ervine's own experience, achieves literary success in London, where he mixes in progressive political circles, and comes to Dublin before the Rising. Like Ervine, too (it seems), the experience of the Rising impels Quinn to enlist in the British army. Ervine joined up in 1917 and lost a leg on the Western Front before returning to London where he was theatre critic of the *Observer* for twenty years.

In later life Ervine gained a deserved reputation for unswerving and ostentatious allegiance to the Ulster Unionist cause.[2] But he was not always thus, as the tone of this account testifies. Ervine describes himself as being an 'Irish Home Ruler', and, seeking 'to apportion blame for the rebellion', he concludes that it was so widely distributed 'that in the end one could only say, "We are all to blame; we Irish people, old and young, are all at fault."'

This vivid piece of reportage was first published in an American journal, and the American spelling of words such as 'theater', 'laborers' and 'defenseless', has been retained.

The Story of the Irish Rebellion, by St John G. Ervine[3]

On Easter Sunday, after an absence of several weeks, I returned to Dublin from England, and in the evening I walked down to the Abbey Theater to obtain my letters. There was an air of festival in the town, for the rigors of Lent were at an end, and the people were making ready for such merriment as is possible in time of war to those whose men are in very present danger in Flanders and France; and as I crossed O'Connell Bridge and stood for a moment or two to look at the high reaches of the golden sky which are everywhere visible in Dublin it seemed to me that the 'peace...which passeth all understanding' had settled on this old, distracted city. There had, indeed, been murmurs and mutterings and marches of drilled men, and now and then one met an anxious official, full of foreboding, who spoke desperately of danger; but these were disregarded. One had stood on the pavement to watch the volunteers go by, and had treated them lightly. How could that tattered collection of youths and boys and hungry-looking laborers ever hope to stand against the British army!

One saw them, on St. Patrick's day, marching up Westmoreland Street to College Green, some of them dressed in a green uniform that, except in colour, was a replica of the khaki uniform of the British soldier. Most of them had no uniform, and their cheap, ready-made clothes had an extraordinarily unwarlike look that was made almost ridiculous by the bandoleers and the long, obsolete bayonets and the heavy, out-of-date rifles they carried. The mind, remembering tales of France and Flanders and the Dardanelles, of guns that fired shells a ton in weight for many miles, of an extraordinary complicity of invention whereby men may be slain by men who have never seen them – the mind, remembering these things, found something supremely comical in the spectacle of young clerks and middle-aged laborers steeling their hearts and fitting their bodies with the worn-out implements of war in the hope that they might so disturb the British race that all they desired would instantly be conceded to them.

It is easy now to pitch blame on Mr. Birrell and to say that he should have known this and that he should have known the other; but I doubt whether many men, seeing the procession of volunteers on St. Patrick's day, would have felt any alarm. At most, one imagined, there would be a brawl in the streets, quickly and easily suppressed by a small force of police.

Such was my mood on Easter Sunday when, coming away from the Abbey Theater, I encountered, on Eden Quay, a company of volunteers marching toward Liberty Hall. They had been, I think, in the mountains all day, drilling and marching, and now, tired and hungry, were nearly at the end of the day's work, in a moment or two to be disbanded for the night. They were just such a company of men and boys as I had been accustomed for months past to see parading about the streets: middle-aged, spare-looking laborers in whom the brutalities of the 1911 strike had left deep bitterness,[4] young clerks and shop assistants and school teachers, full of generous ideals and emotions that were unchecked by the discipline of wide knowledge and experience; and boys, vaguely idealistic and largely thrilled by the desire for romantic enterprise, and the hope of high happenings. And with them, as intent and eager as the men, were a few women and little girls.

I stood on the pavement to watch them go by. The captain of the company was a man, I had known slightly, a modest, quiet, kindly man of honest desires, called Sean Connolly, unrelated, save in the comradeship of arms, to James Connolly. I nodded to him, and he waved his hand to me. The next day he was dead, killed in the street fighting for some ideal that dominated and bound his mind.[5] I remember, too, seeing the Countess Marckevitz [sic] in the ranks that Sean Connolly commanded. I had met her twice very casually and did not recognise her in the half-light of the evening, but someone standing by said, 'That's the countess,' and I looked, and I saw a tired woman that would never admit that she was tired, stumping heavily by in a green uniform, oblivious of the comments, many of them mockery, that the onlookers were making.

It is not my business here to explain the rebellion or to describe the causes of it. An adequate explanation would fill too much space, and the causes of it were varied. Some of the volunteers were men belonging to the citizen army which had been formed in 1911 by James Larkin and James Connolly and Captain White, the son of Sir George White, the defender of Ladysmith, during what was probably the most brutally conducted strike (on the part of the employers) in the history of industrial disorder.[6] I have no knowledge of what was in these men's minds, but I do not doubt that the rebellion meant to them less of an opportunity to establish an Irish Republic than an opportunity to avenge their outraged humanity. Others were men who remembered, no doubt, that the gun-running practised by their side was treated with a severity that ended in death, whereas the gun-running practised by the followers of Sir Edward Carson was treated as an admirable exploit.[7] Others, again, and these were the majority, were men who loved Ireland and sought to set her free, If one were to set out to apportion blame for the rebellion, one would find that it must be distributed over so many people that in the end one could only say, 'We are all to blame; we Irish people, old and young, are all at fault.'

But while one does not set out to explore the causes of the rebellion, one may briefly say that the origin of the volunteers lay in the necessity which some Irishmen felt for an effective defence against the volunteers who had been created in Ulster by Sir Edward Carson. The extent of that necessity was made plain when what is called the Curragh Camp incident happened. On that occasion a number of officers refused to obey an order (so it is said) to proceed to Belfast and keep the Unionist volunteers in control. I do not believe that any reputable Irishmen wished to see the Ulster volunteers terrorized or put to death by British soldiers; but the incident set a number of Nationalists wondering what sort of defense they would have if the Ulster volunteers made an attack on them. The temper of the soldiers at the Curragh indicated that they could hope for little from that quarter, and there was no other defense, apart from the police. So they set up volunteers of their own, under the leadership of John [*sic*] McNeill, a professor at the National University. The purpose of these volunteers was, first, to defend themselves against attack, and, secondly, to make a display of force if Home Rule was not conceded to Ireland. After the outbreak of the war this purposes was extended to prevent the imposition of conscription on the Irish people.

The reader, remembering these purposes of the volunteers, may now wonder why the rebellion took place, seeing that an attack was not made by the Ulster volunteers, that Home Rule in law had been conceded to Ireland, and that the Irish people were expressly excluded from the scope of the Military Service Act. The answer to such speculation is that the great majority of the

Irish volunteers firmly believed that the Home Rule Act would be annulled after the war. They were convinced that the Liberal government would quit office in the conclusion of peace, and be succeeded by a Conservative government, which would make as little of the Home Rule Act as the Germans of the treaty guaranteeing the neutrality of Belgium; and they were confirmed in this belief in the tone of an obstinate English newspaper. A further factor was the treatment of the Irish regiments in Gallipoli, where although they bore the brunt of the fighting, they were disregarded by the commanders in a thoroughly incomprehensible manner. One of strange features of the Gallipoli campaign is the fact that Admiral de Robeck forgot to mention the names of the Irish regiments which took heroic part in the landing on the peninsula, although he remembered to mention the names of all the other regiments concerned in it![8]

The causes, then, which led up to the rebellion were many and varied, but the dominant cause was this suspicion that once again the English Government was about to betray the Irish people. I belong to a school of Irish Home-Rulers who believe that the destines of Ireland and England in the world are as inseparable as the waters of the Liffey and the Mersey in the Irish Sea, and I do not believe that these suspicions of English perfidy were justified; but I can readily understand why men of an impatient temperament, in whose hands the wrongs of their country had made an indelible impression, were quick to suspect treachery where they should only have seen the petulance of irresponsible and impotent politicians and journalists.

When the history of the Irish rebellion is written I suppose people will notice particularly how completely it surprised everyone, even the officials who had fears of it happening. I do not imagine that any of the company of volunteers whom I saw on Easter Sunday evening had the slightest idea that there was to be rebellion the following morning. I know that the Countess Marckevitz was not aware of the proposed outbreak until it actually began, and I know of one volunteer who did not know what was about to take place until he heard the sound of rifle-fire. It is obvious that the strictest secrecy as to intention had to be preserved, otherwise the plan would have been betrayed. A secret that is committed to several thousand persons ceases to be a secret. The Irish secret service knew that a rising had been planned, but they did not suspect that it would take place so soon. Indeed, at that moment when the very rebellion began a council was actually being held in Dublin Castle to determine what steps should be taken to cope with the insurrection when it took place. The secret service, I understand, expected the attempt to be made on Whit Monday. The result was a state of un-preparedness that is almost incredible. General Friend, who was in charge of the troops in Ireland, had left the country on Easter Saturday, and was in England when he heard news of the outbreak. The lord lieutenant had arranged to pay a visit to Belfast on official affairs, and was making ready to start when the news came to the viceregal lodge that the Sinn Féiners had revolted. There was a race-meeting at Fairy House, and many of the officers and soldiers were there. Very few troops were stationed in Dublin, and many men were on leave. It is said in Dublin that if the rebels had known, they could have taken Trinity College and the headquarters of the Irish command with ease, there were so few persons of the premises to defend them. Easter Monday is a bank-holiday, therefore the shops and business offices were closed.

That was the state of Dublin when suddenly a small body of armed men came out of Liberty Hall and marched along Abbey Street into O'Connell Street and thence to the general post-office. Simultaneously other men marched into strategic points such as Westland Row railway station and the road leading to Kingstown, along which troops from England would be obliged to pass. Another company of men set off to take Dublin Castle, where some harassed officials, as I have stated, were wondering what they should do to cope with the rebellion that they believed to be likely to take place on Whit Monday. The Countess Marckevitz led a company of men and boys and women and girls to Stephen's Green and the College of Surgeons. Considerable knowledge of strategy was displayed by the rebels, together with some strategic ineptitude. It was, for example, extremely foolish to seize St. Stephen's Green Park, which was exposed on every side to attack, and had to be abandoned on Easter Tuesday, when the soldiers arrived and began operations.

All the men were disposed at the points of vantage, and about 11 o'clock on the morning of Easter Monday the rebellion began. The post-office was seized, St. Stephen's Green Park was occupied, the College of Surgeons was entered, and private houses on roads of consequence was taken. The attempt to seize Dublin Castle failed after the policeman on guard outside it was murdered; and the rebels then took the offices of the Dublin 'Daily Express,' which are near the castle, and ejected the reporters and staff from it.

There was to be a matinee at Abbey Theater on Easter Monday. We were to produce Mr. W. B. Yeats's little vision of Ireland, 'Kathleen ni Houlihan,' together with a new play by a new author, 'The Spancel of Death' by Mr. T. H. Nally. There is something odd in that conjunction of plays, something almost anticipatory of what was about to happen; for *Kathleen ni Houlihan*, the poor old woman, is the figure of Irish dispossessed and calling to her children to regain her inheritance for her.

'What is it that you want?' the young man says to *Kathleen*, the daughter of *Houlihan*, when she comes to his home on the evening of his marriage.

'My four beautiful fields,' she answers, 'and the hope of driving the stranger out of my house.'

I had gone down to the theatre from my home in St. Stephen's Green about nine o'clock that morning so that I might deal with my correspondence before the matinee began, and while I was working in my office a stage-hand came to me and said that he thought we would not be able to hold a performance. I said 'Why?' He replied:

'I think there's a rebellion or something on. The Sinn Féiners are out.' I laughed.

'Listen!' he said, and I listened. I could hear distinctly the dull sound of rifle-firing,

'Oh, that's only some skylarking,' I answered. But it wasn't skylarking.

A man came into the theatre while I was wondering about the thing. He was pale and agitated.

'I've just seen a man killed' he said brokenly.

'Is it true?' I interrupted.

He nodded his head.

'I was outside the castle,' he went on. 'The policeman went up to stop them, and one of them put a rifle up and blew his brains out. The unfortunate man!'

'But – but what's it all for?' I asked feebly. 'What's it all about?'

'God knows,' he answered.

I went to the front of the theater and looked into the street. I could see little knots of men and women and children at the corners of the streets that run at right angles to O'Connell Street, and every now and then some one, suddenly alarmed, would run away. There was a heavy feel in the air, that curious physical sensation of waiting for something to occur which precedes all dreadful events, and, disturbing it ominously, the flat rattle of distant rifle.

There were no policemen anywhere. Mysteriously and swiftly, the whole of the Dublin Metropolitan Police had vanished from their beats.

'Well, this is damned funny,' I said.

There is a wide lane at the side of the Abbey Theater which runs parallel to the Liffey and ends at the side of Liberty Hall. While I was standing outside the theater, wondering whether I ought to abandon the performance or not, I heard shouting and the rumbling of heavy carts, and looking up the lane, I saw a precession of wagons approaching me. Each wagon was piled high with cauliflower, and was guarded by armed youths. I began to laugh again. There was something irresistibly comical about those wagon-loads of cauliflower, the commissariat of the rebels. We had not yet realized that serious things were about to happen, so we made jokes! There were funny jokes about interminable meals of cauliflower – breakfast, dinners, teas, and suppers of cauliflower. I remember how sick the soldiers of France and Flanders became of plum and apple jam, and wondered how long it would be before the rebels become bored of cauliflower.

People turned up at the door of the theatre, unaware of anything that had happened. Some of the players, unable to catch a tram, came to the stage-door bewildered.

'What's up?' they said, and I answered jocularly:

'Oh, don't you know? There's a rebellion on, and we're all republicans now!'

In every tragical happening there is an element of the ridiculous, and it is the business of the artist to strip the ridiculous from the tragical, and leave only the essential tragedy. The realist, such a realist as Mr. Bernard Shaw, insists on showing everything, the ridiculous and the tragical; and so it is that one is puzzled by disturbing laughter in so beautiful a play as 'Androcles and the Lion.' There was much that was ridiculous in the Dublin rebellion, and all who lived through it can tell many funny stories. I think now of the woman who telephoned to me at the theatre to enquire about a friend.

'What's up?' she asked when I had told her that her friend had left the theatre to go home, and when I told her that a rebellion was 'up,' she exclaimed: 'Oh dear! What a day to choose it! Easter Monday! The people won't enjoy themselves a bit!'

I told the attendants to shut the theatre, and went into O'Connell Street. Crowds of people were wandering up and down or standing about in an expectant manner. All around me I could hear men and women asking the question which was general that day in Dublin, 'What's it for?'

I looked across the street, and saw that the windows of the post-office had been broken. Furniture and sacking were pilled up behind every window, and stretched on top of these were boys with rifles, lying there, waiting. Some of the rebels were distributing bills, in which the heads of the provisional government announced the establishment of an Irish republic. Some one began to deliver an oration at the base of the Nelson pillar, but the crowd had no taste for oratory, and it did not listen long. There were two flags on top of the post-office, a green one, bearing the words 'Irish Republic,' and a tricolour of orange, white and green; and that was all. One saw volunteer officers, carrying loaded revolvers, passing about their duties, instructing pale boys who were acting as sentinels; and when one saw how young they were, there came again into the mind that sense of the ridiculousness of it all, and one thought, 'This is all very well, this playing with rebellion and establishing a republic; but wait – just wait until the police catch you at it!' One thought of them as boys who had let their lark run away with their wits. All this joking had gone too far, and presently there would be trouble, and some sorry people would be mumbling excuses to a magistrate. It was as if boys, letting their imaginations feed too fat on penny dreadfuls, had forgotten that they were only pretending to be wild Indians attacking Buffalo Bill, and had suddenly scalped a companion or halved his skull with a tomahawk.

'It'll be over when dinner time comes,' some one said to me. We were all extraordinarily lacking in prescience. We still thought of this thing as a kids' rebellion, a school-boys' escapade. 'Silly young asses!' people were saying, 'they'll only get into trouble.'

I got tired of hanging about O'Connell Street, and so I went home. At the top of Grafton Street I crossed over to the park, and saw the gates were closed, and barricaded rather ineffectively. A man was standing inside the gates, holding a rifle and looking intently down Grafton Street. Some girls were chaffing him, and asking him if he was not scared to death, and what would his mother say if she could see him, and was he not afraid that she would give him a beating. But he paid no heed to their chaff, though now and then, when someone obscured his vision of the street, he gruffly ordered them away and, if they did not move speedily, threatened to shoot them, 'G' long with you!' they would say, still chaffing, but a little uncertain. After all, he might shoot.

I walked along the side of the green toward the Shelbourne Hotel. Inside the railings I could see the boys digging trenches and throwing up heaps of earth for shelters. Other boys were stretched on the turf, with their fingers on the triggers of their rifles, and they, too, like the boys at the post-office, were waiting. I heard a man say to one lad who was digging into the soft earth.

'What in the name of God are you doin' there?' and the lad replied:

'I don't know, I'm supposed to be diggin' a trench, but I think I'm diggin' my grave.'

It is said, and I believe it to be true, that none of these lads knew what was to happen that day. Some of them had come up from the country to take part, they imagined, in an ordinary demonstration, a route march. It is said that some of them who were deputed to capture Westland Row station – their task was not told to them until they had reached the station – that when they heard what was to be done, they sent for a priest, made their confessions to him, and received the host. They told the priest that they were ignorant until that moment about what was about to take place, and he advised them to drop their rifles and uniforms and when dusk came to go to their houses.

'Oh no,' they answered; 'we joined this thing, and we ought to go on with it.' There was much of that kind of young chivalry in Dublin that week. I doubt whether many of the volunteers funked when the moment came, although they must have felt like they had been led into something like a trap.

At the Shelbourne Hotel there was a barricade across the street, composed of motorcars and vans taken from their owners by the volunteers. Inside the green there was much hurrying to and fro. At each gate there was a small group of armed sentries, who challenged every vehicle that passed. If the vehicle was found to be above suspicion, it was allowed to pass on. If the driver of it failed to halt when challenged several times, he was fired on.

I went into the house where I was living. It overlooks the green, and from my bedroom window I had as clear a view as was possible to anyone. I saw women walking about inside the green, and I saw three little girls who could not have been more than fifteen years of age running busily about. They were members of the Countess Marckevitz's corps of Girl Guides and they were acting as messengers. On the opposite side of the green I could the tricolour of the republic floating over the College of Surgeons.

A man came to see me.

'Will there be a performance at the Abbey tonight?' he said, and I answered: 'I don't know. You'd better turn up anyhow. Perhaps it will be all over by eight o'clock.' I was told later that the D'Oyly Carte Opera Company, who were to begin a fortnight's engagement at the Gaiety Theater that day, did not abandon their intention until a few minutes before the hour at which the performance was due to begin.

After tea I walked round the park. On one side of the green, near the Unitarian Church, there was a pool of congealed blood. I almost sickened at the sight of it. On this spot a second policeman had been murdered. I use the word 'murdered' intentionally. It is, I think, true to say that the rebellion was conducted by its leaders as cleanly as it is possible to conduct any rebellion, and many high and chivalrous things were done by them and their followers. They strove to fight, as closely as they could, in accordance to the laws of civilized warfare. But the killing of these policemen at the castle and the Unitarian church were acts of murder, for these civil servants were unarmed, defenseless, while their opponents carried loaded rifles. I believe indeed, that much of what we call atrocity in warfare, civil or international, is largely the result of fright and nervous strain, the panic attack of men who are 'rattled'; and it is very probable that the murder of the policemen was due to an attack of nerves. But whatever the cause of it may have been, it stained a singularly clean record. The behaviour of the rebels to their prisoners was exemplary. An old colonel who was in their hands for the better part of a week subsequently stated that he had been treated with exceptional kindness, and a subaltern who was interned in the post-office asserted that his captors were very considerate to him.

It was while I was looking at the pool of congealed blood that I saw Francis Sheehy Skeffington. I had known him fairly well for some time. He was a man of immense energy and vitality. Once he walked into Dublin from Wicklow and back, covering fifty miles in one day. His honesty was superlative, and his courage was leonine. I think of him as a man overruled by intellect. He was governed by logic, and he seemed incapable of understanding that life is a wayward thing, that men are moody, that humanity cannot be set out in terms of an equation; and this submission of his intellect robbed him of any capacity to act practically in affairs. Had he been a witty man, he would have resembled Bernard Shaw. But he was not a witty man; he was almost totally devoid of any sense of humour. I think, too, he was completely devoid of any feeling for tradition, any sense of reverence. Once when I was living in a Welsh village I met him. I went one day with him to see a cromlech outside the village, and when we reached it, he looked at it for a few moments, and then, to my disgust, took a bill out of his pocket and stuck it in a crack in the stones. 'I may as well do a little propaganda,' he said. The bill had 'Votes for Women' on it. But when all the small irritations one had in his presence were accounted for, there remained this, that he was a man of great integrity and courage, and men of integrity and courage are so rare in the world that it is a calamity to have lost this man in the miserable way in which he was lost.

He came up to me, and we talked about the rebellion. I was full of anger, because I saw in it the wreck of the slowly maturing plans of the better ordering of Irish life; but his emotion was different.

'I'm against all this fighting,' he said. 'More and more I am inclined toward the Tolstoian position.' He spoke of the rebellion as, 'folly, but it's noble folly,' and declared that it was a hopeless enterprise. He went off, walking in that habitual quick, nervous way of his, which seemed to indicate that he could never walk with sufficient swiftness. I went home, and sat in the window, looking out on the park and the passing people. The dusk gathered about the trees in the green, and a film of blue mist enveloped us. Behind the College of Surgeons, which faced my side of the green, the setting sun sent shafts of golden light shimmering up the heavens. There was hardly any wind, and the tricolour on the college fluttered listlessly. The evening became quiet. The crowds which had moved about the city in a holiday mood, treating the rebellion as jolly entertainment provided by benevolent persons for their amusement, had dispersed to their homes, carrying with them not the mood of merriment, but the mood of alarm, and of anxious anticipation.

One could hardy have felt otherwise then. All day the rebels had been in possession of the city. The Government seemed to have thrown up the sponge. There was not a policeman to be seen, or a soldier or any person in authority. At ten o'clock that morning there had been a Government and policemen and soldiers; at eleven o'clock all these had disappeared. There was looting in O'Connell Street, some of it extraordinarily ludicrous. There was one looter who had stolen a dress-suit from a shop near O'Connell Bridge. He went into an abandoned tram-car stripped his rags off, and then put on the dress-suit. When he reappeared, swaggering up and down the street, he was wearing brown boots, a dress suit, a Panama hat, and he was carrying a lady's sunshade. The rebels tried to prevent looting. I saw them making the attempts, but their attempts were ineffectual, and all that day (Monday) and all Tuesday the looting went on ridiculously.

Although the Government had mysteriously vanished, and there were no policemen to arrest the looters, one did not feel that victory was with the rebels, nor did they themselves think that victory was with them. That anxious, waiting look had marked the rebels' faces all day, and now something of dread came to the larking crowd; and as the night fell, the jokes ceased, the laughter died out, and silence came. At seven o'clock the streets were nearly empty. I looked out of my window and saw shadow-shapes moving swiftly homeward, huddling close to the houses. The rebel sentries still guarded the gate of the green which faced toward Merrion Street, and through the gloaming I could detect the figures of boys and women hurrying about their business in the camp. A cab came down the east side of the green, and the sentries challenged the driver; but he would not stop, thought they called 'Halt!' a dozen times. Then they fired on him. The horse went down instantly, and the driver, abandoning it, leaped from the box of his cab and flew down Merrion Street. The poor beast, sprawled on its haunches, tried to struggle to its feet, but fell back as often as it rose. While it lay there, struggling and kicking, a motor-car came down the side of the green, and the driver of it, too, was challenged, and he, also, refused to halt, and again the sentries fired. I was leaning out of the window to see what happened, and I laughed, for the man who was in the car yelled out the moment he was hit:

'Oh, I'm dead! I'm dead!'

The car stopped suddenly, grating harshly on the roadway, so that one's blood curdled for a few seconds. Then the wounded man was taken out. The sentries gathered round him. 'Why didn't you stop when you were told?' they said reproachfully, and added, 'Take him to Vincents',' the hospital a little way up the street. While they were supporting toward the hospital, the man went on moaning: 'Oh, I'm dead! I'm dead!' It was the worst imitation of death I had ever witnessed. They did not take him to Vincents'. They changed their minds, and took him into the green and treated him there. His wound was obviously slight; he could not have yelled so lustily or walked so well as he did if it had been serious. There was no dignity in him, only foolish bravado that speedily turned to squealing; and so one laughed at him.

After that there was a queer silence in the green. In the distance one heard the occasional rifle-firing, but here there was this ominous quietness. It became difficult to see, and so I closed the shutters; but before I did so, I looked toward the wounded horse. It was lying in the middle of the street not making any movement. 'Thank God, it's dead!' I said to myself, and then drew the shutters to.

There was a dreadful feeling of strain in the house, and I moved about restlessly. I got out the manuscript of a play on which I am working and began to revise it, but I could not continue it long. I tried to read a book by H. G. Wells, called 'An Englishman Looks at the World.' I had opened it at the chapter entitled 'The Common Sense of Warfare,' but I found that the war outside proved conclusively that there is no common sense in warfare, so I put the book down and tried to play a game of patience. I played three games and then I went to bed.

I slept in small dozes that were more exhausting than if I had not slept at all. The desultory rifle-fire had increased during the night, and it seemed to me that shooting was proceeding from the Shelbourne Hotel. At four o'clock I got up and looked out of the window. I was sleeping in the front of the house, and I had left the shutters of my bedroom open. It was not quite light enough for me, who have poor sight, to distinguish things clearly, but I could see a huddled heap lying in front of the gate where the sentries had been a few hours before. And the horse was not dead. While I looked, it made a feeble struggle to rise, and then fell back again. 'Why don't they kill it?' I said to myself, and I went back to bed. But I did not sleep. There were people moving about in the next room, fidgeting and fidgeting. I got up and began to dress, and while I was doing so I heard the sound of heavy boots on the pavement below, echoing oddly in that silence; and then I heard shots, followed by a low moan.

One's mind works in a queer way in moments of unusual happenings. I knew that someone had been shot in the street outside my home, and if I had been asked before the thing happened what I was likely to do, I think I should have never guessed correctly. I stood there counting the dying man's moans. He said, 'Oh!' four times, and then he died. I went to the window and looked out. It was now about six o'clock, and I could see plainly. The huddled heap outside the gates of the green was the body of a dead Sinn Féiner. The horse in the roadway was now quite still. Just off the pavement, in front of the door of my home, lay the body of an old man, a labourer, evidently, who had been stumping to his work. I suppose he had not realized the rebellion was a serious one, and had started off on the usual routine of his life; and then Death had caught him suddenly and stretched him in the road in a strangely easy attitude.

I came down-stairs, and the maids gave me breakfast, apologizing because there was no milk. It seemed to them that one could not drink tea without milk. These minds of ours are amazing instruments. Outside the door lay the body of an old man, a little farther off, wearing a fawn-colored overcoat, lay the body of a dead Sinn Féiner; at the corner of the street a horse had died in pain; and we were wondering about milk. Had the milkman funked?

*

I think it was between eight and nine o'clock that the ambulance came and took away the two dead men. The horse was dragged, I do not know how, to the pavement, and it lay there, offensive to the eye and nostril, for a week. People came to one and said, 'Have you seen the dead horse?' In whatever way conversation began, always it seemed to end with that question, 'Have you seen the dead horse?'

I remember now standing with a friend on the stairs, so that my eyes were on a level with the fanlight over the hall-door, and looking into the bushes just inside the green railings. I could see a young Sinn Féiner, rifle in hand, crawling on the ground; and then the soldiers at the Shelbourne saw him and let a volley at him, and he rose and ran, and we saw him no more.

Later on people came out of their houses and began to walk about. No one was allowed to cross the road to look into the green, and it was impossible to say whether any Sinn Féiners remained in it. The foliage obscured the view. There were rumours that many of the Sinn Féiners had been killed in the night, and that those who had remained had fled from the green and taken refuge with their comrades in the College of Surgeons; but there was no confirmation of these rumours, and it is doubtful whether they were true.

Toward ten o'clock the street filled. A few soldiers had been smuggled by back ways into the Shelbourne Hotel, and these commanded St. Stephen's Green. Other soldiers, few in number, were stationed in various parts of the city; but to all intents and purposes Dublin was as completely in the hands of the rebels on Easter Tuesday as it was on Easter Monday.

I went down to O'Connell Street and found that during the night the Sinn Féiners had been busy. Each of the streets running at right angles to O'Connell Street was barricaded, in most instances ineffectively. Barbed wire was stretched across O'Connell Street in such a way as to form a barrier on each side of the general post-office. And on Tuesday, as on Monday, one saw the pale, 'rattled,' and very tired looking young rebels preparing for attack. On the other side of the barbed wire, beyond the Nelson pillar, were some dead horses that had been killed while being ridden by soldiers. One heard rumours of desperate fighting in other parts of Dublin. Some of the veterans' corps, who had been drilling in the mountains on Monday, had been shot dead by Sinn Féiners when they returned home in the evening. The lord lieutenant, the rumour ran, had been taken prisoner, and was now immured in Liberty Hall. The wildest talk was being uttered. It was said that the pope had committed suicide on hearing of the rebellion. It was said that Archbishop Walsh, the Catholic Archbishop of Dublin, had killed himself. It was said that the Orangemen were marching on Dublin in support of the Sinn Féiners.

It was on Easter Tuesday that the worst looting took place. Men and women and children surged up from the foulest slums in Europe and rifled the shops, stripping them almost bare. Some harsh things have been said about the looting, perhaps no harsher than ought to have been said, but I doubt whether in similar circumstances in any city in the world there would have been so little looting as there was in Dublin on those two days. One tries to imagine what London would have been like if it had suddenly been abandoned for two days to the mercy of the mob. I think a Whitechapel mob would have sacked it in that time.

While I was standing in O'Connell Street, Francis Sheehy Skeffington came up to me. He had half a dozen walking sticks under his arm, and he said to me: 'I'm trying to form a special constabulary to prevent looting. You'll do for one,' and he offered a walking-stick to me. I looked at the stick and I looked at the looters, and I said, 'No.' It was characteristic of 'Skeffy,' as he was called in Dublin, that he should behave like that. The pacifist in him would not permit him to use force to restrain the looters, though one might have thought the logician in him would have regarded the walking-stick as a weapon; but the hero in him compelled him, for the honour of his country, to do something to restrain them. On the previous day he had harangued them from the top of a tram-car, reminding them that they were Irish, and bidding them not to loot for the sake of Ireland's honor; and they had stopped looting – until he had gone away. To-day his proposal to overawe them with walking-sticks. Here indeed, I could not but think, was *Don Quixote* charging the windmills yet another time!

I imagine that he was unsuccessful in his efforts, for later on in the afternoon I saw him pasting slips of paper onto the walls of O'Connell Bridge. The slips bore an appeal to men and women of all parties to attend the offices of the Irish Suffrage Society in Westmoreland Street and enrol themselves as special

constables to maintain order. I never saw Francis Sheehy
Skeffington again. That evening he was taken by a lunatic officer
and shot in Portobello Barracks.

By this time the soldiers in Dublin had been reinforced, and
troops were already hurrying from England. All that evening, as
far as I could see, there was no stir in the green, but the firing
was heavier than on the previous day, and all over the city there
was the persistent banging of bullets. The windows on the
ground floor of the Shelbourne were full of bullet-holes, and the
wall of the Alexandra Club on the west side of the green was
covered with the marks of bullets. That afternoon I had seen a
dead Sinn Féiner lying inside the gate of the green that looks
down Grafton Street, lying face downward in a hole in the earth,
and I wondered whether he was the man I had seen the day
before, intently watching, while the girls chaffed him.
    And while I was peering through the railings at the dead
man, someone came up and said to all of us who were there:
    'Poor chap! Let's get him out and bury him!' There were three
women from the slums standing by, and one of them, when she
heard what he said, rushed at him and beat him with her fists
and swore at him horribly.
    No, you'll not get him out,' she yelled. 'Let him lie there and
rot, like the poor soldiers!'
    That speech was typical of the general attitude of the Dublin
people toward the Sinn Féiners. Popular feeling was dead
against them. Here was a singular rebellion, indeed! Men had
risen against a power which they could not possibly beat in
behalf of people who did not wish for their championship!
Wherever I went in Dublin in the first days of the rebellion I
heard the strongest expressions of hatred for the Sinn Féin
movement. There was a feeling of remarkable fury against the
Countess Marckevitz, remarkable because this lady had spent
herself in feeding and succouring poor people during the 1911
strike, and one would have imagined that some feeling of
gratitude would have saved her from the insults that were
uttered against her. A strange, incalculable woman, born of an
old Irish family, she had thrown herself into all kinds of forlorn
hopes. It was said that her most ardent desire was to be the Joan
of Arc of Ireland, that she might die for her country.
    On Easter Tuesday night, about ten o'clock, the soldiers on

the top floor of the Shelbourne began to use machine-guns, and the fire from them went on, I think, for an hour. Up to then we had heard only the sound of rifles, and it was a very unimpressive sound. If this was war, we thought to ourselves, then war is an uncommonly dull business. We became bored by bullets. When the surprise of the rebellion was over, most of us became irritable. We could not get about our ordinary affairs, we could not take our customary pleasures, and the rebellion itself had become flat.

But the rattle of machine-guns made us all sit up. The marrow in our spines seemed to be crawling about in search of a hiding place. I do not know what to compare the sound that a discharging machine-gun makes. Some said to me that it resembles the sound of a lawnmower which has been turned upside down; but to me it sounded like the noise made by a stick which is drawn rapidly along railings. One sat there, frankly afraid, and imagined a perpetual flow of bullets pouring across the green, killing and wounding and terrifying. One wondered, too, whether the wooden shutters were stout enough to keep out ricocheting bullets. The sensible thing to do, of course, was to keep to the back of the house, or, at all events, as far from the front windows as possible; but one does not do the sensible thing in such times. Instinctively, one rushed to the window to look out when a shot was fired, as instinctively as the crowds in London, despite official warnings, rush into the streets to look at the Zeppelins. The overmastering desire to see what was happening will draw the most craven to the scene of disaster, and that accounts, no doubt, for the fact that people went every day to 'see the fighting' in Dublin, and could not be persuaded to keep indoors until the rebellion had been suppressed.

That night, that Easter Tuesday night, was, I think, the worst of all the nights. It was the first time we had heard the noise of machine-guns, and it was the only night that a lengthy spell of fighting took place in this part of the city. If rebels remained inside the green, their terror must have been akin to madness. I wondered vaguely what had happened to the three girls who I had seen busy there on Monday. I suppose they had been sent away on Monday, but if they had endured that rake of fire –

I cannot remember now on what day the great fire of Dublin began. I think it was on Thursday. There were rumours that the

Helga had come up the Liffey and had shelled Liberty Hall and I was told that the Abbey Theater was lying in ruins; but it was impossible to get near O'Connell Street or obtain any reliable information as to what had happened. There were soldiers on the roof of Trinity College, commanding the general post-office and also the rebel strongholds in Dame Street, and the fire from their rifles and machine-guns made the approach to O'Connell Bridge a no-man's-land. One went down to the firing-line every day, and repeated all the rumours that one had heard on the way.

And then the fire began. I stood at the window of my bedroom and looked at the sky that was scarlet with flame. The whole of O'Connell Street and many of the contiguous streets were like a furnace, roaring and rattling as roofs fell in a whirlpool of sparks the splashed high in the air. The finest street in Europe was consumed in a night.

All this was in the center of the city. In outlying places fierce fighting continued, and many men on both sides were killed and wounded; but of these things I knew nothing beyond what I subsequently read in the newspapers. I was bound inside the city, just beyond the zone of flames, and here there was little firing left. I could still see the republican flag floating over the College of Surgeons, but those who were inside the college were keeping very still. Now and then the soldiers in the Shelbourne fired spasmodically, and we could hear the sound of heavier and more regular firing further off; but for us, there was chiefly the flames flowing skyward from O'Connell Street. Almost one was glad that the looters had secured some stuff that would otherwise have been fuel in that terrible fire. No one can tell what caused the fire. Some say that it was started by looters, either intentionally or accidentally, and some say it was caused by the explosion of shells or ammunition. It is, I think, more likely that a careless looter began it.

In a few days Dublin became a city of nurses and doctors and ambulances. Wherever one went, one saw them with Red Cross badges on their sleeves, hurrying continually. Motor-cars, with large Red Cross flags flying at their sides, rushed about the town, laden with nurses and doctors and medical students, and every now and then an ambulance came swiftly to a hospital door, and some wounded man or woman or child was carried from it.

On the Saturday following the beginning of the rebellion, I walked out of Dublin to see a friend, and when I was returning in the evening I heard that some of the rebels had surrendered. A man came along the road, riding a bicycle furiously, and as he passed he leaned forward a little and shouted, 'They've surrendered!' and then went on. We had been heavy in our minds till then. The rebellion was getting on our nerves, and we were pessimistic about the future of Ireland. News had come to us, too, that a friend, a man of unique value to Ireland, had narrowly escaped death by accidental shooting. He had miraculously escaped all injury, but the shock of his danger hurt our spirits. And then came the news of the surrender, and suddenly the heaviness lifted. We doubted the truth of the news, but even in that state of dubiety there was relief. It seemed to us that the air became clearer, and there was a noticeable look of recovered happiness everywhere. When we came to the outer suburbs of the city we saw groups of people standing at corners, talking animatedly. 'it must be true,' we said, and hurried to join one of the groups; but as we hurried we heard the dull noise of rifles being fired, and the joy went out of us, and our pace slackened.

But the news *was* true. Some of the rebels had surrendered. Thomas MacDonagh and P. H. Pearse, finding themselves in an impossible plight, decided to surrender, and thus prevent the loss of more lives. A friend of mine, a member of the viceregal court, who witnessed the surrender told me afterward that Thomas MacDonagh came to the surrendering-place as coolly as if he were going for a stroll of a summer evening. P. H. Pearse was rather 'rattled,' and his head rolled from side to side, He was, perhaps, a more emotional man than Thomas MacDonagh, and he was frightfully tired.

I never saw P. H. Pearse, but I met Thomas MacDonagh once. He was interested in the Independent Theater of Ireland, and one evening I went to see the tiny theatre in Hardwicke Street to see some performances he and his friends were giving there. I had only lately come to Dublin, and I knew none of the people connected with the Independent Theater. A friend introduced me to Thomas MacDonagh. I remember him chiefly as a man who smiled very pleasantly. There was a look of great gentleness about him. He sat beside my friend for a while, and I was so placed that I saw his face easily.

He was a man of middle height and slender build. His high, broad brow was covered with heavy, rough, tufty hair that was brushed cleanly from his forehead and cut tidily about the neck, so that he did not look unkempt. His long, straight nose was as large as the nose of a successful *entrepreneur*, but it was not bulbous, nor were the nostrils wide and distended, as are the nostrils of many business men. It was a delicately shaped and pointed nose, with narrow nostrils that were as sensitive as those of a race-horse: an adventurous, pointing nose that would lead its owner into valiant lengths, but would never lead him into low enterprises. His eyes had a quick, perceptive look, so that he probably understood things speedily. And the kindly, forbearing look in them promised that his understanding would not be stiffened by harshness, that it would be accompanied by sympathy so keen that, were it not for the hint of humour they had, he might also have been mawkish, a sentimentalist too easily dissolved in tears. His thick eyebrows hung closely over his eyes and gave him a look of introspection that mitigated the shrewdness of his pointing nose. There was some weakness, but not much, in the full, projecting lower lip and the slightly receding chin that caused his short, tightened upper lip to look indrawn and strained; and the big, ungainly, jutting ears consorted oddly with the serious look of high purpose that marked his face in repose. It was as though Puck had turned poet and then had turned preacher. One looked at the fleshy lower lip and the jutting ears, and thought of a careless, impish creature; one looked at the shapely, pointing nose and the kindly, unflinching eyes, and thought of a man reckless of himself in the pursuit of some fine purpose.

When the news of his execution was proclaimed, a woman wept in the street.

'Ah, poor Tom MacDonagh,' she said. 'And he wouldn't have hurt a fly!'

I do not know what dreams these men had in their minds, but this much is certain, their was nothing unclean or mean about their motives. I think that they were foolish men, and I think that they did incalculable harm to their country; but whatever was their belief, they were prepared to suffer the hardest test for it – the test of death.

'We did not come here to surrender,' some of the rebels said to an envoy, carrying a white flag, who came to demand their surrender; 'we came here to die.' And when their stronghold was subsequently taken, only one man out of twenty-three was still alive, and he died soon afterward.

The rebellion was virtually over on the Saturday following Easter Monday, but for the best part of the succeeding week there was still some difficult work to be done in rounding up the snipers who had taken to the roofs of houses. In places like Merrion Square they were virtually immune from discovery. They could run along the roofs, hidden by parapets, and fire at the troops with a minimum chance of detection; but their position was a hopeless one. Death or discovery was inevitable, and in a few days the last of the snipers were taken.

About the middle of the second week I was able to get across O'Connell Bridge into O'Connell Street. The official name of O'Connell Street is Sackville Street. A soldier told me that Ypres was not much worse than O'Connell Street was. An American lady who had seen Louvain said that that town was not more battered and broken than the heart of Dublin. One saw a huddle of torn walls and twisted girders and rusty rails and stones and ashes. I went hurriedly to Marlborough Street, and found that the Abbey Theater had been marvellously untouched, though the houses immediately facing it were in ruins. The Royal Hibernian Academy, where an exhibition of pictures was being held, was a heap of cinders. One had to walk warily because the ground was covered with hot ashes, and if one was not careful, one sank into them and was burned.

One wall of a house near the theatre still stood, and it contained the fireplace. There was a kettle sitting on the hob, and on the mantelpiece there were two delf ornaments, uninjured, and a clock; and by the side of the fireplace a photograph frame was hanging, a little askew. The post-office was gutted; the Imperial Hotel and the offices of the 'Freeman's Journal' were level with the street. One looked around that pitiful pile of broken shops and houses, at the broken wires and burned-out tram-cars and shattered walls, and wondered what was to be the end of it all. High-minded men had led the romantic boys to a futile enterprise, and the end of their work was a smashed city and a ruined population.

Thomas MacDonagh, they say, was urgent against the rebellion, and so was The O'Rahilly, but the voting went against them, and they submitted to overruling and joined their friends. The O'Rahilly was killed in the fighting at the post-office. Thomas MacDonagh died, as he had lived, with a high heart. So did they all.

One thinks of three big rebellions in Ireland and of their failures. The first failed because there were no leaders good enough for the followers they had; the second failed because the followers were not good enough for the leaders they had. In this third rebellion leaders and followers were worthy of one another, matchless in spirit and devotion; but they had not the people behind them, and they had to fight an immeasurably superior force. And the third rebellion is, we pray, the last rebellion. MacDonagh and Pearse and all who followed them had found their highest aspiration in the desire to die for Ireland. There are other Irishmen who turn away from that ambition and look hopefully to a harder fight in which they shall spend themselves not in the hope of dying for Ireland, but in the hope of living for her.

That fortnight of ruin and rebellion was passed in sunshine and sweet mountain airs. One looked at the trees in St. Stephen's Green, and saw them spreading out their fresh foliage, and wondered how men could be content to lurk in their shade with loaded rifles in their hands. Now and then the wild fowl in the lake cluttered in fright; but mostly they flew about their domain, untroubled by the hatred of humans. The warmth of spring was everywhere except in human things; and when the rebellion was over, suddenly the skies slackened, and there was heavy rain for three days. The end of all that misery has not come yet. A man said to me that MacDonagh had no hope of a military success, but that he had every hope of a spiritual success. One wonders, and, wondering, thinks that so much devotion and generosity of ideal and high purpose might more worthily have been used. There is an old, ignoble phrase which has often been bandied about by Irish politicians: England's necessity is Ireland's opportunity. It is hardly an exalted sentiment even when one allows for the circumstances of Irish history, and it is the tragedy of this rebellion that noble-minded men sought to prove the truth of that mean phrase. Perhaps in a different way than that for which they hoped their ideal may be achieved, and Ireland yet come to unity, joined in honourable friendship with England.

Notes

1. Headlam, *Irish Reminiscences*, p. 49.
2. Ervine's role as a prominent apologist for Northern Ireland is explored in Gillian McIntosh, *The Force of Culture: Unionist Identities in Twentieth-Century Ireland* (Cork: Cork University Press, 1999).
3. From *Century Magazine* (1917), pp. 22–39.
4. '1911' appears to be a mistake. Ervine was probably recalling the great Dublin lockout which ran from August 1913 to the end of the year, and was accompanied by much violence.
5. Sean Connolly (no relation to James), an actor and officer in the Irish Citizen Army, was killed at the City Hall on Easter Monday.
6. Again, '1911' is wrong. The ICA was founded in 1913.
7. Four people were killed at Bachelor's Walk by British troops in the aftermath of the Howth gun-running on 26 July 1914. Ervine contrasts this with the Ulster gun-running of 24-5 April 1914, which passed without any interference from the authorities.
8. An observation which is given added point by the fact that de Robeck came from a family of Swedish nobility who had lived in County Kildare since the late eighteenth century. For the Irish at Gallipoli, see Keith Jeffery, 'Ireland and Gallipoli', in Jenny Macleod (ed.), *Gallipoli: Making History* (London: Frank Cass, 2004), pp. 98–109.

9 Rounding Up the 'Usual Suspects'

The main document in this chapter is the 'Report on the cases of Irish civil servants suspended in connection with the recent rebellion', by The Right Hon. Sir Guy Fleetwood Wilson, GCIE, KCB, KCMG, and Sir William P. Byrne, KCVO, CB, of 16 August 1916.[1] The committee had been set up by the Home Secretary, Sir Herbert Samuel, in response to the concerns of Arthur Hamilton Norway, and possibly other senior civil servants in Ireland, that government employees suspected of complicity with the Rising might be dismissed simply on the word of the military authorities. As is clear from the report reproduced below, Wilson and Byrne took their task very seriously, and were anxious even to distance themselves from the Dublin Castle administration. The Home Secretary thought that the report should be published, and consulted the heads of Irish departments for their views on the matter. T. W. Russell of the Department of Agriculture and Technical Instruction was generally in favour of publication, although he predicted 'a good deal of adverse press criticism of the – to my view – needlessly apologetic tone of the first page of the Report'.[2] The Chief Secretary for Ireland (in succession to Augustine Birrell), Henry Duke, felt that publication would 'probably do more harm than good',[3] and in the end Samuel decided against publication. The report is published here for the first time.

Part of the potential government embarrassment following publication, might have stemmed from the evident gulf between what Wilson and Byrne conceived to be a proper civil servant attitude, and that which was expressed by some of the individuals they examined. 'We have been struck', they wrote, 'by the readiness with which a considerable number of those inculpated air views quite incompatible in our judgment, with their position as public servants'. Nevertheless, they clearly gave the benefit of the doubt (at least) to nearly half of the forty-two persons whom the military had named. Among those whose dismissal they confirmed, however, were some who had been active on the rebel side. Two such were Martin King and A. J. Fitzpatrick, who were employed in the Engineering Department, and, according to R. M. Fox, were members of the Irish Citizen Army and Volunteers respectively.[4] Fox describes how King and Fitzgerald 'made a careful survey of the various cables and manholes in the city, with special attention to important trunk lines'. Plans had been made to cut 'cables and poles in key positions', but in the end these were not carried out. According to King, this was 'not the fault of the Citizen Army men but was due to that section of the Irish Volunteers who failed to mobilise and so prevented the carrying out of the joint operation as planned'.[5]

The records of the Wilson-Byrne committee in the United Kingdom National Archives are accompanied by what appear to be the working papers prepared for each individual case. Sets of papers concerning four Post Office employees are reproduced below, which together show a range of engagement with, and activity during, the Rising.

Report of the Wilson-Byrne Committee[6]

The Right Honourable Herbert Samuel, M.P.,
Secretary of State for the Home Department

On 26th of July, 1916 you commissioned us to proceed to Dublin and there to investigate the cases of certain Civil Servants whose conduct during the Rebellion had caused suspicion.

The terms of our reference were as follows:-

'To consider the cases of Irish Civil Servants who have been suspended from their duties owing to their suspected complicity with the recent Rebellion and to advise how they should be dealt with.'

We arrived in Dublin on July 27th and remained there till August 15th, during the whole of which time we were engaged upon our investigation.

We interviewed 14 heads of Departments and 42 Civil Servants.

We append a list of both.[7]

Arrangements had kindly been made by Sir Robert Chalmers[8] for our holding our investigation in the Castle, but we considered it better to avoid all connection with the Castle, feeling that the Civil Servants of the humbler ranks might be disinclined to approach the Castle and even suspect the neutrality of our attitude, if the enquiry were held there. For the like reason we denied ourselves all secretarial, clerical and stenographic assistance, although this materially added to our work and difficulties. We were very desirous that the incriminated civil servants should feel that we wished them to make out the best possible case for themselves, and that it would be a genuine pleasure to us, as civil servants ourselves, should we find ourselves able to recommend their re-instatement.

We so informed every civil servant who came before us, and we hope and believe we succeeded in convincing them of our sincerity. We allowed everyone the fullest latitude and allotted to each a very considerable amount of time. In some cases the interview extended over several hours.

Everyone was informed of the terms of the terms of reference and was told that he was at perfect liberty to decline to answer any of the questions put to him. Every civil servant was made acquainted with the nature of the charge against or suspicion held regarding him, and he was encouraged to tender the fullest explanation he could in respect of either or both. We afterwards compared his verbal statement to us with the Departmental, Military and Police documentary evidence placed at our disposal, and, when it seemed necessary or advisable to do so, we called for further information from, or confirmation by the Authorities cited.

In one or two instances we allowed men to refresh their memories at home or to obtain further evidence and to communicate with us again.

We have been assured by the Heads of Departments of the undoubted loyalty of the general body of their staffs.

We had greatly hoped that no cases, or only isolated instances of evident disloyalty would come before us, but we regret to have to state that in a good many cases we felt it our duty to recommend removal from the service, the confession of faith of the suspect was often tendered freely, frankly and unblushingly. Briefly it amounted in many cases to a declaration that so long as the individual in question discharged his official duties satisfactorily during office hours, he was fully entitled to do as he pleased out of office hours, even if it involved violence which might lead to the killing of troops or police officers. This view was expressed not by the lowest ranks only. In more than one instance the allegation that a man engaged in military operations had not actually fired at a soldier was advanced as sufficient justification for re-instatement. We have been struck by the readiness with which a considerable number of those inculpated air views quite incompatible in our judgment, with their position as public servants. In no instance were we altogether satisfied that such Civil Servants as actually took active part in the rebellion, under alleged compulsion, could not have withdrawn at an early stage of it.

In only one instance was formal notice of resignation of membership of the Irish Volunteer Corps tendered, and it is to be noted that whilst some ex-volunteers were apparently distrusted by the Rebels and only used as orderlies, others were so fully trusted that rifles and ammunition were served out to them and they were posted as sentries at, and as defenders of points of strategic importance.

Owing to the peculiar political situation in Ireland, we did not, broadly speaking, judge men <u>only</u> from the standpoint of their continued connection with the Sinn Féin movement. We were guided by their activities, their explanation thereof, by their mental attitude towards the rebellion, and by their expressed intention in the future to subordinate or otherwise, their loyalty as public servants, to their political creed.

The compilation of a list of persons in the employment of Government suspected of complicity in the Sinn Féin rebellion, did not come within our province. Such a list was furnished to us by the Assistant Under Secretary, Dublin Castle, and we dealt with it on the following lines:-

(a) We have judged within the terms of our reference the conduct of only those Civil Servants who came within the correct and accepted interpretation of that term, excluding unestablished men on weekly rate of wage.

(b) We have considered the cases from the point of view of possible re-instatement, only of such Civil Servants as were under suspension by the order of the Heads of their Departments, whether they had been before the Sankey Advisory Committee[9] or not.

(c) We have assumed that all Civil Servants, whether suspended or not, who have been deemed to deserve continued internment by the Sankey Advisory Committee shall ipso facto be considered unfit for retention in the Public Service.

We have been unable to trace any circular or general notification issued by Irish Departments to Civil Servants, as a class, not to remain members of the Irish Volunteers or to belong to 'an organization of which the avowed object was to thwart and injure the Government'[10] and all the Heads of Departments and the Civil Servants who came before us repudiated knowledge of any such general circular or of any general instructions as to loyalty and discretion given to entrants to the Civil Service or to existing civil servants in the view of the unrest in Ireland.

We append a circular letter (appendix 6[11]) which is all we have been able to obtain in this connection. It will be seen that it is for use in individual cases only, where a personal warning is deemed to be needed.

We advocate the issue of a general circular, drafted for use in the Irish Departments, on the lines of the Home Office circular herewith (appendix 7[12]) and in view of the evidence that has come before us we may be allowed to express our strong conviction that legislative sanction should be sought for requiring all Civil Servants throughout Great Britain and Ireland to take the oath of allegiance, just as soldiers and sailors are called upon to do.

In all cases of re-instatement we advise that the civil servant be made to sign an undertaking of good and circumspect conduct in the future.

Advantage should be taken of the present situation, by serious and combined effort on the part of all concerned, to instil a higher tone in the ranks of the Irish Civil Service and to require a more distinct recognition of the obligations which properly attach to Public Service. We believe that much good would result in increased interest were shown in, and if friendly advice were more freely tendered to, young Civil Servants by their Chiefs.

In view of certain suggestions made to us, we consider that we should put our opinion on record that only in very special cases transfer to offices outside Ireland might be sanctioned so as to remove very young Civil Servants from a bad entourage; but we greatly disapprove of any suggestion to transfer Civil Servants, unfit for service in Ireland, to service in English or Scottish offices. Such a course, we are confident, would be injurious to the service and subversive to the discipline.

We will now deal with the cases which we have been called upon to consider, recording our recommendations in each instance.

Rebukes, forfeiture of pay for a period of suspension, withholding increments of salary and arresting promotion, in the case of re-instated civil servants, are matters for Departments to deal with, and we offer no remarks thereon.

Department	Name	Recommendation
Local Government Board	Kenny, J. P.	To be dismissed
"	McElligott, J. J.[13]	To be dismissed
Customs and Excise	Cox, J. E.	To be retired on pension
"	Calnan, J.	May be re-instated
Customs and Inland Revenue	Horan. M.	May be re-instated
Irish Land Commission	Belton, P.	May be re-instated
"	Sheehan, P.	To be dismissed
"	Kelly, P. J. (Patrick)	To be dismissed
"	Coughlan, F. X.	To be dismissed
"	Rooney, R.	To be dismissed
"	O'Hehir, H.	To be dismissed
Reformatory and Industrial Schools	McNeill, Margaret	May be re-instated
Board of Agriculture and Technical Instruction (Museum)	Gogan, W. J.	To be dismissed
(Library)	O'Connor, P.	To be dismissed
Congested Districts Board	Cox, E. J.	May be re-instated
"	O'Connor, R.	May be re-instated
General Post Office	Hayes, J.	To be dismissed
"	de Loughrey, D.	May be re-instated
"	Heery, J. M.[14]	To be dismissed
"	Archer, W.	May be re-instated
"	Darcy, J.	May be re-instated
"	McDonnell, P. J.	To be dismissed
"	O'Neill, M. Joseph	May be re-instated
"	O'Neill, John	May be re-instated
"	McCarthy, F.	May be re-instated
"	Tyrrell, J.	To be dismissed
"	Collins, M. J.	To be dismissed
"	Byrne, F.	To be dismissed
"	O'Callaghan, J.	To be dismissed
"	Larkin, W.	May be re-instated
"	Henigan, J.	To be dismissed
"	Byrne, J.	To be dismissed
"	King, M.	To be dismissed
"	Hughes, P.	May be re-instated

"	Pollard, F.	To be dismissed
"	Fitzpatrick, A. J.	To be dismissed
"	Kehoe, P.	May be re-instated
"	Murphy, J.	May be re-instated
"	Breslin, J. F.	May be re-instated
Stationery Office	Kavanagh, M. J.	To be dismissed
Board of Trade	Somers, C. D.	To be dismissed
"	Connelly, A. J.	May be re-instated

Cases dealt with	. . . 42
To be dismissed	. . . 23
To be pensioned	. . . 1
May be re-instated	. . . 18

In conclusion we desire to express our very genuine thanks to Sir Robert Chalmers and to Sir Edward O'Farrell,[15] to the heads of the Civil Departments and to the Military and Police Authorities n Dublin, all of whom freely placed their documentary evidence at our disposal and rendered all the assistance in their power.

(Signed) GUY FLEETWOOD WILSON
W.P. BYRNE.

August 16th, 1916.

APPENDIX NO. 1

List furnished by the Under Secretary, Dublin Castle, of persons in the employment of Government who are suspected of complicity in the Sinn Féin Rebellion, and whose cases are to be investigated by the Rt Hon. Sir Guy Fleetwood Wilson, GCIE, KCB, KCMG, and Sir William Byrne, KCVO, CB.

Office	Name	Rank	Remarks
Congested Districts Board	Roderick O'Connor	Clerk	Arrested, deported and released and subsequently suspended.
"	Edward J. Cox	"	"
"	Joseph Bracken	"	Arrested and deported. (Not a civil servant).

Local Government Board	J.J. McElligott	Higher Div. Clerk	Arrested, deported and released and suspended
"	J.P. Kenny	Asst. Clerk	In custody.
Board of National Educ.	Joseph Neary	Servant at Marlborough Hall, Glasnevin	Deported, and subsequently dismissed.
Department of Agriculture andTechnical Instruction	G.N. Count Plunkett[16]	Director of National Museum	Arrested and subsequently deported to England by Military Authorities where he is compelled to live under Art. 14 of D.R.R.[17]
"	Wm. J. Gogan	Asst. Keeper National Museum	Arrested and released and subsequently suspended.
"	Patrick O'Connor	Attendant National Museum Library	Interned in England.
"	John Daly	Assistant Agricultural Overseer, Co. Leitrim	Interned in England.
"	Mr O'Reilly	Manual Instructor employed by Co. Galway (Joint) Technical Instruction Committee	Interned in England (not a Civil Servant)
"	Bartholomew Bowen	Science teacher under Clonmel Borough Technical Instruction Committee	Interned in England. (not a Civil Servant)
"	R. Cotter	2nd Div. Clerk	Interned in England.
Irish Land Commission	R. Rooney (dismissed)	Minor Staff Clerk	Arrested on release, allowed to resume duty but subsequently suspended.
"	P. Sheehan	2nd Div. Clerk	"

	(dismissed) Patrick J. Kelly (dismissed)	"	"
"	Hugh Hehir, or O'Hehir (dismissed)	Asst. Clerk	In custody and suspended. Subsequently released and suspension continues.
"	Peter J. Kelly	" (interned)	In custody and suspended.
"	C. Murphy	"	"
"	M. Sheppard	" (interned)	"
"	M. Flanagan	"	"
"	J. Derham	" (interned)	"
"	M. Lynch (interned)	"	"
"	F. X. Coghlan (dismissed)	"	Arrested and on release suspended.
Reformatory and Industrial Schools	Miss Margaret McNeill	Lady Inspector	Suspended.
High Court of Justice In Ireland	Edward Price Rules Office, King's Bench Division	2nd Class Clerk,	In custody in England.

POST OFFICE IRELAND

POSTAL OFFICIALS SUSPECTED OF COMPLICITY IN RECENT REBELLION

Name of Official	Rank	Office	Remarks
Richard J. Mulcahy	Clerk	Engineering Dept. Dublin	In Military custody
John O'Callaghan	Clerical Assistant	"	"
A. J. Fitzpatrick	"	"	"
James J. Tyrell	"	"	"
James Byrne	"	"	"
John J. Twamley	"	"	"
Francis Byrne	"	"	"
Martin King	"	"	"
Francis Pollard	Youth	"	"
Joseph Lyons	Second Division Clerk	G.P.O. Dublin	"
Patrick O'Keeffe	Sorter-Tracer	"	"

Name	Position	Location	Status
John Hayes	Sorting Clerk & Telegraphist	"	"
M. J. Collins	"	"	"
James F. Breslin	"	Ferns	"
Philip Murphy	Postman	Enniscorthy	"
Thomas Maher	"	"	"
M. Smith	"	Athgarvan, Newbridge	"
Christopher Caulfield	"	Athenry	"
Patrick Ryan	"	Cloghran, Dublin	"
Patrick O'Leary	Boy Messenger	Dublin	"
Daniel Buckley	Telephone Attendant	Maynooth	"
Dr Edward Dundon	Medical Attendant	Borris, Co. Carlow	"
William Archer	Sorting Clerk & Telegraphist	Dublin	Under Suspension
Michael J. O'Neill	"	Ferns	Arrested, deported and released. Suspended
John O'Neill	"	Enniscorthy	"
P. J. McDonnell	2nd Division Clerk	Dublin	"
John Darcy	Postman	Dublin	"
James M. Heery	Clerical Assistant	Dublin	"
James Haugh	Sorting Clerk & Telegraphist	Waterford	Under Suspension
P. C. Mahony	"	Dungarvan	"
Michael McSweeney	Clerk	Waterford	"
William Larkin	Postman	Wexford	Arrested by Military but immediately discharged. Now under suspension.
Patrick Kehoe	Auxiliary Postman	Bridgetown, Wexford	Arrested and released. Now under suspension.
John Murphy	"	"	"
John Stafford	"	Ballymitty, Wexford	"
D. M. de Loughry	Sorting Clerk & Telegraphist	Kilkenny	Under suspension
F. McCarthy	"	"	"
Michael Cremen	3rd class Clerk	Stores Branch	Arrested, deported and released. Restored to duty.

William S. O'Doherty	Assistant Clerk	"	"
John McGinn	Postman	Rockcorry, Monaghan	Arrested and released. Restored to duty.
F. H. Clarke	"	"	"
Joseph, Patrick and Chris. Kenny	"	Rathangan, Co. Kildare	Arrested, deported and released. Restored to duty.
*Pat Hughes	Sorting Clerk	Dundalk	
*J. Henigan	Auxiliary Postman	Cork	

*These were added by Mr Norway, Secretary, Post Office, Dublin. (They were not in the Castle List).

Department	Name	Rank	Remarks
Board of Works, Dublin	Christopher Duffy	Temporary Labourer, V[ice] R[egal] Lodge, Dublin	Deported.
Customs and Excise	James Calnan	Preventive man, Waterford	Under suspension.
"	M. O'Connell	Unattached Officer, Dublin	In custody, suspended.
"	John E. Cox	Reserve Surveyor, Dublin	Arrested, deported and released. Not re-employed on the Reserve since arrest.
"	P. F. Burke	Officer of C. & E., Carrickmacross (Retired).	Deported
Inland Revenue	Matthew Horan	Assistant Clerk Stamps and Taxes Office, Customs House, Dublin	Deported
Board of Trade, Labour Exchange, Dublin.	Chas. D. Somers	Temporary Assistant	Arrested and released. Suspended.
"	A. J. Connolly	Clerk	Deported
" Wexford	William Fortune	Temporary Assistant	Arrested, deported and released.
" Loughrea	B. J. Fallon	Local Agent	Arrested and deported. Not a Civil Servant.

Stationery Office	M. J. Kavanagh	Assistant Clerk	Deported and released. Now under suspension.
National Health Insurance Commission	T. Cotter	"	Arrested and deported.
"	F. J. Shouldice	"	"

CASES REPORTED BY MR ROBERTS

Department	*Name*	*Rank*	*Remarks*
National Health Insurance Commission	B. Maguire	Temporary Clerk	Deported.
"	P. Moore	Temporary Messenger	Deported.
"	Thomas Croke	Temporary Porter	Deported and subsequently released.

<u>The places of the above men have been filled.</u>

APPENDIX NO. 2

LISTS OF HEADS OF DEPARTMENTS AND OTHERS INTERVIEWED IN DUBLIN

Sir Henry Robinson	Local Government Board
Sir George Stevenson	Board of Works
Dr. Flinn	Reformatory and Industrial Schools
Messrs. Barlas	Local Government Board
" Micks	Congested Districts Board
" Langan	Customs and Excise
" Green	Land Commission
" Norway	Post Office
" Hanrette	Board of Trade
" Houlihan	National Health and Insurance
" Simpson	Inland Revenue
" Coyle	Board of Agriculture and Technical Instruction
" Chapman	Stationery Office
Professor Lowry	Trinity College

APPENDIX NO. 3

LIST OF SUSPENDED CIVIL SERVANTS EXAMINED
IN DUBLIN

O'Connor, R.	Congested Districts Board
Cox, E. J.	"
MacNeill, Magaret	Reformatory and Industrial Schools
Calnan, J.	Customs and Excise
Cox, J. E.	"
Horan, M.	Customs and Inland revenue
Breslin, J. F.	General Post Office
Archer, W.	"
Darcy, J.	"
Heery, J. M.	"
McDonnell, P. J.	"
O'Neill, J.	"
O'Neill, M. J.	"
de Loughrey, D.	"
McCarthy, F.	"
Collins, M. J.	"
Tyrrell, J.	"
Byrne, F.	"
Larkin, W	"
Henigan, J.	"
O'Callaghan, J.	"
Kehoe, P.	"
Murphy, J.	"
Fitzpatrick, A. J.	"
King, M.	"
Byrne, J.	"
Pollard, F.	"
Hayes, J.	"
Hughes, P.	"
Kavanagh, M. J.	Stationery Office
Somers, C. D.	Board of Trade
Connolly, A. J.	"
Belton, P.	Land Commission
Sheehan, P.	"
Kelly, P. J.	"
Rooney, R.	"
O'Hehir, H.	"
Coghlan, F. X.	"
Kenny, J. P	Local Government Board
McElliogott, J. J.	"
Gogan, W. J.	Board of Agriculture
O'Connor, P.	"

Papers relating to individual civil servants as provided for the Wilson-Byrne Committee[18]

1. William Archer, Sorting Clerk and Telegraphist, GPO Dublin

Did not present himself for duty on or after the 24th ultimo. No explanation was received from him and enquiry was made at his house on 9th May. His father was met with there and stated that Mr. W. Archer had left home on the evening of the 24th to report for duty and that nothing more was known of his movements until rumours reached his home that he had been wounded on his way to the Office and was a patient in Hospital. The Post Office Medical Officer was then requested to visit Mr. W. Archer and found him with one of his toes amputated, Mr. Archer explaining that he had been injured in the foot by a stray bullet.

The Police were them asked to make an enquiry and as a result the following report was received.

'With reference to the attached, I beg to report that the above named is a son of Mr. Edward J. Archer, 16 Shandon Road, a retired inspector of G.P.O. messengers.

He is at present a patient in the Richmond Hospital and has had the second largest toe of the right foot amputated.

I have had an interview with William Archer in Richmond Hospital and he made the following statement:- "On 25th ultimo, I was passing along Church Street, about 11 a.m., going in the direction of he Four Courts when I was struck by a bullet. I could not tell where it was fired from. I was struck in the right foot. I cried out I was shot. I was brought into the Father Matthew Hall and dressed by the Volunteer Ambulance. I remained there from Tuesday to Thursday and was carried on a stretcher by the Volunteers to the Richmond Hospital".

When asked what he was doing out at the time, he replied: "I was only rambling about the city, sight seeing."

I subsequently saw his father, who informed me that his son, William, was at home on Easter Monday, went out with his brother, Robert L. Archer, an employee of the A.O.H., was home on Easter Monday night, went out on Tuesday morning and he heard nothing of him further until the news of his having been wounded and a patient in the Richmond Hospital reached him, but he could not state on what date he received this information.

The father states he has no knowledge of his son, William, being connected the Volunteers, and the son denies being a member of that body.

On making confidential enquiry, in the neighbourhood, I was informed that the Archer family are bosom friends of the O'Hanrahans, 67 Connaught Street, notorious rebels, one of whom was shot and the other sentenced to Penal Servitude in connection with the recent Rebellion.[19] I also learned that William Archer's brother, Charles J. Archer, 1 Enniskerry Road, a G.P.O. Sorting Clerk, is married to a sister of J. Richmond, 275 North Circular Road, who was arrested in connection with the recent rising and deported to Knutsford Detention Barracks on 2nd instant. (Please see "Sunday Irish Times" of 20th instant).

It is freely rumoured in the district that William Archer was out with the Volunteers, but I am unable to obtain any confirmation of the rumour. He was in civilian clothes when brought to the hospital and had no boots. It is rather strange that he should be sight seeing in Church Street going towards the Four Courts at such an early hour on this particular date.

(Sd) J. Fagan
Detective Sergeant.
27 May 1916'

It will be noticed that while Mr. Archer's father stated to the Officer of the Post Office who called at the house that nothing was known of Mr. W. Archer after Monday evening he told the Police that he was at home that night, and disappeared the following day.

An explanation of his movements from noon on Saturday 22nd April to noon on Monday, May 1st furnished by Mr. W. Archer runs as follows:-

'The Secretary,

On Saturday, April 22nd, having made arrangements for the performance of the evening portion of my duty I went home and remained there till tea-time. I then went for a walk as far as Merrion returning about 10.30 p.m. I slept at home on that night. It was my original intention to go for a motor cycling trip through Co. Wicklow with my brother for the weekend starting on Sunday morning, but we were forced to abandon this trip owing to a breakdown to his machine. I spent some time with him on Sunday morning endeavouring to fix it up but without success. I passed the afternoon in the Phoenix Park. That evening I walked as far as Donnybrook returning home about 11 p.m.

On Monday morning having fixed his machine we left home about 11 a.m. for a trip round Malahide and Skerries, but the machine again broke down on the Clonliffe Road. We succeeded in getting home on it and spent part of the afternoon mending it. Hearing that a revolt had been started in the City by the Volunteers we left home and spent some time watching their movements on the N.C. [North Circular] and Cabra Roads. I slept at home that night. The following morning at about 9 or 9.30 I left home to se the state of the City. Various rumours were current and I wished to see for myself what had happened. I went down to N.C. Road, Berkeley Road, Blessington Street, and by Dorset Street and North King Street into Church Street some distance beyond Church Street Chapel and while walking towards the Four Courts I was struck in the foot by a bullet. A couple of Volunteers on seeing I was shot helped me up to their Hospital in Father Matthew Hall, where I was attended by their ambulance staff, and detained there during that day and Wednesday. On Thursday I was removed to the Richmond Hospital where one of my toes was amputated. I have been detained a patient there since then.

W.A. Archer, S.C. & T.'

It should be mentioned perhaps that the Church Street and Four Courts area was a lively centre of the disturbances.

<u>Note signed by Mr Norway, 5 July 1916</u>
Mr Archer's official conduct was good, and he discharged his duties satisfactorily. Nothing is known in the Post Office as` regards his political views or (possible) activities.

2. Paul James McDonnell, Second Division Clerk, GPO Dublin

Mr. P. J. McDonnell, Clerk, Accountant's Office, G.P.O., Dublin was arrested on 10th May and deported. He was released and reported himself in person for duty on 26th May but was not allowed to resume He made a written statement as follows:-

26 May 1916

The Accountant,

I was arrested on 10th instant, as you are aware, at the insistence of the Military Authorities, presumably on suspicion of having taken an active part in the recent Rebellion in Ireland.

When interrogated at the Town Hall, Pembroke, by a Military officer, I admitted the following facts:- That I had joined the Irish Volunteers at their inception in December 1913 under the presidency of Eoin MacNeill; that at the so-called 'split' about a year later, I thought it consistent on my part to remain with the original body under the same leadership as before, their objectives having, to my mind, undergone no change at all, namely, 'to defend and maintain the rights common to all the people of Ireland;' and that I continued as such until Easter Monday 1916. On that day about 2 p.m. I heard, with surprise, on the course at Fairyhouse (about 15 miles from Dublin) a rumour to the effect that an outbreak had occurred in the city, and this was confirmed on my return there at 7.30 p.m. I reached my home by a circuitous route, avoiding the danger zone as far as possible, at 9.30 p.m.

The situation was fully discussed with my brother who was at the races with me, and was likewise an Irish Volunteer. We now realised, for the first time, that the organisation to which we belonged was not a purely defensive organisation, as we had supposed, but a revolutionary one. (In view of later information, it would have been more accurate to consider the Irish Volunteers as dominated by a secret revolutionary organisation). We, therefore, definitely severed our connection with the Irish Volunteers that night, by parting with our arms and ammunition by plunging them into an adjacent quarry at Milltown, for we always held that to be an Irish Volunteer meant an Armed Volunteer.

It is necessary to mention that for some time previous to Easter Sunday, we had been warned of mobilisation on that day at 4 p.m. for inspection of equipment, and possibly for something in the nature of a route march or simple manoeuvre afterwards. Preparations were made accordingly, and such would doubtless have taken place, but for an order which was published, over the signature of Mr. MacNeill, in a newspaper of that morning, the 'Sunday Independent', that all Irish Volunteer parades, arranged for the Easter, were thereby cancelled.

On the Bank Holiday my brother and I left home at 10.30 a.m. to proceed, by tram and train, to the Races at Fairyhouse, our usual plan of spending Easter Monday for some years past.

A belated attempt was made to mobilise me for a 10 o'clock parade on the Monday by a caller (unknown) arriving at my house at 11.15 a.m. after I had left.

It has been suggested to me that my visit to the Races was made so as to avoid taking part in the Rising, of which I was assumed to have previous knowledge, and my obvious duty, had such been the case, was pointed out to me. I have denied the truth of such statement and I repeat the denial. It is not clear by what process I could have suspected a mobilisation on that day.

These matters have been thoroughly investigated by the Military Authorities during my detention in Wandsworth Prison, London, and as a result, my release therefrom was ordered on 25th instant by Head Quarters, Dublin, and confirmed by Director of Personal Services War Office – (signed 'Reginald Brooke, Lt-Colonel, Commandant, Wandsworth').

I reached home to-day and respectfully await your instructions.

P. J. MacDonnell.

The Police Reports concerning him are as below:-
Detective Sergeant Ahern, D.M.P., says:- I beg to report that the above named lives with his mother who keeps a Spirit Grocer's shop at 91 Upper Rathmines. At the commencement of the Irish Volunteers he joined that organisation with his brother Frank who is an assistant in his mother's shop. Almost on every Sunday since then when any meetings were being held P. J. MacDonnell was observed cycling from his home dressed in the uniform of the Irish Volunteers and having a rifle strapped across his shoulders. It is said that he belonged to the Camden Row Battalion. He is well-known to Sergeant Megahy and Constable Devine E. Division.

As far as I can ascertain Frank who is an assistant in his mother's shop, and the man in question were at Fairyhouse Races on the Easter Monday returning home that night. They were missing on the Tuesday, Wednesday and Thursday following, and it is believed they were out during that period assisting the Rebels. P. J. McDonnell was arrested by Constable Devine, E. Division, on 10th May 1916, and on the following day he was handed over to the Military. After his arrest he admitted to the Constable being a member of the Irish Volunteers and said his rifle and ammunition were buried in a pond in the River and that his mother burned his uniform.

He is well known to the Police at Rathmines Station as being a Sinn Féiner and a member of the Irish Volunteers.

7th June 1916.

Sergeant Megahy reports as follows (16/6/16):-

With reference to attached file I beg to report that on 10th May last I accompanied Captain Tucker of the Military Department Ballsbridge, to McDonnell's residence where we saw Francis McDonnell and [Thomas] Birmingham referred to in said file. These two men admitted being members of the Irish Volunteers and stated they threw their guns into a quarry pond in the neighbourhood and burned their uniforms in a grate in the back room of their residence which they pointed out, and that they were at Fairyhouse Races on the day the Rebellion broke out and took no part in same. When questioned as to where they spent the remainder of the Rebellion week they said they were out walking in the District. Frances McDonnell said that what applied to him also applied t his brother Paul McDonnell now in question.

It was then about 4.30 p.m. and Paul was to return home from business around 5 p.m.

Captain Tucker took the first-mentioned into custody and conveyed them to Ballsbridge and directed Constable Devine 129E who was also present to remain about and when Paul McDonnell arrived home to arrest him. The Constable accordingly carried out his directions.

The pond where the guns were supposed to be thrown into was searched by the Police but no trace of guns could be found, and the grate where the uniform was alleged to have been burned bore no trace of a fire having been in same for some time past.

These three men were well-known Sinn Féiners in this District, and weekly attended the Parades carrying guns.

They were, however, I believe at Fairyhouse Races on Easter Monday but there would appear to be some doubt as to their movements during the remainder of same week. Although there is no conclusive evidence of their having taken any part in the fighting Mr. Free, Post Office, Upper Rathmines, which is a few doors distant from McDonnell's residence states he did see Paul about the Thursday evening of Easter week, that he passed his door and entered 5 Fitzwilliam Terrance, Upper Rathmines, which is the residence of a Mr. Burgess who was an officer in the Volunteers, and is now a patient in Castle Hospital suffering from wounds received during the Rebellion. Mr. Free, who does not wish his name mentioned, also states that it is said in the neighbourhood that the McDonnells had their guns buried in their garden and have now removed them to some unknown place. He believes their action during rebellion week was in the way of carrying information to the Rebels. He also states that prior to the Rebellion large supplies of food was seen to be delivered at Mr. Burgess's residence as above.

Petition of Paul McDonnell, Francis McDonnell and Thomas Birmingham is worded as follows:-

'All were members of the Irish Volunteers organisation up to the date of the rising, but neither of them at any time understood that they should have to take part in any rising against the armed forces of the Crown, and had they known that such were expected of them each of them would have ceased to have any connection with the organisation.

They were all present at Fairyhouse Races on Easter Monday, and were unaware until after the Races that any rising had taken place in Dublin. They immediately came home and having taken their evening meal at 91 Upper Rathmines went out with the three rifles which they had respectively belonging to the Irish Volunteers and a small quantity of ammunition for the same which they were also possessed of, and they proceeded to Milltown Quarry and there threw in the three rifles and the ammunition.

They took no part in the recent rising, and remained at home within the district of their own house for the succeeding week. They were arrested on Wednesday, 12th April [corrected to 10 May in margin], and lodged in Richmond Barracks from whence they were sent on Friday 14th April [corrected to 12 May in margin] to the Detention Barracks in England where they are now.

The annexed six letters and three affidavits are furnished by Petitioners with a view to having the facts enquired into and when found correct that an order may be made for their early release.'

22nd May 1916. Mr. A. P. Hughes, General Post Office, swears he saw Mr. McDonnell at Fairyhouse.

22nd May 1916. Mr. J. W. P. Pope, 102 Rathmines, swears he knows Paul and Francis McDonnell from their infancy, always considered them respectable and well-conducted young men, and saw them very frequently in the district of their own home upon Easter Wednesday and the succeeding seven days.

22nd May 1916. Patrick Gorman of 82b Upper Rathmines, swears that he is well acquainted with the three men, and he saw them on 25th April many times passing about the district of their home. Again saw them on many occasions during that week, and is satisfied they took no part in the recent rising. Knows each of them for a considerable time, and is satisfied that they were not in any way connected with those members of the Irish Volunteers who raised in Armed Rebellion though the accused persons were members of the same organisation.

Mr. George Curran, Post Office Accountant's Office, Mr. T. J. Healy, 34 Finglas Road, and Mr. P. Horan, Gate Lodge, Mount Tallant Monastery, Harold's Cross, all certify that they met Mr. McDonnell at Fairyhouse Races on 24th April 1916.

Mr. O. Breakey, 2 Park View, Upper Rathmines, and Mr. P. Moore, 3 Rathmines Avenue, certify that they were with McDonnell brothers at Fairyhouse Races on 24th April 1916, and that they were about with them continually up to the time of their arrest, and that they can say they took no part in the disturbances.

It should be mentioned that one of Mr. Mc Donnell's relatives (a sister) in referring to his absence from Dublin at the Fairyhouse Races stated that Mr. McDonnell on the morning of that event offered the observation that 'Dublin was no place for him today'. This would imply a knowledge of coming events, but in this statement of 26th May Mr. McDonnell denies the possession of any such knowledge. The point was put guardedly to Mr. McDonnell when he reported himself for duty; hence the reference to it in his statement.

<u>Note signed by Mr Norway, 5 July 1916</u>

Mr H. Albery, Board of Works' Surveyor, informed the Post Office Accountant that he or some member of his family had seen Mr P. J. McDonnell in the neighbourhood of his home frequently during the period of the outbreak. Access to the Accountant's Office was impossible during the time.

Mr McDonnell's official character is good, and he performs his duties satisfactorily. Nothing more is known in the Post Office as to his political views or (possible) activities.

3. *John Darcy, Postman, Dublin*

Mr. John Darcy, Postman, 17 Ballsbridge Terrace, Dublin, was arrested on 27th April and deported. Was released and reported himself for duty on 1st June but was not allowed to resume.

The Police Report reads as follows:-

With reference to this File, I beg to report that John Darcy was a member of the Irish Volunteers, prior to the Rebellion, and so stated in his application for release from Military custody.

There is no evidence that he took part in the Insurrection.

On .27th April, he was arrested at his residence, by the Military, who found there an Irish Volunteer Uniform, a revolver and a quantity of ammunition.

Geo. Love,
Inspector.

Copies of an appeal from Mr. Darcy and of official reports concerning him are attached.

The Inspector,
I beg leave to make this claim to be allowed to resume my work as postman. I was at my work each day during the revolt up to the time when I was arrested by the Military which occurred on Thursday, 27th April at my home. I was a member of the Volunteers, but had actually given them up about a month before the outbreak. I took no part in the revolt of even the slightest kind; nor at any time while I was a member, did I think that anything of the kind was intended. I was detained by the Military for a month and three days, and during the greater part

of that I was treated with great severity, and coupled with the anxiety of my mind it is hardly possible to believe what I have suffered. I was released from Lewes Detention Barracks because the Military Authorities were satisfied that I was innocent as soon as they went into my case. I earnestly request that I may be allowed to resume my work at the earliest possible moment, as it is nearly six weeks since I received my wages, and we are finding it very hard to live. I am a member of the Postal Service since April 1893, and I believe have a good record. Trusting that I will be allowed to resume work at an early date.

> I remain,
> Yours obediently,
> John Darcy, Postman,
> 31/5/16.

The Controller,

Submitted. Mr. Darcy called here yesterday evening and informed me that he had been released by the Military Authorities, but had no document to this effect in his possession. I have called for a full report in his case from the Asst. Inspector in charge of Ballsbridge District Office where Mr. Darcy was employed and when received it will be duly submitted.

It is well known that Mr. Darcy was a member of the Irish Volunteers in which he held rank and wore uniform, and nothing whatever is known here regarding his statement that he severed his connection with that body.

> P. J. Sweeney,
> Inspector i/c,
> 1st June 1916.

Mr. John Darcy, Postman, arrested in connection with Volunteer Rebellion.

– -

The Asst. Inspector,

Ballsbridge D.O.

Please report so far as you are able all the circumstances relating to this case, the position occupied by Mr. Darcy in the Volunteers, and any other information you may have obtained since his arrest.

Although he has been released from custody he should not be allowed to resume duty until further instructions are received in his case.

> P. J. Sweeney,
> Inspector i/c,
> 1st June 1916.

The Inspector,

As a matter of common knowledge, Mr. Darcy, Postman, was a member of the Volunteers in fact I can go as far as to say I saw him in the uniform at the funeral of the late O'Donovan Rossa. Since his arrest I have made from time to time discreet enquiries respecting this man but could not obtain any useful or definite information beyond the fact that he had been a member of the above.

Mr. Darcy was not due for duty on Easter Monday the 24th of April nor did he perform any duty n that day.

According to record the last time he attended here was on the 26th of April from 6.0 p.m. to 9 p.m.

The last paragraph of your endorsement has been noted.

> E. Smith,
> Asst. Inspector,
> 2nd June 1916.

The Controller,

Submitted. Mr. Darcy was not due for duty on Easter Monday but he attended for duty of Tuesday 25th and Wednesday 26th April and has not since given any further attendance.

> P. J. Sweeney,
> Inspector i/c,
> 2nd June 1916.

– -

Mr. John Darcy, Postman, arrested during recent Insurrection.

Mr Nutty,

(Ballsbridge D.O.)

Please note that Mr. Darcy should not be allowed to resume duty until instructions to that effect are received.

Have you anything further to report in connection with his case?

P.J.S.
6/6/16.

Mr. Sweeney,
Read and noted. I have nothing further to report other than Mr. T. Sands, Postman, says he was speaking to Mr. T. Clare, Postman, Parcel Office, and the latter told him he was speaking to Mr. Darcy in College Green on Monday the 24th April (Bank Holiday) between 9 and 10 a.m. and he, Mr. Darcy, was then in the Volunteer Uniform. Mr. J. P. Moffett, Acting Head Postman, informs me that he was informed by Miss Simpson, Clerk at the Branch Office, that she saw Mr. Darcy in a hack car on Easter Monday in the same uniform.

E. Smith
Asst. Inspector,
8th June 1916

The Controller,
Submitted. When Mr. Darcy called to me he denied having been with the Volunteers on Easter Monday, and stated that he did not leave his bed until about 10 a.m. that day, while he further stated that he had severed his connection with that body over a month previously.

P. J. Sweeney,
Inspector i/c,
8/6/16

Note signed by Mr Norway, 5 July 1916
Mr. Darcy's official character is good, and he has discharged his duties satisfactorily.

4. James Michael Heery, Clerical Assistant, Post Office Engineering Branch

Mr J. M. Heery, Clerical Assistant, Post Office Engineering Branch, Dublin, was arrested and deported. He was released about the 14th June and applied to be allowed to resume duty. This permission was not given.

The facts are as follows:-

The Police say that he was not known to be a member of the Irish Volunteers or of the Citizen Army prior to the outbreak. The Military cannot say where or by whom he was arrested, but he was one of a large number of men brought into Richmond Barracks when the general surrender of rebels took place. He has made no statement; and given no explanation of his proceedings; and the Military have released him on the ground that they have nothing against him, i.e., he was not, so far as is known, a Volunteer, they cannot prove he was a participant in the Rebellion, and they do not know where or how he came into their custody. These reasons are not given in writing on the records, they were stated verbally by the officer who authorised the release.

It has to be noted that in addition to making no statement to the Military, Mr. Heery made no representation to the head of his Department until he found himself at liberty, although he was in custody for more than six weeks. Moreover a card of membership of the Irish Volunteers was found in his lodgings when enquiry was made there by a member of the Staff of the Post Office on the 3rd May with reference to Mr. Heery's resumption of duty (See copy of report which follows):-

The Superintending Engineer,

In accordance with instructions from Mr. Black, I visited Mr. Heery's lodgings at 40 Fitzroy Avenue, yesterday. His landlady, Mrs. Jauncey, informed me that he had not been seen since between 6 and 7 p.m. on the 24th April, when he is stated to have gone out for a walk after his tea. His present whereabouts are not known at his lodgings.

His landlady is under the impression that Mr. Heery was a member of the 'Irish Volunteers' and she holds what appears to be his card of membership.

Mrs. Jauncey also handed me a quantity of Post Office stationery which is detailed on the attached list.[20] I found on examining the items in detail, on my return to the office, that 1 rifle cartridge, 1 revolver cartridge, and two private letters were included.

Sd. by Mr. Colthurst,
5th May 1916

Mr. Heery left his lodgings between 6 and 7 p.m. on 24th April 1916, and did not return. It may be mentioned that the Military say that the names of surrendering persons were taken on the spot by the officer in charge of the troops at each particular place, and that false names were given in some cases. Hence if a man when in the Barracks and allotted for deportation then gave his right name it would not be apparent how or where he was actually taken as the slips handed in by the arresting officers were bundled together and each particular individual in the drafts of prisoners could not be identified. Mr. Heery might have been one of those who gave false names, and so identification would in his case fail.

A statement has since been made by Mr. Heery and is as follows:-

Garristown,
Co. Dublin
20/6/16

Sir,

I am in receipt of your kind acknowledgement of the 18th instant with reference to my application for reinstatement as Clerical Assistant. I have since been advised by a friend to state fully my whereabouts on Easter Monday last. At 11 a.m. I went for a walk along the Canal Bank, which I frequently do, to Lucan and returned about 4 p.m., when I had my dinner. I went out again about 5 p.m. and near Nelson's Pillar, was forced by two armed men into the General Post Office and was kept a prisoner by rebels until the surrender to the Military took place.

I was then deported to Stafford Detention Barracks, from which I was released on Wednesday last the 14th instant without being tried for any charge whatsoever. Therefore it is clearly evident that I was entirely innocent of any connection directly or indirectly with the insurgent movement.

Mrs Jauncey (my landlady) 40 Fitzroy Avenue, Drumcondra, who is a good loyalist can verify as to my going to and returning from my lodgings.

I trust therefore when the above facts are placed before you they should aid the investigation of my case now being enquired into, and that I will soon be restored to my former position.

J. M. Heery.

Note signed by Mr. Norway, 5 July 1916
Mr. Heery's official character is good, and he performs him
duties satisfactorily. Nothing is known in the Post Office as to his
political views or (possible) activities.

Notes

1. TNA, CO 904/25/1. The entire document is reproduced below apart from Appendixes 4-6, respectively comprising a list of civil servants interviewed by the Sankey Committee; a list of papers relating to Irish civil servants provided by the Home Office; and a pro forma Home Office letter designed to be sent to civil servants alleged to be members of the Irish Volunteers.
2. Russell to Sir Edward O'Farrell (Assistant Under-Secretary to Lord Lieutenant), 25 Aug. 1916 (TNA, CO 904/25/1).
3. Duke to Samuel, 2 Sept. 1916 (ibid.).
4. R. M. Fox, *The History of the Irish Citizen Army* (Dublin: James Duffy, 1943), p. 172. In his detailed commentary of Fox's book, Diarmuid Lynch (a Volunteer officer who had been involved in the planning to cut communications) disputed that King was a member of the ICA: 'I'm pretty sure King was one of my men' (Lynch, *The I.R.B. and the 1916 Insurrection*, p. 81).
5. Fox, *History of the Irish Citizen Army*, pp. 172–3.
6. TNA, CO 904/25/1.
7. See Appendixes 2 and 3 below, pp. 199–200.
8. Joint Secretary to the Treasury, 1916–19, and Under-Secretary for Ireland, May-Sept. 1916.
9. A committee, chaired by Mr Justice Sankey, was appointed to review the cases of all the prisoners interned in England after the Rising.
10. As asserted in paragraphs 13 and 14 of evidence given before the 'Hardinge Commission' (the Royal Commission appointed 'to investigate the facts surrounding the rebellion in Ireland').
11. Not reproduced. The letter was for issuing to a civil servant whom it was alleged was 'a member of the Irish Volunteers under the leadership of a Committee presided over by Mr John McNeill', an organisation 'hostile to recruitment in the Forces of the Crown and generally to the Government'. The letter called on the individual, under threat of dismissal, 'to cease all connection with the Irish Volunteers, or any other organization pursuing similar objects'.
12. Not reproduced.
13. McElligott, having resigned from the Volunteers in 1915, claimed that he had been forced at gunpoint by some former Volunteer colleagues to join the rebels in the GPO. He resumed his civil service career after independence and was head of the Department of Finance from 1927 to 1953 (Eunan O'Halpin, *The Decline of the Union* (Dublin: Gill & Macmillan, 1987), pp. 127–8).

14. See below, pp. 201–14, for detailed papers about his case, and those of Archer, Darcy and McDonnell following.
15. Assistant Under-Secretary to the Lord Lieutenant, 1908–18, who had been appointed principally because he was a Catholic and a nationalist. He has been described as 'a hopeless civil servant, without energy, ideas or ability' (O'Halpin, *Decline of the Union*, p. 94).
16. Father of Joseph Mary Plunkett, signatory of the Proclamation and executed after the Rising. Standing as a representative of Sinn Féin, Count Plunkett won a famous by-election in Roscommon North in February 1917. He was later a member of the First Dáil, and served successively as Minister of Foreign Affairs and Minister of Fine Arts.
17. The 'Defence of the Realm Regulations', which gave sweeping wartime powers to the government across the United Kingdom.
18. TNA, CO 904/26.
19. Michael O'Hanrahan was Quartermaster of the Irish Volunteers, and fought in the Jacobs' factory garrison during the Rising. He was executed at Kilmainham Gaol on 4 May 1916. His brother Henry had worked as a clerk in the Volunteers' headquarters.
20. Not in the file.

Index